C000139048

LET'S ST
JOHN

Let's Study

JOHN

Mark Johnston

THE BANNER OF TRUTH TRUST

THE BANNER OF TRUTH TRUST
3 Murrayfield Road, Edinburgh EH12 6EL, UK
P.O. Box 621, Carlisle, PA 17013, USA

*

© Mark Johnston 2003
First Published 2003
ISBN 0 85151 833 8

*

Typeset in 11/12.5 pt Ehrhardt MT at the
Banner of Truth Trust, Edinburgh

Printed in Great Britain by
Bell & Bain Ltd.,
Glasgow

Scripture quotations are from THE HOLY BIBLE,
ENGLISH STANDARD VERSION, © Copyright 2001 by
Crossway Bibles, a division of Good News Publishers.
Used by permission.
All rights reserved.

For

Derek and Rosemary,
longstanding friends to whom
I owe an enormous debt
of gratitude

Contents

Contents

Publisher's Preface

*L*et's Study John is part of a series of books which explain and apply the message of Scripture. The series is designed to meet a specific and important need in the church. While not technical commentaries, the volumes comment on the text of a biblical book; and, without being merely lists of practical applications, they are concerned with the ways in which the teaching of Scripture can affect and transform our lives today. Understanding the Bible's message and applying its teaching are the aims.

Like other volumes in the series, *Let's Study John* seeks to combine explanation and application. Its concern is to be helpful to ordinary Christian people by encouraging them to understand the message of the Bible and apply it to their own lives. The reader in view is not the person who is interested in all the detailed questions which fascinate the scholar, although behind the writing of each study lies an appreciation for careful and detailed scholarship. The aim is exposition of Scripture written in the language of a friend, seated alongside you with an open Bible.

Let's Study John is designed to be used in various contexts. It can be used simply as an aid for individual Bible study. Some may find it helpful to use in their devotions with husband or wife, or to read in the context of the whole family.

In order to make these studies more useful, not only for individual use but also for group study in Sunday School classes and home, church or college, study guide material will be found on pp. 275–301. Sometimes we come away frustrated rather than helped by group discussions. Frequently that is because we have been encouraged to discuss a passage of Scripture which we do not understand very well in the first place. Understanding must always be the foundation for enriching discussion and for thoughtful, practical application. Thus, in addition to the exposition of John, the additional material provides questions to encourage personal thought and study, or to be used as discussion starters. The Group Study Guide divides the material into twenty-six sections and provides direction for leading and participating in group study and discussion.

Foreword

There are different ways in which we can benefit from the Bible. We can simply listen to it being read in public worship, or read it for ourselves in some quiet setting. This in itself is a great privilege and blessing. We are not listening to mere words of men but to the Word of God. We can also memorize Scripture, storing it away in our minds so that it will always be accessible, even in unlikely circumstances. Then again we can have it explained to us, either through preaching, or else in guided study of its message. All of these approaches to the Bible – and others besides – are sure to be beneficial to us as we are exposed to its truth.

Another vital, yet much neglected use of Scripture is personal study: cultivating the habit and discipline of daily reflection upon some passage or other. The first Psalm reminds us that fruitful and effective Christian living is inseparably linked to delighting in and meditating on God's Word each day (*Psa.* 1:1-3). Far from being a cold, mechanical exercise, this ushers us into the living dynamic of interaction with the living Word of the living God.

That truth brings us to the conviction that underlies this contribution to the *Let's Study* series. The title of each volume invites you to delve more deeply into the Bible. Not so deep that you feel you are starting to flounder, but deep enough to appreciate the riches God has placed in our possession in this book.

Let's Study John is not intended to provide a verse-by-verse commentary on the text. The approach instead is to identify and follow the main threads running through the text. That means that there will inevitably be questions that are left unanswered and for which more detailed commentaries will be needed. Some of these are listed on page 302.

This particular volume engages in such a study of the Gospel according to John. It is designed for use either in private, or in a small group setting. There is a brief study guide at the end together with questions on each section. These may be used for guided interaction with the text.

The study is based on the text of the English Standard Version of the Bible, though in places it will offer alternative translations to bring out more fully what a particular passage is saying.

It is a thrilling exercise to be able to 'search the Scriptures' with more than just a cursory fascination. They constitute God's Word to the world – the message that tells of salvation and mends broken lives. It is the message of Christ our Saviour!

While writing this book I have been conscious of my debt of gratitude to many people who have taught me over the years what it means to handle carefully God's Word of truth. Although many could be named, I want to single out one dear friend who, perhaps more than anyone else, shaped my convictions about the importance of exposition: Derek Thomas. This volume is dedicated to him and to his wife Rosemary as a small token of appreciation of all that their friendship and prayers have meant to me over the years.

MARK JOHNSTON
Grove Chapel
Camberwell
February 2003

Introduction

There are two ways to appreciate an Art Gallery. You can either do a swift tour, surveying all it contains, or else you can select a number of key exhibits and spend a longer time appreciating in detail the beauty of each one. Both approaches have value; indeed it may be argued that the best way to get the most from the gallery is to combine them.

This illustration helps us to answer the first question that arises when we start reading John's Gospel: 'Why is it different in character from Matthew, Mark and Luke?' It is fairly obvious, even to people who are not used to reading the Bible, that the fourth Gospel has certain traits that set it apart from the other three. It is not that its content conflicts with the account of Jesus set out by the other evangelists, but rather that the way John has arranged and presented his account of Jesus and his work has its own distinctive flavour.

UNIQUE CHARACTERISTICS

John is selective when choosing the details he records about the Person and work of Christ. Out of a total of thirty-five miracles of Jesus recorded in the Gospels, John relates only eight, seven of which are designated 'signs'. He records none of Jesus' parables that form a significant part of the other Gospel records. Instead, he devotes a significant amount of space to key sermons or discourses delivered by Jesus in various settings.

The first three Gospels have been dubbed 'the Synoptics', that is, they provide an overview of the life and work of Jesus from the same general perspective. But John takes a different perspective.

Like the visitor to the Art Gallery who selects a few works for more detailed perusal, John chooses particular aspects of Christ and his work for close consideration. His is the reflective Gospel, the one which takes us by the hand and leads us into the depths of the mysteries of Christ's Person and the wonders of all he has accomplished for his people and for the world.

Its character is such that it is said that this is the Gospel in which 'a child may paddle and yet an elephant can swim!' In that sense it provides not only a point of entry into the Bible for someone who is new to the Christian faith, but also a favourite haunt for those who know and love the Bible well.

BACKGROUND DETAILS

It is always helpful when we study any part of Scripture to try and find out the historical background and circumstances in which it was written. This is true in particular for the fourth Gospel, not least because it has been the subject of much debate over the years. Despite all the energy that has been expended arguing over various details of John, the general consensus on key points of background has not altered.

Who was John? The Gospel never explicitly identifies its author, but refers repeatedly to 'the disciple whom Jesus loved' (13:23; 19:26; 20:2; 21:7, 20) in a way which suggests it was this disciple who wrote it. Piecing together the clues in each of these references strongly suggests that John, the brother of James and son of Zebedee, was the disciple in question.

This is confirmed by other internal features which are in accord with an authorship by John the Apostle. His knowledge of the Jewish way of life; the local geography of Palestine; and the details of events which only an eye-witness could have known, all point to his being John, the brother of James. This view of authorship has a good pedigree among the writings of the Early Church Fathers, especially Irenaeus, Tertullian, Clement and Origen and continues to command respect even among contemporary scholars.

As to when the Gospel was written, there is good reason to believe that this must have been late in the first century, perhaps in the late eighties, or early nineties AD. Although an earlier date is possible and has arguments in its favour, the more fully developed reflections on the life and work of Christ that are a feature of the Gospel are consistent with a later date of authorship.

Although none of these issues significantly affects the message of the book and its timeless relevance, it is worth bearing in mind the circumstances that provided its original setting.

PURPOSE AND STRUCTURE

Why did John write? What particular purpose did he have in mind that would warrant another record of Christ and his coming? (There can be little doubt that he would have been aware of the existence of the other Gospels, even if the date of writing was earlier than has been suggested.)

John answers that question for us. He states plainly that the things he has recorded in his book 'are written so that you may believe that Jesus is the Christ, the Son of God, and that by believing you may have life in his name' (20:31). His purpose, then, is twofold: that his readers might be brought into a relationship with Christ through genuine faith, and that in this relationship they might discover the fullness of life which can only be found in living fellowship with God through his Son. The purpose of John's account is not at odds with those of Matthew, Mark and Luke. It serves rather to complement their witness to Christ and to reinforce the message of how Christ has come to bring about a total transformation in the lives of those who trust him.

Even as the apostle wrote, at this very early stage of Christian history, the identity of Jesus and the story of his life, death, resurrection and ascension had become encrusted with myth and mystery that was damaging to the gospel. Hence John writes to set the record straight, not just in relation to the facts, but also with regard to their significance.

John's account of Jesus and his mission is structured in such a way as to demonstrate the wonder of what God has done in bringing salvation to our world. It places key emphases on certain themes and events in order to underline where the heart of human need really lies. It also structures the record in such a way as to highlight the crux of God's answer to that need: the saving work of

Jesus Christ. From the very outset of the Gospel, the themes of world, flesh, darkness and death, all demonstrate the fact that, left to their own devices, people cannot save themselves.

By contrast, the themes of light, life, love and the divine sonship of Christ, all proclaim a salvation that has entered our world from above. Here is the good news: Jesus has come, not to tell us how we might save ourselves, but actually to bring salvation and offer it freely to all who will believe.

With that in mind, the account that John provides begins, not in time, but in eternity; taking us to the very heart of God's eternal purpose for the world (1:1–18). This prologue – unique to the fourth Gospel – sets the scene for the first major section of the Gospel: some eleven chapters charting the public ministry of Jesus (1:19–11:57). After this, almost half of the Gospel is devoted to just one week of Jesus' life: the week in which he was put to death (12:1–19:42). This division of the book speaks for itself with regard to the biblical emphasis on the nature of Christ's work. There follows the record of the resurrection (20:1–31) and a closing section which paves the way for our understanding of how the message of Christ began to spread, and has continued to spread throughout the world and down through history (21:1–25).

The scene is set then for us to proceed into the Gospel itself and discover all that it says about God's promise of eternal life for all who truly believe in his Son, Jesus Christ.

I

The Beginning

In the beginning was the Word, and the Word was with God, and the Word was God. ² He was in the beginning with God. ³ All things were made through him, and without him was not any thing made that was made. ⁴ In him was life, and the life was the light of men. ⁵ The light shines in the darkness, and the darkness has not overcome it (John 1:1–5).

Perhaps the most important question we can ever ask ourselves in life is, 'Who am I, where have I come from and where am I going?' It is a question about origin and destiny. Popular answers to that question have been shaped by the theory of evolution and the notion that the origin of the world and the human race is the product of blind chance. Such a view of how it all began has a profound impact upon the way we live. The Bible gives us an altogether different insight.

The opening words of John's Gospel take us immediately into the realm of origins, and connect that realm unequivocally with God. In a way that clearly echoes the first verse of Genesis, John makes a statement about Jesus. (The fact that 'the Word' (1:1) is a title for Jesus is made clear when we are told that he 'became flesh and dwelt among us' (1:14)). Without apology or qualification, John goes back in time beyond Bethlehem where Jesus was born, and Nazareth where he was conceived, indeed back beyond the beginning of time itself, and allows us a glimpse of a glorious person who has an eternal existence.

It is as though we are being taken up a mountain to its peak and allowed to catch a glimpse of the breathtaking view from the top.

We are then taken back down to its base in order now to climb with a sense of anticipation and appreciation. The Gospel begins at that point where John wants us to end: with an understanding that Jesus Christ is God. At the close of the Gospel, as Thomas the sceptic comes face to face with the resurrected Jesus, he falls down in worship and cries out, 'My Lord and my God!' (20:28): where it ends is where it all begins.

The opening section of John's Gospel is often called 'the Prologue' because it sets the scene for all that is to follow. It provides a context for understanding Jesus that is infinitely bigger than that of first-century Palestine, or even that of the history of the world itself. It introduces the Christ of time as none other than the God of all eternity. The first five verses confront us with four crucial truths about Jesus which we need to grasp if we are to appreciate truly who he is and all that he has done.

1. Who He Is

It would be foolish for anyone not to consider the question 'Who is Jesus?' Even a complete atheist is forced at least to wonder what it was that made practically every nation in the world act in unison as the clocks struck midnight in the passage from 1999 to the year 2000. What was the great anniversary that inspired such celebration? The answer: the celebration of the anniversary of the coming of Christ. Whoever he was, Jesus Christ has had an impact on world history that has never been equalled. If anyone merits some serious thought and reflection it is Christ.

John links our understanding of Jesus to our understanding of God and his relation to the world. 'In the beginning . . .' (1:1–2). The echo of the opening words of the Bible itself is a signal that what is being revealed in and through Jesus Christ is but a continuation of what God had revealed through the Old Testament. For his Jewish readers, John is saying that message of Jesus is not in conflict with the message of the Hebrew Bible; it is the continuation of that message. Indeed, it is the consummation of Old Testament revelation, because God was making himself known through Jesus in a way he had never done so before.

The fact that Jesus is called 'the Word' is significant. For the original readers of this Gospel in the first century AD, this was a title that would resonate with Jew and Gentile alike. Jewish readers were sufficiently familiar with Old Testament descriptions of creation to realise that 'Word' and 'world' were closely connected. God spoke and the world came into being (*Gen.* 1:3–31, see also *Psa.* 33:6). For his non-Jewish readers, the Greek concept of *Logos*, or 'Reason' as the cause of all that exists was widely acknowledged. John takes both the Jewish and Gentile understandings of the term on to a different plane.

He says, 'In the beginning *was* the Word.' What to our eyes may seem a fairly innocuous verb is in reality a monumental statement. It is saying in effect, 'When the world had its beginning, the Word was already in existence!' The Word does not by nature belong to the sphere of time and space. John uses an expression of timeless existence. We might paraphrase it by saying, 'In the beginning there was Someone who had no beginning.'

We are not, however, left with a vague and shadowy impression of this Someone. We are told explicitly that, 'the Word was *with* God, and the Word *was* God.' That he was 'with God' (literally, 'towards God') indicates that this is a distinct person in his own right. That he 'was God' indicates that his nature was divine.

John chooses his words carefully to express this inexpressible truth. It reads, literally, 'and God was the Word.' The point he is making was not that Jesus was 'a god' (as, for example, the Jehovah Witnesses try to argue), but that Jesus possesses the very essence of deity.

Not surprisingly, this is a statement that defies human logic and understanding, but then again, is it such a strange thing to be confronted with the fact that God is above us and beyond us? Can we expect to be able to squeeze him into the confines of our mind? John is not telling us something he has discovered by scientific investigation, but rather that which has been given to him by revelation. Just as Moses, when writing Genesis, was able to describe matters with which he had no direct involvement, because he was being carried along by God's own Spirit (*1 Pet.* 1:21), so here with the apostle.

Who is Jesus? He is God. Ever one with God in sharing the essence of deity, yet ever distinct in that his existence is one of eternal relationship within the Godhead. These truths should have us catching our breath in wonder and in worship as we glimpse on earth realities which the angels gaze upon in heaven.

2. What He Did

We are immediately whisked from the realm of eternity to that of space and time, from a world that is not familiar to us to one which is. We are told, 'All things were made through him' (1:3). Here is an equally staggering statement. The totality of the world and the universe – all things visible and invisible – owes its existence to him. This brings us back to the great question of origins which confronts all people everywhere. How do we account for the world, the universe and everything? More importantly, how do we account for ourselves as human beings?

The great gap in the theory of evolution is not the lack of evidence for 'the missing link', but the lack of explanation for what lies behind it all. Those who preach the theory of the 'Big Bang' have no answer to the simple question, 'What banged?'

The complex theories of mathematical probabilities which are paraded to support the concept of life evolving by itself over millions of years have a hollow ring to them when confronted with the wonder of the world, the universe, and the complexity of the human race. You cannot have something out of nothing.

It is anything but simplistic to attribute the entire order of existence to a powerful and personal Creator. To do so makes infinitely more sense of the world and, moreover, offers real hope to the world. The One who made the world is the very One who has entered it, and John calls us to turn and look at him.

3. How He Relates to Us

The Maker of the world and the universe is not some impersonal force. Nor is he detached from his creatures. 'In him was life, and the life was the light of men' (1:4). He has a relationship with humanity. What he is by nature – 'life' – has, in some sense, a universal impact on the human race.

It is not that John is advocating pantheism – the idea that everything is God. Rather he teaches that all life is touched by God, and the lives of human beings are touched very particularly by God. Genesis tells us that men and women are made in the image of God (*Gen.*1:26–27). Human beings are different from the animals: their lives have the stamp of God upon them. Although that image has been defaced and damaged because of our sin, it remains sufficiently intact for all people everywhere to realise that we cannot understand humanity unless we first appreciate deity. To borrow John Calvin's expression, every human being has 'a sense of God'.

All people, whether Christian or not, bear some relationship to God, some sense of accountability. By nature we suppress that fact (*Rom.* 1:18), but when confronted with Jesus Christ, we are reminded of it. The truth that the eternal Word is also the everlasting Creator means that we his creatures have an interest in him, just as he in turn has a profound interest in us.

4. WHY HE MATTERS

Jesus is not just one idea among many, just one more theory in the market place of theories that spans the course of history. John dares to say that he is '*the* light.' (1:5). This great claim will be taken up by Jesus himself later on in the Gospel (8:12; 9:5), but here at the outset, John declares him to be the ultimate and true light which continually shines in the world. There is a bold exclusivism in the gospel. It does not sit easily with a world that celebrates a pluralistic view of life, but it cannot be deleted from the message about Jesus nor from the claims that he makes.

John acknowledges that even in his day this was not a popular assertion to make. He sets the light against the darkness – the God who is light and the world which is in spiritual darkness are not in harmony with each other – and then he says, 'and the darkness has not overcome it.' This is the first of many word-plays in this Gospel. John uses a word that can mean either 'understood' or 'overcome'. In so doing he demonstrates two things about God and Jesus: we cannot understand him through human reason alone, and, even though he has been consistently opposed by our race, he never has and never will be overcome. He is the light that can never be extinguished.

[5]

John was reflecting on some fifty years of opposition and persecution that had not extinguished the light of Christ in the gospel. The subsequent two millennia that have passed bear out that same assertion. Jesus will not go away, we cannot escape from him and we will one day give account to him.

The scene is set. Jesus is presented, not in the obscurity of a stable in Bethlehem, but as he was from eternity, in all his glory and majesty: the Maker of the universe and the Light of all mankind.

2

The Light in the Darkness

There was a man sent from God, whose name was John.
[7] He came as a witness, to bear witness about the light, that all
might believe through him. [8] He was not the light, but came to
bear witness about the light.
[9] The true light, which enlightens everyone, was coming into
the world. [10] He was in the world, and the world was made
through him, yet the world did not know him. [11] He came to his
own, and his own people did not receive him. [12] But to all who
did receive him, who believed in his name, he gave the right
to become children of God, [13] who were born, not of blood
nor of the will of the flesh nor of the will of man, but of God
(John 1:6–13).

It is becoming more and more popular to provide crash-courses
in language study by means of the so-called 'Immersion
Technique'. Instead of following the traditional approach of starting
with simple grammar and basic vocabulary, students are immersed
in the language from the outset. The theory is that after the initial
shock, they will begin to pick up what is involved in the language
and proceed to use it quickly and effectively.

It might be said that John is employing a similar technique in these
opening verses of his Gospel. Having plunged us into the mystery
of Christ in the realm of eternity, he now tells us, a mere six verses
later, how this eternal being entered time and space and made himself
known in human history.

Even in John's day the thought of such a supernatural
manifestation might easily be dismissed as the stuff of private fantasy,

or an over-active imagination, so the writer supplies independent, supporting testimony. He wants us to grasp what happened when Jesus came into the world. But he also wants us to see that this event at one point in history will impact on people's lives throughout history, according to their response.

The Witness

Having told us about the Light that 'shines in the darkness' but which has not been overcome (1:5), John now informs us of a person who was sent to explain and proclaim that light to the world. This person was John the Baptist – mentioned in all four Gospels. He was the figure who, as foretold by the prophets (*Isa.* 40:1–5, *Mal.* 3:1),was to precede the promised Messiah and announce his arrival on the stage of world history.

The literal meaning of the text is that 'there *appeared* a man' (1:6). John is signalling a movement from the realm of eternity to the realm of time: from the realm of faith to that of the senses. His gospel is not about religious ideas, but about historical reality. The Christ of eternity steps on to the stage of the world, and his forerunner, John the Baptist, is there to herald the event.

John comes as 'a witness, to bear witness about the light' (1:7). He is sent by God to announce that the light of heaven has dawned in the darkness of the world and to explain how this momentous event is to be understood.

Testimony and witness are key concepts that recur throughout this Gospel. They are legal terms and have to do, not with a person's subjective opinion or experience, but with objective fact. A witness at a trial is asked to testify to what he or she actually saw or heard, not what they thought, or may have speculated. Quite simply, they are to tell the truth. In an age when so much in life has been reduced to the level of what is relative and subjective, the Bible brings us face to face with facts that are of towering significance. Thus, John's prime concern in bearing testimony to this light was 'that all might believe through him' (1:7).

In order to emphasize the point, the Gospel writer makes it clear that John the Baptist was not himself the promised light, but that the One to whom he pointed was (1:8–9). The light that penetrates the spiritual darkness of a world in rebellion against God does not dawn from within. It comes from without; from God himself. Jesus Christ is 'the true light which enlightens everyone'.

What does this mean? There are three possible interpretations. The first is that Christ is the light of God who makes 'everyone' without exception aware of God and of his accountability before God. The second is that Jesus provides inward illumination to all kinds of people without distinction so as to bring them to salvation. The final option is to view this statement as an objective fact: Jesus Christ embodies the ultimate light of God's self-revelation to the world. All three options are possible and all three relate to strands of thought running through this Gospel. The point is that John relates the promise of light for the world (*Isa.* 9:2) to the coming of Christ.

Neither Recognized nor Received

What kind of reception would mark the arrival of such an important figure in the world? Every culture has its own way of welcoming dignitaries from other countries, but how would the world respond to a visitor from heaven? John tells us in the starkest of terms: 'He was in the world, and the world was made through him, yet the world did not know him' (1:10). Picking up on the universal consciousness of God mentioned in the previous verse, John tells us that this awareness of God had been so damaged by sin that the world did not naturally recognize God when he entered this world in the person of his Son.

Worse than that, when Jesus came, not merely to the world but especially 'to his own' (1:11) – that is, the people of Israel, even they did not welcome him. The very nation that had been prepared for the hundreds of years of its history for the coming of the Saviour did not rejoice to see that day when it dawned.

John's description of the reception given to Jesus when he entered our world through the incarnation is not just an indictment of the human race or of the Jewish people at the time of Christ's coming, it is an indictment of us all. Sin has so darkened our understanding (*Eph.* 4:18) and made us instinctively hostile to God and to his truth (*Rom.* 1:18), that no-one in and of themselves can recognize and receive Jesus in a way that will truly honour him. Here is God's indictment of the human heart.

GOOD NEWS

Some of the most beautiful words in the Bible are its smallest words! We are given hope that we can be delivered from the crushing condemnation of our rejection of God in Christ by a word which is just two letters in the Greek and three in its English translation: 'But' (1:12). God does not deal with us in the way our sin deserves; he provides a way of escape.

God graciously holds out the title to a place in his family for all who receive Christ, all who 'believe in his name'. Here is God offering adoption papers to those who by nature are aliens and outcasts. To those who are his enemies, God offers the opportunity to become his children, and all of this on account of Christ and of what he has done. Simply by trusting in Christ, rather than in ourselves and our own merits, we become beneficiaries of the grace of God in salvation.

But there is a catch surely! If we have been following the logic of what John has declared to us so far, we know enough to realise that we are all by nature so opposed to God and his truth that none of us will look to Christ in this way. That is indeed the case, but it is not the end of the story as far as God and his gospel are concerned. Those who receive the grace of adoption into the family of God are also the people who receive the grace of new birth. Their response to God's Son and their admission to God's family are not the consequence of the natural processes of human procreation, but rather the result of their being 'born of God' (1:13).

The good news of the gospel is that God not only shows people the door into his household, he personally carries them over the threshold. What we can never do by ourselves – namely recognize Jesus for who he is and trust in him – God enables us to do by his grace.

3

The Word Became Flesh

And the Word became flesh and dwelt among us, and we have seen his glory, glory as of the only Son from the Father, full of grace and truth. ¹⁵ *(John bore witness about him, and cried out, "This was he of whom I said, 'He who comes after me ranks before me, because he was before me.'")* ¹⁶ *And from his fullness we have all received, grace upon grace.* ¹⁷ *For the law was given through Moses; grace and truth came through Jesus Christ.* ¹⁸ *No one has ever seen God; the only God, who is at the Father's side, he has made him known* (John 1:14–18).

The great beauty of a symphony, or a tapestry is simply that the more we listen to the music and look at the design, the more we appreciate and admire. The skills of composer and weaver are seen in the way that people are captured and enraptured by their work and by the way in which as artists they have revealed something of themselves in what they do. So it is with the incarnation of Jesus Christ. Not only the works of God but God himself in his triune glory, is revealed in human flesh. As John concludes his introduction the spotlight shines on the way in which the revelation of Jesus Christ lays hold of those who receive it by faith.

He wants us to do more than simply stand in awe of the God who has made himself known through Jesus. He wants us to grasp the fact that all that we need for life and salvation is actually found in Jesus and is freely offered to us by him.

The God Who Came to Save

We are taken to the dizzy heights of the truth of this message right at the very outset. We see Jesus, not with his glory veiled and his true identity concealed, but as he really is: the infinite God who stepped into our finite world, taking upon himself the flesh of our humanity.

John brings his readers to the same conclusion as that arrived at by the other Gospel writers, but by a different route. Matthew, Mark and Luke tell the story of Jesus as it happened. They bring out the wonder felt by the disciples and the crowds as it began to dawn upon them that the One they thought was merely the carpenter's son from Nazareth was in reality the Son of God from heaven. So, for example, in Mark's Gospel, the climax comes at the end in the confession of a Roman centurion, 'Surely this man was the Son of God!' (*Mark* 15:39). For John, however, the climax comes at the beginning and, as we have noted, is then reinforced at the end. He confronts us immediately with the mystery of what happened when Jesus came, and then proceeds to explain the mystery and to show how it touches the lives of all.

One word sums up all that has taken place: 'glory!' It is not just that in the incarnate Christ the glory of God's majesty is set on display in this world (though that is surely the case) but it is ultimately the fact that the glory of God's grace is seen. This majestic God has stooped down to come to us; but more than that, he has come to us in order to save us.

Some people have the wonderful ability to make each person to whom they speak feel special, because they focus all their interest and attention on them. It is something even more amazing that is found uniquely in Jesus Christ and to which John directs our attention. Using language that clearly echoes the request of Moses to God in Exodus, 'Please show me your glory', and God's subsequent answer when he appeared, proclaiming, 'The LORD, the LORD, a God merciful and gracious' (*Exod.* 33:18-34:7), John tells us that this same God has now come in person. The 'love and faithfulness' of God declared to Moses (*Exod.* 34:6) are now seen in the 'grace and truth' revealed in Christ. The majesty of God is enhanced by the fact that he is willing to mingle with the crowds of a fallen humanity and with the express purpose of proving his love for them in salvation.

The remaining verses of John's opening section are given over to explaining precisely for whom Christ came and why.

1. HE CAME FOR THOSE WHO LONG FOR CERTAINTY

It is easy for us to believe that our age is uniquely an age of confusion and uncertainty. We live in a global market place of religions and ideas, and people inevitably want to know which are right and how it is that we can ever be sure of anything. The truth is, of course, that the same essential problem has always been present, the only difference is that we see it today on a larger scale than ever before.

In Jesus' day there was a multiplicity of ideas and religions in the world. The cosmopolitan character of the Roman Empire created widespread exposure to competing and conflicting claims about life and the gods. The quest for an assured certainty was as much of a struggle then as it is today. So John takes time to state again, as he will do repeatedly, that the things of which he is speaking are not merely true, but are the ultimate truth.

What John the apostle has to say about Jesus is entirely consistent with the testimony of John the Baptist. The fact that we are told 'John testifies' [present tense] (1:15) is interesting in that though the Baptist himself was long since dead, his testimony lived on with abiding force. In a strikingly unusual way for a society in which rank was associated with seniority, John's witness is that the One who comes *after* is the One who is greater. Then, with words that were bound to have raised eyebrows, he attributes the reason for the greatness of Jesus to the fact that 'he was before me.'

This remarkable statement bears out the testimony of the apostle when he says that the glory seen in Jesus was that of 'the only Son' or, 'the Only Begotten' (1:14). The concerted witness of these two men was to the fact that Jesus is unique because Jesus is God. He is set apart from the mêlée of the world's religions and philosophies because he is from outside this world.

Our faith is being directed, not to one among many, but to the One who stands alone.

2. He Came for Those Who Long to be Filled

Jesus also meets our need for fulfilment. The emptiness of the human soul is met by the fullness of Jesus Christ. Thus in verse sixteen John states, 'And from his fullness we have all received, grace upon grace.' That is, the deepest needs of the many who have come to trust in this Christ have been more than adequately met by him.

This statement again brings us back to the great summary statement at the start of this section: 'The Word became flesh.' In one sense John could have chosen a more dignified word to describe what Jesus took to himself when he entered this world. 'Flesh' has an earthiness about it that seems alien to the glory that belongs to the Son of God. Yet it is the very earthiness of the word that John uses to make his point. Once more it carries echoes of the account in Genesis 2 of how God created. Breaking with the pattern of creation established in the first five-and-a-half days of that extraordinary week, God does not simply speak Adam into existence, he enters into the act of creation in a much more intimate fashion.

Adam was fashioned out of the dust of the earth and God then 'breathed into his nostrils the breath of life' (*Gen.* 2:7). That too has an undignified air about it; as though God bent down and pressed his face into the face of this form he had made, breathing not just natural life but spiritual life into it, thus making something that was uniquely human.

Given that one of the main threads of Old Testament teaching is the fact that sin has seriously impaired our humanity as creatures made in the image of God, the gospel in the New Testament announces the recovery of true humanity through the incarnation of Jesus Christ. He takes flesh, real human flesh, but does so in a way that breaks the chain of fallenness that our race had shared since the sin of Adam.

If our fallen nature has reduced our humanity to the level of spiritual vagrants, burrowing through the bins of life for scraps of spiritual food – all of which leave us empty – Jesus Christ is the One in whom the full dignity of our humanity is restored. It is one of the most thrilling facets of the gospel. In an age when human degradation and worthlessness seems to be sinking to depths lower than could ever be imagined, and when emptiness is the badge of every life, Jesus brings true hope.

John tells us that Jesus is the climax of all that God has given, for, from him 'we have all received, grace upon grace'. The best way to understand this rather unusual turn of phrase is simply to see it in its original setting as addressed to first-century converts whose only Scriptures were those of the Old Testament. John wanted those readers to grasp that: 'Yes, the Old Testament is indeed full of God's grace, but it is superseded by the grace that God reveals and pours out through the coming of Christ.' We must never get stuck in the Old Testament; but must rather be carried along in its ever-deepening flow of grace until we find ourselves in Christ.

The fullness that we so desperately need and long for in life – the fullness of a fulfilled humanity – can be found only in fellowship with the One who is the supreme demonstration of God's grace to sinners: the Living Word incarnate.

3. He Came for Those Who Long for Freedom

John continues this train of thought in the following verse, 'For the law was given through Moses; grace and truth came through Jesus Christ' (1:17). They 'came' through Jesus in the sense that they were realized, or reached their fulfilment through him. It would be wrong to think that John was trying to set the New Testament over against the Old, or suggest that there is some kind of antithesis between grace and law. Rather, he was demonstrating the fact that what was already there in the Old Testament reaches its fruition only in the New.

In the same way as the blossom on a flower is but a fuller expression of what was there in the bud, so also is the progress of God's revelation in the Scriptures. It is striking to note the strong dependence of the New Testament on the Old. This is seen in the frequent allusions and direct quotations made and is borne out most obviously perhaps in the book of Hebrews. There we are told explicitly that Old Testament believers could not be made complete apart from their New Testament counterparts (*Heb.* 11:40).

We cannot fail to see the connection between the fulfilment John describes in this verse and the freedom that comes with it, to which Jesus alludes later on in his Gospel (8:32). The transition from an age in which God dealt with his people through the medium of many external laws, regulations and rituals to one in which that relationship became more direct and personal through the mediation of his Son, was a liberation in itself. Paul, when writing to the Galatians, describes the transition in terms of moving from spiritual childhood to adulthood – from a stage of life when much external constraint was necessary, to one in which greater maturity and knowledge allows for greater responsibility (*Gal.* 3:23-25).

If we want to find genuine freedom in life, it must come, not through seeking licence to live as we please, but through entering a new and transforming relationship with God through faith in his Son. Religion cannot liberate (the Jews in the time of John and Jesus were learning that the hard way); but a relationship that lives through the grace of God most surely will.

4. HE CAME FOR THOSE WHO LONG TO KNOW GOD

If this freedom comes through knowing God, how then is that knowledge to be acquired? Men and women have searched for God in many ways, from the rigours of Islamic religion to New Age mysticism, and yet have been disappointed. These, and every other attempt to construct a pathway to God through man-made religious techniques, are bound to fail, because they originate from below and are therefore inherently flawed. The unique difference and distinctive of the Christian faith and gospel, as John declares it, is that it originates from above – not merely with a message from heaven, but with a personal visitation from God himself.

He tells us in self-evident terms, 'No-one has ever seen God'. No-one, that is, 'the only God, who is at the Father's side' (1:18). He it is who has made the Father known.

Again and again the Bible tells us that God is beyond the reach of men and women in their natural fallen state. He cannot be found by searching (*Job* 11:7), man cannot understand him in his natural sinful condition (*1 Cor.* 2:14). If God is to be known, it can only be as he is made known by Someone who already possesses true knowledge of him. Jesus is that Someone. Because of who he is – the eternal Son of God – he is uniquely qualified to reveal God.

Jesus speaks from the vantage point of the intimate and eternal communion of the Godhead. He reveals God, not so much in terms of the absolute truth about him - such a revelation would be more than any human being could bear – but in the sense rather of explaining God. He makes the God who is beyond all human comprehension accessible to us and does so without subtracting anything from what God is.

There is a depth and complexity to what John says that takes our breath away. The very attempt to convey something of what it means in simple language is almost impossible! At the same time there is a beautiful simplicity to it all. If we are to know this infinite, eternal, incomprehensible God, we need simply to know Jesus. This is because to know him, as Jesus will tell us later, is to know the Father and to enjoy life eternal (17:3).

4

How Great a Salvation

And this is the testimony of John, when the Jews sent priests and Levites from Jerusalem to ask him, "Who are you?" [20] *He confessed, and did not deny, but confessed, "I am not the Christ."* [21] *And they asked him, "What then? Are you Elijah?" He said, "I am not." "Are you the Prophet?" And he answered, "No."* [22] *So they said to him, "Who are you? We need to give an answer to those who sent us. What do you say about yourself?"* [23] *He said, "I am the voice of one crying out in the wilderness, 'Make straight the way of the Lord,' as the prophet Isaiah said."* [24] *(Now they had been sent from the Pharisees.)* [25] *They asked him, "Then why are you baptizing, if you are neither the Christ, nor Elijah, nor the Prophet?"* [26] *John answered them, "I baptize with water, but among you stands one you do not know,* [27] *even he who comes after me, the strap of whose sandal I am not worthy to untie."* [28] *These things took place in Bethany across the Jordan, where John was baptizing.* [29] *The next day he saw Jesus coming towards him, and said, "Behold, the Lamb of God, who takes away the sin of the world!* [30] *This is he of whom I said, 'After me comes a man who ranks before me, because he was before me.'* [31] *I myself did not know him, but for this purpose I came baptizing with water, that he might be revealed to Israel."* [32] *And John bore witness: "I saw the Spirit descend from heaven like a dove, and it remained on him.* [33] *I myself did not know him, but he who sent me to baptize with water said to me, 'He on whom you see the Spirit descend and remain, this is he who baptizes with the Holy Spirit.'* [34] *And I have seen and have borne witness that this is the Son of God"* (John 1:19–34).

People instinctively cluster around great leaders or popular icons in the hope that they will find something of lasting worth – something that might make a difference to their life. They may not always be able to articulate precisely what they are hoping for. Whether it is an Ayatollah, the Dalai Lama, a pop star, or the Pope, people will flock in their droves to them in the hope that these might provide what they are unconsciously seeking. That instinct in man has always been there through the ages. It amounts to a kind of messianic longing and it will only be satisfied when the One who possesses true messianic credentials is found.

In the months immediately prior to Jesus' public ministry, there was an unusual upsurge of spiritual concern among the Jewish people. It focused on a preacher in the desert: John the Baptist. His 'testimony' is now related as John the apostle unfolds his gospel message.

The intensity of interest in John's ministry in the Judean wilderness was striking, given the fact that there had been some four hundred years of national spiritual decline among the Jews. During this time the voice of God in prophecy had been silent. Suddenly, here was a message about sin, repentance and cleansing, that touched the hearts of an entire cross-section of Jewish society. It is hardly surprising that people began to wonder if this Elijah-like figure in the desert could be the long-awaited Christ.

John's testimony began on a negative note: 'I am not the Christ' (1:20). He vigorously directed popular attention away from himself. His role was not to save but rather to point people to the One who could. Two things happened as a result. Firstly, he sharpened people's understanding of who the Messiah was and what he would be like. Secondly, he prepared the way for Jesus – the true Messiah – to step into public view. We see this happening in several ways.

RAISING HOPES ABOUT SALVATION

John picks up the story of the ministry of John the Baptist at a later stage than do the other evangelists. He begins at that point where the Baptist's ministry and its impact are reaching their climax. John was generating such interest that the Jewish authorities sent a delegation from Jerusalem to ascertain who he was. John responded that he was not the Christ, nor Elijah, nor the prophet that Moses had said would one day come (1:19–21, see also *Deut.* 18:15). Instead John identified himself as 'the voice of one crying out in the wilderness, "Make straight the way of the Lord!" ' (1:22–23).

John's reply was telling. The suggestions the Jewish leaders had made about John's identity referred to great figures from their past whom God had used for their deliverance. These suggestions reflected the ongoing hope that someone would come to deliver the Jews again. John dismissed each of those options in turn and instead identified himself by means of a prophetic statement from Isaiah (*Isa.* 40:3). He was forcing these men to think again as to the meaning of salvation and therefore as to the means by which true salvation was to be found.

What was needed was a salvation of a different order from anything that could come through a Moses or an Elijah. (The popular longing for deliverance among the Jews of that day was more political than spiritual.) Hence the Messiah-Saviour they needed would have to be of a different order as well.

The Messianic hope raised by Isaiah over six hundred years before was for the coming of the *Lord* to bring deliverance. John was announcing that the Lord was indeed coming and that when he did so he would bring salvation in the highest sense.

When it comes to looking for deliverance, the hopes of every generation are set too low. For many, the hope is of economic deliverance achieved by just a little more prosperity. For others, it is social, political, or merely psychological deliverance – something to make life in this world a little more bearable. The gospel makes us think again as to the real nature of our need. In essence our need is spiritual: the problem of a sinful heart. What we need is a salvation that can deal with sin in all its ramifications. To realize this forces us to think again as to who or what can save us.

By Whose Authority?

It is easy to make great claims and raise people's expectations. But who gives us the right to do so?

Some astute Pharisees in the delegation from the capital asked John precisely that question: 'Then why are you baptizing, if you are neither the Christ, nor Elijah, nor the Prophet?' (1:24–25). What was the warrant for his ministry? Credentials are all-important when someone is claiming to speak as an ambassador for God and is making promises about forgiveness and salvation.

Once more John responded with self-effacing humility. He pointed away from himself to the One who would follow after him. Although the Messiah was already among them in the crowd (1:26), these men did not know him. John said that he himself was not worthy even to untie the strap of his sandals; such was the rank of the One who was to come. His authority was the kind that really mattered. It would be seen in the baptism that he would ultimately provide when he poured out the Holy Spirit (1:33).

John was telling these men, 'Watch this space!' The credentials of his messianic successor would be endorsed through the outpouring of the Holy Spirit upon his ministry, through his resurrection, and ultimately through the gift of the Holy Spirit to the nations on the Day of Pentecost. All of this would, of course, point to Jesus as the One who authentically fulfilled all Jewish expectation.

The Greatness of Our Need and the Greatness of God's Salvation

The next day John made perhaps the most startling statement of his public ministry. The men from Jerusalem had gone home. They missed the announcement that marked the climax, and effectively the completion, of the work God had given him to do.

As he saw Jesus, who was also his relative, coming towards him through the crowd, John said, 'Behold, the Lamb of God who takes away the sin of the world!' (1:29). John was marking a major milestone in the unfolding of God's plan of redemption. He was announcing to the crowds on the banks of the Jordan River that God's moment had come, his promised Saviour was publicly stepping on to the stage of world history.

What is particularly interesting is the way that the announcement was made. Having discussed with the leaders from Jerusalem the question of who Messiah would be and, by implication, the kind of deliverance he would bring, John now spells out those issues in unmistakable terms. He takes all the expectations about redemption and about the Redeemer on to a completely different plane.

He makes it clear that we have no greater need than that due to the problem of sin. It is a universal problem, endemic to the human race: John is talking about the sin of the world. Not only so, it is a deep-seated problem, touching the very heart of our humanity.

In one sense John was not telling his Jewish listeners anything they did not know. The whole Old Testament revelation had impressed upon Israel time and again that at the heart of the problem of sin was the problem of a sinful heart. They were in the grip of a nature that was hostile to God and they were liable to the consequences of the rebellion it produced. Worse than that, they were powerless to do anything about it: unable to change their ways for the future, or to make amends for their past.

Throughout Israel's history, God had emphasized the fact that the only way to deal with sin and the alienation it caused, was by means of sacrifice. There can be no forgiveness of sins unless blood is shed (*Lev.* 17:11), hence the elaborate system of animal sacrifice which lay at the heart of Jewish religion. God also impressed upon his people the fact that, by its very nature, *animal* sacrifice was incapable in itself of making atonement for *human* sin and guilt (*Isa.* 1:11). The ritual sacrifices were designed to foreshadow an ultimate sacrifice that would actually accomplish the real and full atonement they depicted. Indeed, God had prefigured his personal provision of a perfect sacrifice when he provided a sacrificial ram to die as a substitute for Isaac on Mount Moriah. Abraham had given God the name 'Jehovah Jireh' (or 'Yahweh Yireh'): 'The Lord Will Provide' (*Gen.* 22:1–14). The great question was, of course, 'What would he provide and when?'

As John pointed to Jesus, he was answering these questions. But more significantly, he was saying that it was not a 'what,' but a 'who' that God would provide. Jesus was God's sacrificial Lamb.

As they were confronted afresh with the greatness of their need by this unique statement of the Baptist, and by his ministry as a whole, John's hearers were being pointed to God's great provision in the person of Jesus of Nazareth.

Of course John was not merely addressing a relatively small audience at some dim and distant point in history, he was speaking to everyone. We all need to face up to the depth and seriousness of our spiritual condition so that we may grasp the wonder of God's provision in Christ for meeting that need forever. The threads of this truth are woven throughout this Gospel, leading us ultimately to the cross.

QUALIFIED AND AUTHORIZED TO SAVE

We cannot overestimate the enormous gravity of John's announcement concerning Jesus. No-one in Jewish society would dare make a claim like this without being absolutely and utterly persuaded that it was true. If such a claim were made but then proved false, it would spell the end of John's ministry, and also prove his loss of sanity. The fact that later, when he was in prison, John was overtaken by serious doubt about Jesus' identity (*Matt.* 11:1–15), underlines the extent to which the question of Jesus' identity weighed upon him.

Yet here on the banks of the Jordan, John made this statement and stood by it, defending it to himself as much as to the crowds who heard it (1:30–34). He wanted them to know that the claim was not merely his own idea or perception (1:31). It was divine revelation (1:33).

The Baptist explained the significance of his ministry – baptism depicting cleansing from sin – as a preparation. The water of the Jordan could not wash away the sin and guilt of any individual or nation, let alone of the world, but John's baptism paved the way for the coming of One whose blood could do just that (1:31). Perhaps some of his hearers wondered, 'But how could the blood of one mere man accomplish such atonement?' John's testimony provides the answer. It is because Jesus of Nazareth is no mere man. He is publicly attested by the Spirit of God at his baptism (1:33) and he is identified as and declared to be 'the Son of God' (1:34). John was ready to stake everything on that bold assertion.

John pointed to Jesus in this way because Jesus alone is qualified and authorized to bear away the sins of the world. He is qualified because he is not just a man; he is God. In the mystery of his person – God and man in one person – he has the capacity to bear and deal with the sin of the world through his sacrificial death. He is authorized because God himself has 'set his seal' of approval upon him' (6:27).

The testimony of John the Baptist confronts us still today with the burning question of our personal destiny. If our greatest need in this world and the next, is for the forgiveness of our sins and reconciliation to God, to whom can we turn and be assured that he has the qualifications and authorization to grant us such forgiveness? The gospel's answer is: Jesus Christ alone.

5

Overwhelmed by Jesus

The next day again John was standing with two of his disciples, *36* and he looked at Jesus as he walked by and said, "Behold, the Lamb of God!" *37* The two disciples heard him say this, and they followed Jesus. *38* Jesus turned and saw them following and said to them, "What are you seeking?" And they said to him, "Rabbi" (which means Teacher), "where are you staying?" *39* He said to them, "Come and you will see." So they came and saw where he was staying, and they stayed with him that day, for it was about the tenth hour. *40* One of the two who heard John speak and followed Jesus was Andrew, Simon Peter's brother. *41* He first found his own brother Simon and said to him, "We have found the Messiah" (which means Christ). *42* He brought him to Jesus. Jesus looked at him and said, "So you are Simon the son of John? You shall be called Cephas" (which means Peter).

43 The next day Jesus decided to go to Galilee. He found Philip and said to him, "Follow me." *44* Now Philip was from Bethsaida, the city of Andrew and Peter. *45* Philip found Nathanael and said to him, "We have found him of whom Moses in the Law and also the prophets wrote, Jesus of Nazareth, the son of Joseph." *46* Nathanael said to him, "Can anything good come out of Nazareth?" Philip said to him, "Come and see." *47* Jesus saw Nathanael coming towards him and said of him, "Behold, an Israelite indeed, in whom there is no deceit!" *48* Nathanael said to him, "How do you know me?" Jesus answered him, "Before Philip called you, when you were under the fig tree, I saw you." *49* Nathanael answered him, "Rabbi, you are the Son of God! You are the King of Israel!" *50* Jesus answered him, "Because I said to you, 'I saw you under the fig

tree,' do you believe? You will see greater things than these."
[51] And he said to him, "Truly, truly, I say to you, you will see
heaven opened, and the angels of God ascending and descending
on the Son of Man" (John 1:35–51).

John moves immediately from telling us who Jesus is to showing us what Jesus does. He recounts the remarkable story of how five men who would one day be apostles came to be converted. (It is more than likely that the one man not named in the account was actually John himself.) Several things are happening here.

John is giving us a snapshot of the most important work Jesus came to do on earth: seeking and saving the lost (*Luke* 19:10). We will be told many similar stories throughout this Gospel, but the record of five conversions in quick succession in this, the first chapter, powerfully underlines the main task that Jesus came to fulfil. Here is the paradigm of the ongoing work of Christ in the history of the human race. Jesus is in the business of changing lives.

At a slightly more subtle level, John is picking up again on that trace echo from Genesis. He clearly has an emphasis on the succession of days during which these events unfolded (1:29, 35, 43; 2:1). The days of Genesis in Christ's work of creation are shadowed by the sequence of days in his work of re-creation. Out of the realm of spiritual death that had engulfed creation under the domination of sin, the great Saviour-Creator starts bringing to life a new race of new creatures (see *2 Cor.* 5:17).

Yet again we are being made to look at Jesus as the One who, according to John's later testimony, 'makes all things new!' (*Rev.* 21:5). He is unique not only in terms of who he is, but also on account of all that he does.

The One Who is in Control

Notice the way in which Jesus takes control of the situation. Emerging out of the obscurity of the crowd who had come to John for baptism, he is suddenly centre-stage. The movement of the chapter has taken us from what Christ is in eternity, via his earthly herald John the Baptist, to what Christ is and does in history. Clear through it all is the fact that 'Jesus Christ is Lord!'

[26]

The one thing that empowers Jesus to emerge from the obscurity of his background and the obscurity of the crowd and to *take* control of events, is the fact that he supremely is the One who is *in* control.

We see it in the first instance in the way that Andrew and his companion – presumably John – became followers of Jesus (1.35–39). It would have been normal practice in those days for would-be disciples to choose a rabbi for themselves and then to ask if they might attach themselves to him. In this case it is the rabbi who takes the initiative. He quizzes the men about what they want and then he issues the invitation for them to follow him and spend the day with him. Jesus is the Saviour who actively seeks followers and does not wait passively for them to appear.

A second example is seen in Christ's first encounter with Simon, the brother of Andrew (1:41–42). This man who, as we learn from other references, was very much used to being in control, is confronted with a person who takes him in hand in a way he has never experienced before. So much is this so that in this very first meeting Jesus has the apparent audacity to tell Simon that before long his name will be changed to 'Peter'. The striking thing about this is that usually name-changes or the application of nicknames are the result of past behaviour or characteristics. However, in Simon's case, it was based not on what he was, but on what he would become when Jesus had finished with him.

The fact that we see a number of references in John's Apocalypse to Christ's conferring 'a new name' on his people (*Rev.* 2:17; 3:12), points us beyond the immediate change which takes place in a person's life at conversion to the ultimate change that will take place when Jesus Christ returns to complete his work.

The same magisterial authority of Christ also comes out in his dealings with Philip (1:43) and again with Nathanael (1:47). As these men meet with Jesus they are immediately confronted by his overwhelming power and authority.

THE ONE WHO PROBES THE HUMAN HEART

As we reflect more closely on this facet of Jesus' character, we discover that his power is in no sense intimidating as can so easily be the case with someone who simply throws his weight around. Jesus exerts his authority in a gentle, loving and disarming fashion. He does not come as an over-bearing adversary but as a friend.

As the two disciples of John approach Jesus, he asks the question, 'What are you seeking?' (1:38). It is a loaded question. It marks the difference between merely dabbling in religion and genuinely seeking to meet with God. Because of their attachment to John the Baptist, it is evident that these men had already thought deeply about what was involved in meeting with God, but when God himself confronts them, they are stopped in their tracks. Have they any idea of what will lie ahead if they proceed down this road?

This question, 'What are you seeking?' is one that Jesus poses repeatedly in different forms throughout his ministry and in his ongoing work in the lives of his people. We are not free simply to play at being followers of Jesus. To be a disciple involves a deep desire of heart to know God and to follow in his ways.

Christ's discernment is seen again in the way he handles his encounter with Peter. John says, 'Jesus *looked* at him and said . . .' (1:42). Calvin comments: 'Christ sees in a way which is not human.' He sees Simon not just in terms of what he is, but in terms of what he will be. Jesus is able to see beyond the image and facade we construct around our lives for the benefit of others. He sees us as we really are and confronts us with ourselves.

When Jesus first meets Nathanael he greets him in a somewhat unusual manner: 'Behold, an Israelite indeed, in whom there is no deceit' (1:47). Jesus is able to see this man. It seems that what Jesus saw in Nathanael was the fact that he was a genuine believer, in the Old Testament sense of the word. This is the reason for his extravagant recognition and joyful acceptance of Jesus as the Messiah (1:49).

To meet Jesus is to meet the one who knows us through and through, to whom we need not (and dare not) pretend, and in whom we can place our complete trust and confidence. We are happy to place our confidence in a physician who knows us and understands our physical condition, so we trust in Jesus – the Physician of our souls – who knows completely our spiritual state.

THE ONE WHO CAPTIVATES LIVES

Jesus made an immediate, profound impression upon Andrew and his friend, because John records the fact that 'it was about the tenth hour' (1:39). Just as people remember exactly at what time and under what circumstances they heard the news of J.F. Kennedy's assassination, or of the death of Princess Diana, so this moment of history was etched upon the consciousness of these disciples of Jesus. He had utterly captivated them in that first close encounter.

The overwhelming impression made by Jesus upon those he first met is reflected in the extraordinary array of titles accorded to this stranger from Galilee in the space of a handful of verses. He is the 'Lamb of God' (1:36), 'Rabbi' (1:38), 'the Messiah' (1:41), the One of whom Moses and the prophets had written (1:45), 'Son of God' and 'King of Israel' (1:49) and finally, 'Son of Man' (1:51). All of these were epithets impregnated with Old Testament expectation of the coming Saviour whom God had promised. Even though the full meaning of Christ's identity would not become clear for another eighteen months or so, at the time of Peter's famous confession at Caesarea Philippi (*Matt.* 16:18), these men became sufficiently aware of Jesus' uniqueness to set him apart from any other religious leader they had ever encountered.

The crucial test of how we have been affected by people is the way we describe them to others. The less sure we are, the less we will say for fear of embarrassment. Notice, then, that the immediate response of Andrew is to bring his brother to Jesus (1:41–43), and Philip to bring Nathanael (1:45). It was proof that the Saviour had already made a deep impact on their lives that they were eager to tell others of him.

THE ONE WHO CALLS PEOPLE TO FAITH

Perhaps the most significant thing of all about these early glimpses of Jesus seen in this chapter is that he calls people to trust in him. In the overall thrust of the Gospel as a whole, John wants us to realize that it is not enough to know *about* Jesus, we need to *know him* through a real and living faith-relationship.

Jesus has no qualms about being put to the test in order to verify his claims or to prove whether he is indeed worthy of the confidence of his followers. So, when Andrew and John quiz him out of curiosity (1:38), Jesus simply says, 'Come and you will see!' (1:39). Again, as he set out for Galilee on the following day, he finds Philip and says, 'Follow me' (1:43). He does not call for a blind leap of faith from his disciples, quite the opposite. Far from being a 'leap in the dark', faith in Jesus Christ is in reality a leap into the light. He wants us to know who it is that we are trusting and why it is that placing confidence in him is the most sensible thing a person can ever do in life.

The initial response of faith brings the individual into a relationship with Christ that progresses and grows towards an ever-increasing confirmation. So Jesus, after Nathanael had believed, promises him, 'Truly, truly, I say to you, you will see heaven open, and the angels of God ascending and descending on the Son of Man' (1:51). Was John present when Jesus spoke those words? He may well have been, because he repeats them almost verbatim at a time in his own life, decades later, when his faith had been tested to the extreme (*Rev.* 19:11). The Christ who called Nathanael to follow him by faith proved himself faithful to the promises he had made, not only those to Nathanael, but all his promises to all his children.

The words spoken by the prophet Isaiah find their ultimate fulfilment in relation to Jesus: 'Whoever believes will not be in haste' (*Isa.* 28:16), or, as Paul renders it, 'will not be put to shame' (*Rom.* 10:11).

6

A Wedding with a Difference

On the third day there was a wedding at Cana in Galilee, and the mother of Jesus was there. ² Jesus also was invited to the wedding with his disciples. ³ When the wine ran out, the mother of Jesus said to him, "They have no wine." ⁴ And Jesus said to her, "Woman, what does this have to do with me? My hour has not yet come." ⁵ His mother said to the servants, "Do whatever he tells you."

⁶ Now there were six stone water jars there for the Jewish rites of purification, each holding twenty or thirty gallons. ⁷ Jesus said to the servants, "Fill the jars with water." And they filled them up to the brim. ⁸ And he said to them, "Now draw some out and take it to the master of the feast." So they took it. ⁹ When the master of the feast tasted the water now become wine, and did not know where it came from (though the servants who had drawn the water knew), the master of the feast called the bridegroom ¹⁰ and said to him, "Everyone serves the good wine first, and when people have drunk freely, then the poor wine. But you have kept the good wine until now." ¹¹ This, the first of his signs, Jesus did at Cana in Galilee, and manifested his glory. And his disciples believed in him (John 2:1–11).

The account of Jesus changing water into wine at the wedding in Cana of Galilee is a popular choice of text for ministers looking for something to preach on at wedding services. The thrust of such sermons usually runs along the lines of needing Jesus at the centre of a marriage if it is to flourish, or needing his presence at a wedding in order for it to be truly blessed. This sort of counsel is undoubtedly wise and true, but it is debatable whether John intended this passage to be read that way.

The Gospels in general, and John's Gospel in particular, are not random collections of spiritual thoughts about different aspects of life. Rather, they are cogent accounts of the life and work of Jesus Christ. All their details are designed to work together in concert to bring us to a deeper understanding of his significance in the wider flow of biblical revelation.

We have already noted the distinctive approach adopted by John as he sets down his record of the Christ. From the very outset he makes it clear that he wants his readers to reflect on what he is saying. In a way, his is a thinking man's Gospel. That is, the more a person thinks about what John says, the more he or she will appreciate how much is being said about Jesus. There is simply so much to know about him. This characteristic is found again in the account of this first miracle.

It is worth noting a few general things about John's treatment of miracles before we consider the detail of the one recorded in this passage. Out of the thirty-five miracles recorded in the Gospels as a whole, John selects just seven for his account. Clearly he wants to isolate a few and consider them more closely than do his fellow evangelists. All miracles have a shared significance in that they point to the deity of the Christ who performed them, and they are all examples of the intrusion of the powers of the age to come into this present age – foretastes of heaven. However, each miracle has its own unique contribution to make to our understanding of Christ and his saving work.

John brings out the unique meaning and significance of the miracles by placing them alongside related discourses. So, for example, the feeding of the five thousand (6:1–15) is linked with the 'Bread of Life' discourse (6:25-59); the raising of Lazarus (11:1–44) is recorded together with the 'Resurrection and the Life' remarks to the bereaved family (11:21–27). This is further borne out by the word John uses consistently to describe these events, namely, 'signs' (2:11). They are miracles and they are wonders – two other words that describe the same phenomena – but John wants us to realize they are also 'signs.' They are supernatural events filled with supernatural significance. The importance of all this is realized when we consider the fact that it is all too easy to feel like mere spectators when we read of the miracles of Jesus. We consider them as events that happened only when Jesus was on the earth and that they involved only a few privileged witnesses. John wants us to know that they touch the lives of all who read of them and all who embrace the Christ who made them happen.

In John's Gospel therefore, the clues for understanding a miracle are often found in the precise way in which it is described and in the commentary that is discreetly woven throughout the description. Several clues stand out in this passage.

A Clue about the Love and Grace of Jesus Christ

The striking thing about this first miracle of Jesus is the very unstriking place in which it was performed! Cana in Galilee is a place that only John mentions. It was an obscure rural community in a relatively obscure part of Palestine. That in itself may not say very much, but when we remember that John's introduction to Jesus Christ took us to the infinite heights of the eternal glory where he belongs, it is extremely significant that such a person from heaven should be so willing to mingle with such ordinary and insignificant people on earth!

This amazing condescension speaks volumes about the nature of the grace and love that lie behind it. Jesus is more than willing to approach ordinary people with their everyday need (a need which is often much deeper than people realize) and lovingly meet that need by his grace and power.

This is true not just for the nameless 'nobodies' who were there in Cana on that day, but also for all the 'nobodies' all over the world who read of this Jesus and discover who he is and what he came to do. The love of the Father was not the only motivation that brought about the entry of the Son into our world (3:16); the Son's own love was just as powerful.

A Clue about the Reason Jesus Came

What would Jesus do for people when he came into the world? What is the ultimate purpose that lies behind his coming? In many ways that was the burning question for the Jews as they read their Scriptures all through the Old Testament period. They were well aware of God's promise to send a deliverer, but they were not so sure of the supreme reason for his coming. The expectation of many Jews was of a Messiah who would come to patch up the symptoms of life's problems, either by establishing a new political order, or simply by improving the circumstances of life. This deficient expectation may well be the reason for Jesus' apparent reluctance, here (and elsewhere), to perform a miracle too hastily (2:4). He did not want to bolster a false understanding of the reason for Messiah's coming.

In a firm, but gentle rebuke to his mother, Jesus says, 'My hour has not yet come.' This is the first of a number of occasions when Jesus uses this, or a similar expression and it speaks of a moment of destiny towards which Jesus was travelling. There would be many highlights in Jesus' public life and ministry – moments which would be significant and which people would remember. But Jesus did not want these many highlights to eclipse in any way the ultimate highlight: the supreme reason for his coming into the world.

So at this striking moment when the veil over his identity is first drawn aside in a remarkable and public way, Jesus wants to emphasize that this is not the supreme event that people were waiting for. Incredible as it was (for it is very unlikely that even Mary expected Jesus to perform a *miracle* in this crisis) the moment was nothing in comparison to that infinitely greater miracle that would take place on Calvary.

This has a crucial bearing on every reader of the Gospels. Too often people have been side-tracked by the good things that Jesus said and did, and have missed completely the supreme reason for his mission: the 'hour' for which he came.

A CLUE ABOUT THE JOY THAT JESUS BRINGS

When Jesus performed this miracle, an extraordinary thrill, as well as a wave of relief, must have swept through the little band of helpers who had organized the wedding that day. The stark contrast between water and wine said it all. It marked the difference between the mundane and the exquisite. Therein lies the next clue to the significance of this event.

In a prophecy made seven hundred years before, concerning the Messiah and the kind of kingdom he would usher in, Isaiah says,

> On this mountain the LORD of hosts will make for all peoples
>   a feast of rich food full of marrow,
>   of aged wine well refined (*Isa.* 25:6).

The astonishment of the master of the banquet at the best wine being saved till last (2:10) is a commentary, not on the days of the feast, but on the history of the world! God in his dealings with the human race and with his people, had saved the best wine until now – the time when he sent his Son and ushered in his kingdom.

The joy and gladness of God's salvation foretold by the prophet (*Isa.* 25:9) – so obviously linked to the symbolism of wine and feasting – would be found ultimately in Jesus Christ and in the salvation he would bring. So as Jesus begins his earthly ministry, he symbolically announces that the Feast of the Kingdom age has begun. As he changes water into wine he shows that the joy of his salvation has arrived. (The point is emphasized all the more by the passing remark that the water jars were those used by the Jews for 'rites of purification' (2:6) – ritual was giving way to reality!)

The thrill of God's good news in Jesus Christ is bound up with the joy of God's salvation – found uniquely in Jesus Christ his Son.

A CLUE ABOUT THE WAY THAT JESUS CHANGES LIVES

One final detail that throws light upon this event in terms of its abiding significance, is found in what Mary says to the servants, 'Do whatever he tells you' (2:5). Even though he was about to issue an instruction that appeared to be unreasonable – even ridiculous – they were to trust him and act upon all that he said. Their faith was to be rewarded and to their astonishment the wisdom of Jesus would be proved true. The outcome of events would exceed their wildest dreams.

The way that Jesus transformed a wedding party that day provides us with a glimpse of how he transforms lives every day. The gulf between the mess we are in and the new life he can give is spanned by the instructions he issues in the gospel and our response to them. 'What must I do to be saved?' asked a suicidal jailer almost ten years later – 'Believe in the Lord Jesus and you will be saved' replied the apostles (*Acts* 16:30–31). Take him at his word, do all that he tells you to do and your life will be transformed. It was true at the wedding in Cana, it was true also for the jailer in Philippi, and it can be true for you and me as well.

7

Ritual or Reality?

After this he went down to Capernaum, with his mother and his brothers and his disciples, and they stayed there for a few days.
13 The Passover of the Jews was at hand, and Jesus went up to Jerusalem. 14 In the temple he found those who were selling oxen and sheep and pigeons, and the money-changers sitting there. 15 And making a whip of cords, he drove them all out of the temple, with the sheep and oxen. And he poured out the coins of the money-changers and overturned their tables. 16 And he told those who sold the pigeons, "Take these things away; do not make my Father's house a house of trade." 17 His disciples remembered that it was written, "Zeal for your house will consume me."
18 So the Jews said to him, "What sign do you show us for doing these things?" 19 Jesus answered them, "Destroy this temple, and in three days I will raise it up." 20 The Jews then said, "It has taken forty-six years to build this temple, and will you raise it up in three days?" 21 But he was speaking about the temple of his body. 22 When therefore he was raised from the dead, his disciples remembered that he had said this, and they believed the Scripture and the word that Jesus had spoken.
23 Now when he was in Jerusalem at the Passover Feast, many believed in his name when they saw the signs that he was doing. 24 But Jesus on his part did not entrust himself to them, because he knew all people 25 and needed no one to bear witness about man, for he himself knew what was in man (John 2:12–25).

The veiled allusion in Jesus' first miracle to the empty condition of Jewish religion (2:6) gives way to a head-on confrontation between Jesus and the Jews whose lives were wrapped up in ritual. In these events Jesus lays down a marker to distinguish between mere ritual and real religion.

The scene changes radically: from Cana to the capital. The company changes also: from insignificant villagers to people who were involved in the daily life of the Temple. And the mood changes: from celebration to confrontation. All of this is indicative of the power and authority vested in this hitherto unknown figure from Galilee. He sweeps into the lives of these unsuspecting people at the heart of Jewish religion in a way that challenges all that they are and all that they stand for. In much the same way, Jesus comes today with an authority that can neither be ignored nor resisted.

At the beginning of his public ministry, Jesus draws attention to the dangers that can arise due to religion in people's lives, as well as the danger due to irreligion. At first sight, nothing seems more safe and commendable in spiritual terms than being religious. So often such people are admired and respected and are assumed to be the kind of people that God will accept. Jesus does not see it that way. He knows that even the best of spiritual truths and practices can become a tool in the devil's hand to deceive and divert people away from the heart of true religion. The senior devil in C. S. Lewis' famous *Screwtape Letters* informs his junior counterpart, Wormwood, that, 'One of our greatest allies [in the war against true Christians] is the church itself!' There is nothing more dangerous spiritually than the false sense of security that comes from being in a religious environment. Paul soberly warns Timothy that in the last days there will be people who have a form of godliness, but have denied its power (*2 Tim.* 3:5) – their religion has shape, but no substance.

These are the kind of people Jesus encounters during one of the highpoints of the Jewish religious year, the Feast of Passover. Several crucial things begin to crystallise in the exchanges that follow.

A CHALLENGE TO THE HEART OF GENUINE WORSHIP

The first exchange that John records took place in the Temple precincts – probably in the outer court of the Gentiles. Since the miracle in Cana, Jesus had gone down to Capernaum on the shores of lake Galilee along with his mother, half-brothers and his little band of disciples (2:12). It was the time of year when the Passover – the major Jewish feast of the year – was due to take place, so their stay by the lake was short-lived and they made the journey 'up to Jerusalem' (2:13). John uses the traditional Jewish expression to describe the direction of any journey to the spiritual capital of the Jewish world: it was always 'up', no matter what the geography of the journey happened to be. This little detail is a piece in the jig-saw that helps us to understand the mindset of the religious world into which Jesus came: a world that Jesus meets head-on and is in immediate conflict with as soon as he enters the Temple precincts (12:14).

This was not Jesus' first visit to Jerusalem or to the Passover festival; he had seen all this before. The difference this time was that he was entering Jerusalem and attending the Feast in a public capacity. He had stepped out of the shadows in which he had lived for some thirty years and now was commencing his public mission and ministry. He was showing the world the reason why he had come into the world.

It should neither surprise nor unduly disturb us that John describes an event at the beginning of Jesus' ministry that looks remarkably similar to one the other Gospel writers describe as having taken place near the end of his public ministry (*Matt.* 21:12–17, *Mark* 11:15–18, *Luke* 19:45–46). Some commentators have assumed that only one such incident could have occurred and that the Gospels simply disagree over when it happened. But there is no solid reason against believing that two quite distinct events are in view. Indeed, given the flow of logic that we have already noted in John's Gospel, it makes perfect sense that John should pick up on the fact that Jesus stepped on to the public stage in Jerusalem in this fashion. He came to challenge sin, not only in its most obvious forms, but also in its most dangerous forms: disguised as the worship of the true and living God.

Jesus enters the Temple area and is confronted by a veritable street market – stall-holders, money-changers, and the sounds and smells of all their wares filling the ears and nostrils of the crowds that were milling around. Jesus is outraged – not because these people's actions were inherently wrong, but because they did not belong in a place that was set apart for the worship of God. Birds and animals were needed for sacrifice; money had to be changed for purchases and for the payment of Temple tax. But all this activity belonged outside, not inside the House of God!

The place designated for the worship of God had been distorted into a precinct for the gratification of man. The focus was all wrong. It was not the Creator who was at the centre of his own holy Temple, it was his creatures. The place where, more than anywhere else, worshippers were meant to 'be still and know that I am God' (*Psa.* 46:10), was filled with the hubbub of a fallen world. The holy place had become polluted by activities that revolved around human interest and earthly gain. Instead of the temple being a place where people could spiritually step out of this world and into God's world, it had turned into a place where God's world had been invaded by the world of man.

Jesus responds with obvious anger. He drives away the animals and overturns the tables of the merchants and money-changers (2:15–16). His actions remind the disciples of a verse from the Psalms which speaks about consuming passion for the house of God (2:17, see also *Psa.* 69:9). The holy place set apart to be the heart of Old Testament worship and the particular Feast that was designated to celebrate the heart of God's deliverance of his people, must not be desecrated by superficiality.

True worship begins in the heart. It is not a matter of 'doing the right things', but rather of being in the right relationship. What was true of Israel in Isaiah's day was true also in Jesus' day, and is true for many who claim to belong to God in every generation: 'This people . . . honours me with their lips, while their hearts are far from me!' (*Isa.* 29:13). Jesus challenges everyone to see that. Do we come to worship God to pacify our consciences, or to satisfy our souls?

A CHALLENGE TO THE POSTURE OF FAITH IN WORSHIP

Not surprisingly, Jesus' action provokes a reaction from the Jews (2:18–22). Their peace had been disturbed. The 'normality' of practices that had become established and accepted among them for generations had been challenged and they were not pleased.

However, the way they respond to Jesus shows that they realize this is not some deranged maniac that they are dealing with – someone who could be arrested by the Temple guards and be removed from the scene without any further thought. They ask him to produce his credentials (2:18). Far from seeing him as a religious crank, they allow for the very real possibility that he might be a prophet, and if he was, then he ought to be able to prove it.

There was nothing wrong with what they wanted to know – God had made it clear in the Old Testament that a person's claim to be a prophet had to be tested to see if it was genuine (*Deut.* 18:17–22) – but there was something wrong with the attitude they displayed.

They were arrogant and demanding in the way they addressed Jesus. Their attitude betrayed the kind of proud spirit and hard heart to which God is implacably opposed (1 Pet. 5:5). It was an attitude that is synonymous with the very essence of sin: a spirit that rises up against God and dares to challenge him to his face.

It is very easy to point the finger at what we regard as expressions of arrogance: atheism, humanism and rationalism, but Jesus is faced with it in Judaism! The very people who were supposed to be God's people had their hearts set against the God they claimed to worship.

Jesus exposes the true posture of their soul when he responds, '*You* will destroy this temple and *I* will raise it again in three days' (2:19, translated literally). In a single breath he sums up where their attitude and action will lead and where his will lead. Their hearts are set against God and are bent on dethroning him even in his own holy place.

True worship begins in the hidden recesses of the soul with a humble posture that acknowledges both God and his Word and is prepared to wait upon him.

A CHALLENGE TO THE FOCUS OF FAITH IN WORSHIP

John adds a postscript to these exchanges in Jerusalem that is both unusual and unsettling. During the days of the feast, Jesus apparently performed a number of miracles and, in response, many who saw what he was doing 'believed in his name' (2:23). However, 'Jesus on his part did not entrust himself to them' (2:24). Was this a rash reaction on Jesus' part?

John makes it clear that it was not. Jesus was not setting out to win the admiration of the crowds, as if the success of his work depended on attracting mass popular support. Even though his own disciples may well have been saying, 'Isn't this great!', and may have tried to commend the crowd's faith in him, Jesus did not need to hear the commendation of fallen man by other fallen men (2:25). As ever, Jesus 'knew what was in man' (2:25). In the same way that he knew the true heart of Nathanael (1:47–49) – despite Nathanael's scepticism about Jesus – so here Jesus sees through the apparent enthusiasm of these would-be followers and perceives that it was only skin-deep.

As was to happen repeatedly in his public ministry, the crowds were more interested in the miracles than they were in the Messiah (see 6:26). Such faith is misplaced.

Jesus makes it clear all the way through his ministry that our greatest need is to recognize exactly who he is and what it was he ultimately came to do. Great as the trappings of his glory and majesty and power may be, it is not the trappings that we trust, but the One to whom they belong: Jesus Christ, the Son of God and the Saviour of sinners!

8

Your Need Is Greater Than You Think

Now there was a man of the Pharisees named Nicodemus, a ruler of the Jews. ² This man came to Jesus by night and said to him, "Rabbi, we know that you are a teacher come from God, for no one can do these signs that you do unless God is with him." ³ Jesus answered him, "Truly, truly, I say to you, unless one is born again he cannot see the kingdom of God." ⁴ Nicodemus said to him, "How can a man be born when he is old? Can he enter a second time into his mother's womb and be born?" ⁵ Jesus answered, "Truly, truly, I say to you, unless one is born of water and the Spirit, he cannot enter the kingdom of God. ⁶ That which is born of the flesh is flesh, and that which is born of the Spirit is spirit. ⁷ Do not marvel that I said to you, 'You must be born again.' ⁸ The wind blows where it wishes, and you hear its sound, but you do not know where it comes from or where it goes. So it is with everyone who is born of the Spirit."

⁹ Nicodemus said to him, "How can these things be?" ¹⁰ Jesus answered him, "Are you the teacher of Israel and yet you do not understand these things? ¹¹ Truly, truly, I say to you, we speak of what we know, and bear witness to what we have seen, but you do not receive our testimony. ¹² If I have told you earthly things and you do not believe, how can you believe if I tell you heavenly things? ¹³ No one has ascended into heaven except him who descended from heaven, the Son of Man. ¹⁴ And as Moses lifted up the serpent in the wilderness, so must the Son of Man be lifted up, ¹⁵ that whoever believes in him may have eternal life" (John 3:1–15).

Like a master weaver, John is very careful in his choice of the threads to be woven in to his tapestry – this tapestry which will tell us who Jesus is and what exactly he came to do. The themes that had been brought to the fore in a negative way in the encounter with the crowds in Jerusalem are now to be explored in a very positive and personal way. This is done by means of a case-study of a man who embodied the kind of misguided religion that Jesus had been denouncing, but whose life was about to be changed by God.

The fact that there is a very definite link between the end of the previous chapter and the beginning of this one is clear from the connecting word 'And' in the original (translated 'Now' in the ESV). It leads us into a sequence of encounters with a number of different people by means of which Jesus reveals his perfect knowledge of the human heart. We are shown how this same Jesus is able to meet and deal with people in all kinds of circumstances – his salvation is for all.

The first of these encounters recorded by John is significant because it is with a person with whom we would least expect Jesus to begin: a Jewish spiritual leader, Nicodemus. He was not only a Pharisee (a member of a religious grouping which was renowned for its concern for theological orthodoxy and moral rectitude) but also a member of the Jewish ruling council. To all outward appearances he was a man of great spiritual standing, yet by probing more deeply Jesus exposed an underlying need that he alone could meet. It is an education in itself to follow through Christ's handling of this man and of his need.

HE QUESTIONED HIS CERTAINTY

It is often assumed that Nicodemus came to Jesus with a question, but that is not the case. He came with a statement – a statement that reveals the kind of confidence found so often in the spiritually self-assured. He says, 'We know you are a teacher who has come from God' (3:2). Jesus immediately responds with a counter-statement that challenges the whole foundation of this man's certainty, and his very standing before God (3:3). A man regarded as a leading spiritual authority on earth is challenged by the One who comes with true authority from heaven!

As the Apostle Paul was to indicate later, coming to true faith is not only a matter of our laying hold of Christ, but of his laying hold of us (*Phil.* 3:12). He stops people in their tracks and challenges their most basic spiritual assumptions. Do we really know as much as we think we do? Are we really able to understand those issues that relate to God and to salvation? The Bible's answer is 'No', because in our natural spiritual condition we are not able to understand the things of God since they are 'spiritually discerned' (*1 Cor.* 2:14).

Nicodemus' starting point was wrong. He thought he had the wherewithal in himself and his own faculties to grasp these spiritual realities; but he did not, and so his whole understanding of the life of faith was flawed. He was relying on spiritual faculties that were providing false information. When Jesus begins to deal with people, he starts by challenging them on what they think they know and shows them their need of listening to him. The fact that Nicodemus came to Jesus 'by night' (3:1) may be more than just accidental detail, but rather an indication of the moral and spiritual darkness of his soul.

HE CONFRONTED HIS EXPERIENCE

There is a profound connection between knowledge and experience. The Wisdom of the Old Testament rightly teaches, 'As [a man] thinks within himself, so he is' (*Prov.* 23:7, NASB). The way we think shapes and moulds us into the kind of person we become.

So as Jesus presses the point with Nicodemus, he quickly moves from the realm of his understanding to that of his actual experience of life. As he does so, he hits him in the solar plexus of his soul! 'Unless one is born again he cannot see the kingdom of God' (3:3), and, 'Unless one is born of water and of the Spirit he cannot enter the kingdom of God' (3:5). Despite Nicodemus' impressive aura of spiritual experience and stature, Jesus confronts him with the fact that in reality they were non-existent.

As Jesus exposed this man's particular need, he also shifts the focus towards all men by slipping into a plural form, '*You* (plural) must be born again' (3:7). Here is a universal Bible truth: if anyone is to experience life in God's kingdom, then they must be born again. Alluding to the prophecy of Ezekiel that anticipates the inauguration of the New Covenant between God and his people (*Ezek.* 36:26), Jesus shows that true spiritual experience originates with the grace of God and not with the religion of men.

HE CHALLENGED HIS UNDERSTANDING

Jesus begins to probe Nicodemus more deeply, and it becomes clear that the latter's whole understanding of God and his kingdom is questionable. The Pharisee's initial confidence changes to bewilderment and his self-confidence begins to falter.

As Nicodemus wrestles with the concept of being born again it is plain that he cannot rise above the literal notion of re-entering his mother's womb and experiencing the process of birth all over again (3:4). He simply could not understand what Jesus was saying to him, so Jesus therefore spells it out in the simplest of terms. He takes him by the hand, so to speak, and emphasizes to him three things that he needs to grasp if he is ever going to enter this unique life that God alone can give. He needs to grasp our true state as fallen human beings – we are a race with a self-perpetuating problem. 'That which is born of the flesh is flesh, and that which is born of the Spirit is spirit' (3:6). John's main use of the word 'flesh' is to denote humanity in rebellion against God, and the word 'spirit' to denote a heart with new life from God. The point is simple: left to our own devices, we cannot rise above what we are as a race by nature.

Secondly, Nicodemus – and we too – must understand that we have a twofold need before God: the need of a new standing before him and of a new life from him. The background to this, as we have noted already, is the promise of a new covenant relationship between God and his people – one which would meet both of these needs – as foretold by Ezekiel (*Ezek.* 36:25-27). Or, put in other words, the need of God's pardon and God's power.

The third great need that Jesus impresses upon Nicodemus is that of God's free grace to work in his life. He uses the wind as an illustration of something which is there, but which is not at the beck and call of man (3:8). The subtlety of this image could hardly have been lost on this seasoned teacher of the Bible since, in their language, the word for 'wind' and 'Spirit' was the same. As the wind is free and sovereign, so also is the Spirit of God in the workings of his saving grace. Religion cannot manipulate God, it can only respond to him.

As God begins to work in people's lives, he probes deeply into our understanding of ourselves and reveals our spiritual needs to us. He turns our own natural understanding of things on its head.

He Broadened His Horizons

By this stage in the conversation, a different attitude has overtaken the man who came to Jesus by night. He now knows himself to be someone who has nothing to give, but is in need of receiving everything. He no longer behaves as if he was Christ's equal, but as a pupil willing to be taught by him. This is the posture of a soul on the threshold of salvation.

As Nicodemus listens, Jesus broadens his spiritual horizons so as to see things he had never realized before. He does so in two ways. First of all, he shows that salvation does not have to do with what man can do for God, but with what God provides for man.

Nicodemus responds to Jesus by asking, 'How can these things be?' (3:9). It is the question of a man who is genuinely perplexed by spiritual truths that he had never encountered before. Here was a person who had been used to thinking instinctively in terms of himself and his own resources, yet Jesus was taking him beyond the limits of his capabilities. This again is something that must happen whenever God begins the work of saving grace in a person's heart. He must bring home to him the fact that the answer to life's deepest need does not come from within, but from without.

So Jesus takes Nicodemus far beyond the limits of human resources and of what is available in this finite fallen world; he takes him into the realm of heaven itself (3:12–13). He speaks somewhat cryptically of 'the Son of Man' as the One who has come from heaven and is therefore able to reveal truth from heaven to people on earth. It would soon become clear that this phrase 'the Son of Man' was a reference to Jesus himself. He alone is able to bring heavenly truth into the world and into our lives. The uncertainty that is exposed in Nicodemus is met by the overwhelming certainty that is found in Jesus.

He Called for His Response

By the end of the conversation, the scope of Jesus' words has moved beyond the personal need of one man to the universal need of all men everywhere: the need of true redemption. His focus now centres on God's provision for meeting that need and the response he requires for it to be experienced.

Jesus uses an illustration that would have been familiar to Nicodemus as an Old Testament scholar. He refers to an incident in the wilderness wanderings of the people of Israel under Moses when God sent a plague of snakes among them, and then provided a miraculous cure for those who had been bitten (*Num.* 21:4–9). Moses was to set up a bronze snake on a pole in the camp and anyone who simply looked at that snake – trusting the promise God had made – would be healed (3:14). In the same way, argued Jesus, the Son of Man had to be lifted up and all who would look to him in faith would likewise be healed (3:14–15).

Jesus was pointing forward to the climax of his earthly ministry when he would be literally 'lifted up' when nailed to a Roman cross and put to death. He was alerting Nicodemus (and all readers of this Gospel) to the fact that God's salvation is received by trusting in him as the crucified Saviour.

It is interesting that we hear almost nothing else about Nicodemus until the day that Jesus' prediction about his death was fulfilled. It was on that day when this Pharisee stood in the crowd and watched the execution of the Man he had met under the cover of darkness, that for the first time he openly declared his faith in him. It was only at the cross that everything began to make sense and he really understood that his need was infinitely greater than he had ever imagined.

9

Getting to Grips with Grace

For God so loved the world, that he gave his only Son, that whoever believes in him should not perish but have eternal life. [17] For God did not send his Son into the world to condemn the world, but in order that the world might be saved through him. [18] Whoever believes in him is not condemned, but whoever does not believe is condemned already, because he has not believed in the name of the only Son of God. [19] And this is the judgement: the light has come into the world, and people loved the darkness rather than the light because their deeds were evil. [20] For everyone who does wicked things hates the light and does not come to the light, lest his deeds should be exposed. [21] But whoever does what is true comes to the light, so that it may be clearly seen that his deeds have been carried out in God (John 3:16–21).

Although many translations assume these verses continue the words of Jesus, it seems more likely that they form John's own evangelistic commentary on his Lord's teaching that 'everyone who believes may have eternal life'. Since part of his purpose in writing the Gospel is to point his readers to faith in Jesus Christ (20:31), John shows how Jesus' teaching applies not only to Nicodemus ('you' 3:3, 5, 8, 11, 12), but to 'whoever believes' (3:16, 17, 18). At one level he is simply marvelling at the wonder of Jesus' words – here was a salvation that went far beyond the wildest dreams of even the most pious Jew. At another level he is taking what Jesus said to one person and demonstrating its universal application to all kinds of people everywhere. The apostle is taking us into the sheer wonder of God's grace and showing that everyone – not just Nicodemus – needs to get to grips with what it means for life and destiny. He spells it out in logical sequence.

THE REASON

In many ways Jesus' last word to Nicodemus about the Son of Man being 'lifted up' (3:15), must have puzzled him deeply. The very thought of God's special servant being treated in that way was more than he could grasp. Throughout the history of the church Calvary has always been an enigma. Why did the sinless Son of God have to suffer in such a way? John supplies the answer, and his answer is more staggering even than the brutalities of the cross. In what must be the best known words of Scripture, John says, 'For God so loved the world that he gave his only Son, that whoever believes in him should not perish but have eternal life' (3:16). Here is the reason for the sufferings that Jesus had to endure: the indescribable love of God. The verse turns on the little word 'so' – the fact that God's love was of such an order that it led him to do these things. Martin Luther rightly says, 'This is the Bible in miniature!'

The love of God is staggering because of whom it embraces: 'God so loved the *world*.' Love is measured in terms of whom it reaches. It is one thing to love family and friends, but something altogether different to reach out to strangers and outcasts. So it is with the love of God. For Jewish readers to hear that God loved 'the world' would make them think again. They were quite at ease with the thought of God loving Israel, but when it came to Gentiles and pagans, that was a different matter. Yet here is John telling us that God loves the 'world' – a race and creation in rebellion against him – and his love is so great that he sends his own Son to die to bring salvation.

Sometimes Christians become confused over the language John uses in this verse. If Jesus died for 'the world', does this imply that 'the world' (that is, every single individual) will be saved? John is not here thinking about the world in its totality but in its diversity and sinfulness. In other words, 'the world' should be taken to mean 'people from every tribe and nation, not just Jews'. By contrast, Nicodemus probably viewed Gentiles as 'dogs' and believed that the work of the coming Messiah would be for Jews only and not for them.

We can only begin to appreciate the beauty of God's love when we grasp something of the ugliness of our sin. God's love embraces, not those who are his friends, but those who are his enemies.

The wonder of the divine love is seen also in what it does. Love is more than a feeling, or an attitude, it is an action. It is measured by what we do for people. When we apply this criterion to God's love we are overwhelmed by its extravagance. God takes the Son with whom he has enjoyed a unique and eternal relationship and he gives him for the salvation of sinners. He is 'his only Son', or, as older translations put, 'his only begotten Son'. John simply wants to convey the uniqueness of the relationship that in turn demonstrates the cost of God's love in action. He gave the one who was most precious to him. He gave him, not merely *to* the world in incarnation, but *for* the world in crucifixion!

What results is a guarantee of true deliverance. As Frances Jane Van Alstyne expressed it:

> *The vilest offender who truly believes,*
> *That moment from Jesus a pardon receives.*

This loving act of God the Father expressed through the loving obedience of God the Son achieved the deliverance promised from the beginning of time (*Gen.* 3:15). God's great love is the reason that lies behind his great salvation.

THE PROMISE

The intent of God's love is restated in the next two verses in the form of a statement and a promise. In the statement John says, 'For God did not send his Son into the world to condemn the world, but in order that the world might be saved through him' (3:17). The primary purpose of Christ's coming in the incarnation was to bring redemption to a fallen race. Though it is true that Jesus, at the end of the age, will be the Judge of all the world (see 5:22, 27), yet the main purpose of his coming was to be the supreme expression of God's saving grace.

The promise that flows from this is, 'Whoever believes in him is not condemned' (3:17). Whoever puts their trust in Jesus Christ – whatever their race, background, or personal history – has the assurance of pardon from God. Even though they deserve to be condemned for their sin and guilt, they are not condemned. Instead, Christ, the Son of Man lifted up, promises salvation for them.

Here is the gospel in all its simplicity – the good news that there is forgiveness from God for all who put their faith in his Son. There is nothing a person can hear more precious than this.

THE THREAT

It is always the case that in his dealings with the human race in general God issues the promise of a blessing for those who believe in him and the threat of a curse for those who choose to reject. It does not surprise us, then, to see that the promise of blessing is counterbalanced by the threat of condemnation for those who choose not to believe (3:18). Although God takes no pleasure in the death of anyone (*Ezek.* 18:32), there is nothing else he can do with those who refuse to believe. Man's liability to God's judgement is made all the more stark in the light of his rejection of God's gracious overtures to his world.

No-one can afford to be indifferent to the reality of God's threat of judgement – a threat involving not only our future state, but also the present state of all those who have not yet come to faith in Christ. To be outside Christ is to be under condemnation. The only antidote is to turn to him in faith.

THE VERDICT

The logic of John's reasoning again flows smoothly from one step to the next. If it is true that those who have not believed are under God's condemnation already, then the verdict that hangs over people in their natural condition in the world is that of 'guilty as charged'. Christ's coming into the world has served to accentuate that verdict on the present state of the human race. The Light has come into the world and it has exposed the dark and sinful deeds of men and their resultant guilt before God. Those who refuse to come to the light only confirm their tragic state of being condemned before God (3:19-20).

The essence of what John is saying, as he presses his readers to reflect on the effect of Christ's coming into the world, is found also in one of the great conclusions of the apostle Paul's letter to the Romans: 'All have sinned and fall short of the glory of God' (*Rom.* 3:23). Hope for our world and our race cannot come from within, or from below; it has to come from without and from above. Jesus Christ – 'the Light' – is the embodiment of that hope.

THE EVIDENCE

How then can a person know that they are no longer under God's just condemnation? This is not only Nicodemus' problem, as a pious Jew whose faith was in his religion, but also the problem of countless numbers of people whose hope lies in their religion and not in God. John answers by pointing to the evidence of a changed life. The answer lies in the way that they respond to 'the light' (3:21). The evidence of a truly changed life is found, not in the kind of spiritual cosmetic surgery that was the speciality of the Pharisees, but in the fact of their coming to Christ who is the hope of salvation.

This is why John says, 'so that it may be clearly seen that his deeds have been carried out in God'. He draws together the mystery of the two strands of Christ's discussion with Nicodemus: the need for sinners to trust the crucified Saviour, and the need for God to work in them so that they can exercise such faith. A genuine willingness to come to Jesus is so unnatural for sinful, light-hating human beings, that when it happens it proves that God's Spirit has been at work!

10

Further Endorsement

After this Jesus and his disciples went into the Judean countryside, and he remained there with them and was baptizing. ²³ *John also was baptizing at Aenon near Salim, because water was plentiful there, and people were coming and being baptized* ²⁴ *(for John had not yet been put in prison).*

²⁵ *Now a discussion arose between some of John's disciples and a Jew over purification.* ²⁶ *And they came to John and said to him, "Rabbi, he who was with you across the Jordan, to whom you bore witness – look, he is baptizing, and all are going to him."* ²⁷ *John answered, "A person cannot receive even one thing unless it is given him from heaven.* ²⁸ *You yourselves bear me witness, that I said, 'I am not the Christ, but I have been sent before him.'* ²⁹ *The one who has the bride is the bridegroom. The friend of the bridegroom, who stands and hears him, rejoices greatly at the bridegroom's voice. Therefore this joy of mine is now complete.* ³⁰ *He must increase, but I must decrease."*

³¹ *He who comes from above is above all. He who is of the earth belongs to the earth and speaks in an earthly way. He who comes from heaven is above all.* ³² *He bears witness to what he has seen and heard, yet no one receives his testimony.* ³³ *Whoever receives his testimony sets his seal to this, that God is true.* ³⁴ *For he whom God has sent utters the words of God, for he gives the Spirit without measure.* ³⁵ *The Father loves the Son and has given all things into his hand.* ³⁶ *Whoever believes in the Son has eternal life; whoever does not obey the Son shall not see life, but the wrath of God remains on him* (John 3:22–36).

More of the same! More talk about testimony to Jesus! We have already been told about the testimony of different people who provide accreditation for Jesus, so why are we hearing yet more of the same? John's Gospel is full of repetition, but not the kind that is crass and boring. Rather, it is the sort of repetition built into an exquisite symphony by a gifted composer, or into a tapestry by a master weaver. It is there, not merely to make baldly the same point over and over again, but to flesh out and enhance the point that is being made so as to create the biggest of pictures and make the deepest of impressions.

It should not surprise us, therefore, that no amount of testimony about Jesus Christ, the everlasting Son of God who took human flesh and entered our world, will ever complete our knowledge and appreciation of who he is and what he has done. John as Evangelist takes us several steps further into that knowledge and appreciation. He continues to pursue his stated aim of persuading people of Christ's credentials and urging them to embrace him and hold on to him by faith as the only true source of hope and salvation.

There is a clear movement in this chapter taking us from the encounter between Jesus and Nicodemus at the start, to the seemingly unrelated incident involving John the Baptist and his response to Jesus' work of baptizing. Far from being a crude case of 'What Jesus did next', John deliberately highlights this episode (which none of the other Gospels record) in order to make a point and to reinforce what has already been learned from preceding incidents. Three things come to the fore.

A Fresh Reminder of the Depth of the Problem of Sin

If at first glance we find ourselves struggling for a connection as the narrative unfolds, the link is to be found in the references to baptism and ceremonial washing. Nicodemus was part of a religious establishment that placed a high premium on the need for ceremonial washing, but Jesus told him that he needed a cleansing far deeper than that provided by any ritual. He needed to be 'born of water and the Spirit' if he was ever to see, let alone enter, God's kingdom (3:5). That did not mean that ritual washings were of no consequence. But what was necessary was the truth being symbolized. That is the reason John brings us back to the issue of washing.

What was the point of these religious purification ceremonies – whether the time-honoured practice of the Jewish system, or the nonconformist variation introduced by John in the desert? They were God's way of reminding people that he was pure and they were not. In simple and graphic imagery he reveals his essential purity and the absolute necessity of spiritual cleansing for a person to enjoy true and saving fellowship with him. John's preaching, which went hand in hand with his baptizing, was making a deep impression on those who came to him in the desert. They were beginning to realize the difference between ritual and the reality it represented. This was evidenced by the heartfelt changes being produced in the lives of John's followers. So, when Jesus sets up what appears to be a rival baptism (3:22), honest questions are asked and John provides the answers (3:23–36).

John is not drawn into the merits and demerits of the different kinds of washing that were available. He lets the need for these ceremonies stand as a constant reminder of our need of the cleansing to which they point. They provide a testimony to human sin, guilt and uncleanness, and tell us that cleansing our own souls before God does not lie within our power. Thankfully, however, that is not all they have to say!

A POWERFUL DECLARATION OF THE SCALE OF GOD'S ANSWER IN CHRIST

What is most significant about the final third of this chapter is that John the Baptist does not focus on the baptism, but on the Baptizer. More than that, he deliberately turns the gaze of his own devoted disciples away from himself as 'the Baptist' to the new 'Baptist' that has now stepped in to the limelight. In a self-effacing way he says that 'a person cannot receive even one thing unless it is given him from heaven' (3:27). God had given him a special job to do, but it was not the most important job. John could only highlight the need; he was not equipped to supply the answer. Yet again he says, 'I am not the Christ' (3:28).

The answer was to be found in a person, and in such a person as had never before been seen in the world. The ultimate answer to the problem of man's sin was 'from above' and was to be found in the one 'who comes from heaven' (3:31).

He illustrates the point by talking about the difference between the groom and the best man (the friend who attends the bridegroom) (3:29). The latter prepares the way for the former and his greatest joy is to hear the voice of the groom when he arrives, signalling his long-awaited union with his bride. The language here is laden with overtones from Old Testament expectation of the coming of Messiah – the true Bridegroom of God's people. It is also full of New Testament anticipation of others entering into the joy that John experienced – it is when anyone hears (and recognises) the voice of the Saviour in the preaching of the gospel that the joy of a heavenly marriage becomes theirs too.

John had already gained a high and worthy reputation in Israel as 'a man sent from God' (1:6), but to himself, he was nothing in comparison to the One who was coming after him and who was now making himself known. Because of who this coming One was and because of where he was from, it was essential for John that 'He must increase; I must decrease' (3:30). That is, John must retreat into the wings and Jesus must stand to the fore. He alone – the Word made flesh – embodies God's infinite solution to the need of our race.

A POINTED APPLICATION OF THESE TRUTHS FOR ALL PEOPLE

One might be forgiven for thinking that the sheer power of what was being revealed in the person of Jesus Christ should have been enough in itself to bring people flocking into the kingdom, yet the opposite was the case. Despite the credentials that Jesus had and the testimony that pointed to his true identity, and despite the incredible testimony he brought first-hand from heaven, yet, 'no one receives his testimony' (3:32). John clearly did not mean this as a blanket 'no one at all', but rather as, 'no one, relatively speaking'. The importance of the Person serves only to highlight the shame of the response.

When we consider the witness that has been borne to Jesus Christ over the centuries, it is not merely tragic that so relatively few respond, it is also culpable. As John outlines both the testimony of others concerning Christ and the testimony that Christ himself presents, it adds up to a solemn warning to those who hear, but choose to reject. Such persons 'shall not see life, but the wrath of God remains on [them].' (3:36).

In complete contrast we also have the words of assurance that John gives for those who do recognize and do receive Jesus for all that he is. John the Baptist makes it crystal clear that something of enormous significance takes place when a person accepts the testimony of Jesus: 'Whoever receives his testimony sets his seal to this, that God is true' (3:33). What John means is that he (or she) has not merely taken Jesus of Nazareth at his word, he has taken God himself at his word and has actually proved that he is true to his word. Believers are those who recognize that Jesus, God's Messenger, speaks the actual words of God himself. More than that, they find him to be the One who imparts the Holy Spirit without limit to his believing people (3:34).

The impact of all this in terms of application and response could not be greater. As far as the testimony about Jesus is concerned, it comes with the divine *imprimatur* and has consequences that will determine our destiny. The options are stark: reject the Son and remain under God's wrath, or believe in him and receive the promised gift of eternal life. Nothing in all the universe is more important. Nothing else demands a more urgent response.

II

Face to Face with Salvation

Now when Jesus learned that the Pharisees had heard that Jesus was making and baptizing more disciples than John [2] (although Jesus himself did not baptize, but only his disciples), [3] he left Judea and departed again for Galilee. [4] And he had to pass through Samaria. [5] So he came to a town of Samaria called Sychar, near the field that Jacob had given to his son Joseph. [6] Jacob's well was there; so Jesus, wearied as he was from his journey, was sitting beside the well. It was about the sixth hour.
[7] There came a woman of Samaria to draw water. Jesus said to her, "Give me a drink." [8] (For his disciples had gone away into the city to buy food.) [9] The Samaritan woman said to him, "How is it that you, a Jew, ask for a drink from me, a woman of Samaria?" (For Jews have no dealings with Samaritans.) [10] Jesus answered her, "If you knew the gift of God, and who it is that is saying to you, 'Give me a drink,' you would have asked him, and he would have given you living water." [11] The woman said to him, "Sir, you have nothing to draw water with, and the well is deep. Where do you get that living water? [12] Are you greater than our father Jacob? He gave us the well and drank from it himself, as did his sons and his livestock." [13] Jesus said to her, "Everyone who drinks of this water will be thirsty again, [14] but whoever drinks of the water that I will give him will never be thirsty again. The water that I will give him will become in him a spring of water welling up to eternal life." [15] The woman said to him, "Sir, give me this water, so that I will not be thirsty or have to come here to draw water."

[16] *Jesus said to her, "Go, call your husband, and come here."*
[17] *The woman answered him, "I have no husband." Jesus said to her, "You are right in saying, 'I have no husband';* [18] *for you have had five husbands, and the one you now have is not your husband. What you have said is true."* [19] *The woman said to him, "Sir, I perceive that you are a prophet.* [20] *Our fathers worshipped on this mountain, but you say that in Jerusalem is the place where people ought to worship."* [21] *Jesus said to her, "Woman, believe me, the hour is coming when neither on this mountain nor in Jerusalem will you worship the Father.* [22] *You worship what you do not know; we worship what we know, for salvation is from the Jews.* [23] *But the hour is coming, and is now here, when the true worshippers will worship the Father in spirit and truth, for the Father is seeking such people to worship him.* [24] *God is spirit, and those who worship him must worship in spirit and truth."* [25] *The woman said to him, "I know that Messiah is coming (he who is called Christ). When he comes, he will tell us all things."* [26] *Jesus said to her, "I who speak to you am he."*

[27] *Just then his disciples came back. They marvelled that he was talking with a woman, but no one said, "What do you seek?" or, "Why are you talking with her?"* [28] *So the woman left her water jar and went away into town and said to the people,* [29] *"Come, see a man who told me all that I ever did. Can this be the Christ?"* [30] *They went out of the town and were coming to him.*

[31] *Meanwhile the disciples were urging him, saying, "Rabbi, eat."* [32] *But he said to them, "I have food to eat that you do not know about."* [33] *So the disciples said to one another, "Has anyone brought him something to eat?"* [34] *Jesus said to them, "My food is to do the will of him who sent me and to accomplish his work.* [35] *Do you not say, 'There are yet four months, then comes the harvest'? Look, I tell you, lift up your eyes, and see that the fields are white for harvest.* [36] *Already the one who reaps is receiving wages and gathering fruit for eternal life, so that sower and reaper may rejoice together.* [37] *For here the saying holds true, 'One sows and another reaps.'* [38] *I sent you to reap that for which you did*

not labour. Others have laboured, and you have entered into their labour."
³⁹ Many Samaritans from that town believed in him because of the woman's testimony, "He told me all that I ever did." ⁴⁰ So when the Samaritans came to him, they asked him to stay with them, and he stayed there two days. ⁴¹ And many more believed because of his word. ⁴² They said to the woman, "It is no longer because of what you said that we believe, for we have heard for ourselves, and we know that this is indeed the Saviour of the world" (John 4:1–42).

It is a sad indictment of many churches today that they have become middle-class institutions - they require certain social and intellectual abilities before a person can feel truly accepted and participate fully. This stands in stark contrast to the range of people among whom Jesus moved so freely and with whom he worked so effectively. He had no trouble crossing every conceivable social or cultural divide.

John draws attention to this wonderful fact about Jesus and his ministry as he shows us how the Master's work progressed. Having devoted significant space to the meeting between Jesus and one of the social pillars and intellectual giants of the Jewish world of his day, John now tells us of Jesus' encounter with an unnamed social outcast in a Samaritan village. Not, indeed, a mere chance encounter but one that had a definite place in Jesus' divinely ordered mission. When the growing numbers of disciples presenting themselves for baptism drew the wrong kind of attention to Jesus and his followers, he quietly moved on to avoid further misunderstanding (4:1–3). As John describes what happened next, he says, Jesus '*had* to pass through Samaria' (4:4). What is odd about that statement is the fact that there is no geographical constraint or logic that made it so! The necessity of the route through Samaria can only be that of divine necessity: God had a purpose in his going that way. This purpose was soon to become clear in the 'casual' conversation that ensued over Jesus' thirst for a drink.

Jesus lived with a profound sense of destiny. Without being unnatural in any way, he was constantly alert to the purpose and possibilities that would unfold with every turn he took in his journey through this world. That same sense of our lives being bound up in God's plan ought to be a mark of every true child of God. It is a mind-set which has the potential of opening up thrilling dimensions, as we shall see in the unfolding details of this encounter.

Face to Face with Self

The journey for Jesus and his followers had been long and he was weary, so he sat down to rest on the outskirts of a Samaritan village called Sychar. Its only claim to fame was the fact that it was close to a plot of land that Jacob had given to Joseph many centuries before. On this plot was a well. Jesus sat by the well while his disciples headed for the village to look for some food. It was midday and as Jesus waited, a lone figure carrying a water-pot came out from the village.

To Western ears, the conversation that follows might appear totally mundane and insignificant, but in the Middle Eastern culture of Jesus' day this was far from being the case. The very fact that the conversation began at all was shocking on two counts. In the first place, here was a *Jew* initiating a conversation with a *Samaritan*, and secondly, here was a Jewish *man* daring to speak in public with a Samaritan *woman*. Little wonder that the woman overlooks Jesus' simple request and focuses instead on the shock of his having spoken to her (4:9). What is striking is the fact that Jesus relates to her primarily as a person and not as a mere representative of a particular group or type. Such an attitude should be our starting point on any occasion of sharing the gospel with another person.

The initial reason for the conversation was a request for a drink (4:7), the discussion that follows soars from the dusty well in Samaria to the heights of heaven itself (4:9–18). As the woman questions the appropriateness of her giving anything to Jesus, he responds by suggesting that he might have something to give to her - the gift of 'living water.' The woman's thoughts are still firmly rooted in the physical world of wells and buckets, but Jesus gently steers her to the deeper issues of spiritual needs and the way in which they can be met. He speaks of 'the water' that he will give and which will become 'a spring of water welling up to eternal life'. Still the penny does not drop! The woman still thinks only in terms of being freed from the daily drudgery of drawing water. Then Jesus touches the raw nerve of her soul: 'Go call your husband and come back.' Suddenly the woman is face to face with herself. She tries to dodge the question by denying that she has a husband, but Jesus continues by exposing the full truth of the moral ruin of her life.

So long as we doggedly confine our thoughts about life to the world of the physical and the material, we can run from God quite happily and even run from ourselves. It is only when we are confronted with the fact that we are as much moral and spiritual creatures, as we are physical and material - only then do we come face to face with ourselves.

FACE TO FACE WITH GOD

The verbal sparring match that dodged and weaved around the difference between life's physical and spiritual needs now continues, but moves on to a different plane. The woman concedes that she has spiritual needs, but starts to argue about how and by what means they can be met (4:19–26). She concentrates on the historic divergence between the religion of the Jews and that of the Samaritans – a difference that many saw as depending on the location of worship and on the rituals that were employed.

Jesus signals the arrival of a new spiritual era (4:23). An era in which past distortions and confusion over religious practice would be swept away and the truth about God displayed as never before. He reminds her that 'God is spirit'. He is above and beyond any physical location or ritual that might once have pointed to him. Those therefore who wish to worship God truly must do so 'in spirit and in truth'. What he is emphasizing here is not that we need the Holy Spirit and the truth of Scripture to enable us to worship (though that is very true) but that we need honesty and sincerity of heart and mind as we come before God. Just as this woman was standing spiritually naked in the presence of Jesus, so every sinner is spiritually naked in the sight of God. No amount of religiosity can conceal the ugly truth about our spiritual condition.

The woman begins to crumble under the penetrating power of Jesus' argument. In one last desperate move she grasps at the hope, held by both Samaritans and Jews, that one day Messiah would come.

Jesus then declares, with disarming candour, 'I who speak to you am he.'

FACE TO FACE WITH JESUS

The thrill we feel in the way that Jesus reveals himself to this woman arises from his use of the ancient and revered name of God. The actual words here are, 'I myself am . . . ' These are the very words used repeatedly in the Greek translation of the Old Testament in Exodus 2 and 6 when God revealed his Name, the LORD, to Moses. Readers of John's Gospel who knew their Bibles well would not have missed the connection he was making for them. Jesus who now revealed himself to this woman had come to fulfil the revelation of God's Name and character given so long ago to Moses as God worked out his covenant with Abraham, Isaac and Jacob (at whose well they now sat!).

The unseen God of whom he had just been speaking, and the Messiah for whom this woman had been waiting, are both embodied in the Person in whose presence she now finds herself. In the stunned silence that must surely have followed this announcement there is a disturbance – the disciples are returning. The woman slips away, leaving her empty water jar – the symbol of her empty life – behind her. While she hurries back to her village to broadcast the news of this extraordinary man whom she has just met, the disciples suppressing their amazement at seeing Jesus speaking to a Samaritan woman, encourage him to eat the food they have brought back from the village.

This interruption to the encounter provides an opportunity for us to consider the situation from the perspective of the church and its failures. The disciples were already beginning to fall into the trap of allowing their view of 'church' to be conditioned by the cultural and ethnic baggage of their day. Jesus therefore makes them think again. Their surprise at the conversation they had observed was a symptom of the prejudice that lurked in their hearts and of their failure to grasp what Christ's mission entailed.

Jesus' response is to ignore the food they had taken the trouble to bring and to express, in startling fashion, that the 'bread and butter' of his existence was to do his Father's will (4:34). If they became less concerned about their stomachs and more concerned about the souls of the lost, then they too would share in that work. With a measure of rebuke, he says to them, 'Look, I tell you, lift up your eyes, and see that the fields are white for harvest' (4:35). That rebuke to the professing Church reverberates down to the present day. We too need to be less preoccupied with ourselves and our own petty concerns and more concerned with the eternal needs of a lost humanity.

It may well be that there is some significance in the fact that Jesus speaks of the fields being 'white' for harvest. There are no Middle Eastern crops in fact that are actually white when ready for reaping! However, the first thing the disciples saw when they looked up was a crowd of people – clothed for the most part, probably, in white robes – coming towards them (4:30). This immediately made them appreciate what Jesus was saying. It was with a human harvest that they were to be involved – and one that was to include even their traditional enemies! The amazing sight of almost an entire village of Samaritans coming to faith in Christ, and their more amazing testimony, 'We have heard for ourselves, and we know that this is indeed the Saviour of the world' (4:42), is an unprecedented witness to the fact that Jesus is the Christ. The end-point of this circuitous diversion in Jesus' itinerary has been to bring two groups of people – the residents of Sychar and the twelve disciples – face to face with themselves, with God, and ultimately with Jesus in his true Messianic credentials. This also is the end-point of the gospel.

12

Recognizing Jesus

After the two days he departed for Galilee. ⁴⁴ (For Jesus himself had testified that a prophet has no honour in his own home town.) ⁴⁵ So when he came to Galilee, the Galileans welcomed him, having seen all that he had done in Jerusalem at the feast. For they too had gone to the feast.

⁴⁶ So he came again to Cana in Galilee, where he had made the water wine. And at Capernaum there was an official whose son was ill. ⁴⁷ When this man heard that Jesus had come from Judea to Galilee, he went to him and asked him to come down and heal his son, for he was at the point of death. ⁴⁸ So Jesus said to him, "Unless you see signs and wonders you will not believe." ⁴⁹ The official said to him, "Sir, come down before my child dies." ⁵⁰ Jesus said to him, "Go; your son will live." The man believed the word that Jesus spoke to him and went on his way. ⁵¹ As he was going down, his servants met him and told him that his son was recovering. ⁵² So he asked them the hour when he began to get better, and they said to him, "Yesterday at the seventh hour the fever left him." ⁵³ The father knew that was the hour when Jesus had said to him, "Your son will live." And he himself believed, and all his household. ⁵⁴ This was now the second sign that Jesus did when he had come from Judea to Galilee (John 4:43–54).

It is never such a bad thing to turn to the last page of a book from time to time in order to remind ourselves what it is all about! The same is true with John's Gospel. It is there, at the end of his book, as we noted in the *Introduction*, that John spells out categorically the underlying reason for writing this Gospel. Everything he records is geared towards leading people to recognize truly who Jesus is, to understand why he came, and to believe on him (20:31). That rationale for writing needs to be kept firmly in the forefront of our minds as we read. John has indicated in his Prologue that there has never been another historical figure so misunderstood and misrepresented as Jesus of Nazareth. The tragic consequence of such a wrong understanding is that Jesus will be wrongly received, and thus the hoped-for promise of eternal life will not be found. The Gospels therefore must always be the crucial primary sources for revealing to us – not a Jesus of whim or fancy – but the real Jesus of history.

As we bear this in mind, it helps us to follow the flow of events recorded in this section of the Gospel, particularly the little nuances that colour the transition from one scene to another. It also helps us to understand some of Jesus' comments that can be hard to fathom when taken only at face value.

The healing miracle of this passage is described by John as the 'second sign' performed by Jesus (4:54). His purpose in noting it is to bring us one more step along the way of recognizing who Jesus is, of understanding the reason why he came, and of appreciating what it really means to trust in him. John achieves this by contrasting those who truly see and believe with those who think they do, but fail in reality.

An Insight into Spiritual Complacency

After the two-day interruption to his northward journey due to his 'mini-mission' in Sychar, Jesus continues on his way to Galilee (4:43). Almost immediately, John provides a most enigmatic comment: 'For Jesus himself had testified that a prophet has no honour in his own home town' (4:44). He is repeating a remark that Jesus had made previously (*Matt.* 13:57). Scholars and commentators offer many different suggestions as to what Jesus meant by 'his own home town'. The most obvious solution is simply to read the remark in context and see it as a reference to Galilee – the region where Jesus had spent most of his earthly life. The general reaction of this Jewish region to its most famous son stands in stark contrast to that of the

Samaritan region from which Jesus has just come. In effect John is saying, 'As we move to the next episode in the ministry of Jesus, bear in mind his own comment on his native land!' He is deliberately drawing attention to the marked difference between the reaction of the Samaritans to Jesus and that of his fellow-countrymen. Even though the reader may be shocked and surprised by the difference, Jesus is not.

Although at first sight the Jewish reaction seems warm, enthusiastic and commendable – 'the Galileans welcomed him' (4:45) – the reason behind their welcome was less encouraging. The Galilean contingent at the last Passover celebration in Jerusalem had witnessed his deeds there and were now waiting expectantly for more of the same on home territory. What appeared on the surface to be spiritually commendable was quickly exposed as nothing more than a veneer of misplaced curiosity. This curiosity is heightened by the urgent request for healing from a royal official based in Capernaum (4:46–47). Jesus responds by issuing a rebuke – not directed so much at the official as at the watching onlookers. This is evident from the plural language that he uses (4:48). They had completely misunderstood the truth as to who Jesus was and what he had come to do!

Little has changed with the passage of time. There has always been and there will continue to be that same spirit of superficial curiosity, academic interest and spiritual voyeurism in the way that many people perceive Jesus. All such responses fail to touch the essential issues of what it means to come to Christ. And Jesus continues to rebuke such inadequate interest in the sternest of terms.

These reactions in Galilee were poles apart from the events at Sychar a mere forty-eight hours beforehand. As Jesus 'came to his own' – the very people who ought to have known better – he was met with spiritual ignorance and confusion.

A GLIMPSE OF GENUINE NEED

If this had been all there was to the visit to Galilee, the whole episode would have been dismal in the extreme and perhaps not worth recording, but the focus of the passage is not upon the Galileans, but rather upon the royal official. This Capernaum man, with a son who is gravely ill, has heard that Jesus was in the locality and has made the twenty-five mile trek over to Cana where Jesus was staying. He was in desperate need and keenly aware of that need. Everything about him is in contrast to those other Galileans and their attitude to Jesus.

The reason for his coming to Jesus was that his son was sick; his pleadings and persistence were a measure of his desperation. He knew that time was running out for his boy (4:47). Though he was a man of rank and substance, he was powerless to protect and keep the most precious thing he had – the life of his son. There was no one else who could help him. It may well be that he had heard only the slenderest of reports of someone who was able to heal the sick, but yet he is tenacious in his approach. He asks Jesus to help (4:47) and even when Jesus issues his rebuke of the crowd's obsession with signs and wonders, he is still not deterred (4:49). He clings to Christ because he is convinced that there is no one else to whom he can turn. Yet, even in his great desperation, he had not fully appreciated the true depth of his need.

What the official did not realize was that God was using this crisis in his family to expose the deeper need of his soul. He did not come to Jesus and say, 'I am a sinner and I need to be saved', but rather, 'I am a father and my son needs to be healed.' However, as Jesus deals with the surface need, he lays bare also the deeper need and reveals how it can be met. Like a surgeon paring away painful, torn flesh in order to expose a more serious wound beneath, so Jesus pares away the surface symptoms of our fallen lives to expose the deeper sickness that lies beneath. God often uses these presenting symptoms to turn people to Jesus so that they may then see where their true need lies. It was the touch of that spiritual 'Surgeon of souls' that caused the Psalmist to say, 'It was good for me that I was afflicted, that I might learn your statutes' (*Psa.* 119:71).

A Display of True Saving Faith

One of the most moving conversions that I have ever witnessed in almost twenty years of ministry was that of an old man in his eighties. He had been born into a Christian family but since his teens had been running away from God. He afterwards said that all through those sixty years of running away from God, he was always conscious of God's pursuit of him. It reached the point that for a period of two years, he became more and more conscious of his sin and guilt before God. Finally, he said, he could bear it no more. 'I got down on my knees and begged the Lord to save me!'

Just as that man came to Jesus *in extremis*, so also this man from Capernaum. He took hold of Jesus by faith and would not let go of him until his request had been granted. He was utterly single-minded in his conviction that Jesus held the key to the problems in his life. Even when Jesus did not respond with some spectacular display of power, but with a simple word (4:50), his faith does not waver. He set off for home believing that what Jesus had promised would happen.

He did not have to travel the whole way home before having his faith rewarded. His servants came from the house to greet him and, on meeting, they informed him of his son's recovery. When he asked of the time of recovery, he realized that it was the precise moment when Jesus had spoken (4:51–53). This led to an even greater miracle: the miracle of life-transforming grace bringing both the man and his entire household to faith in Jesus (4:53). The turning point in both cases was the same: 'The man believed the word that Jesus spoke to him' (4:50). He took what Jesus said at face value and acted upon his promise.

This is why John describes the event as 'the second sign that Jesus did' (4:54). To all outward appearances – at least as far as the sign-hungry crowd was concerned – nothing had happened other than a few words being spoken. But in reality a miracle had taken place. Jesus is not interested in satisfying crowds who want to be entertained. He is interested in sinners who feel their need and are prepared to take him at his word. These are the people who genuinely recognize Jesus for who he is.

13

What Do You Really Want?

After this there was a feast of the Jews, and Jesus went up to
Jerusalem. ² Now there is in Jerusalem by the Sheep Gate a pool,
in Aramaic called Bethesda, which has five roofed colonnades. ³
In these lay a multitude of invalids – blind, lame, and paralysed.
⁵ One man was there who had been an invalid for thirty-eight
years. ⁶ When Jesus saw him lying there and knew that he had
already been there a long time, he said to him, "Do you want to
be healed?" ⁷ The sick man answered him, "Sir, I have no one
to put me into the pool when the water is stirred up, and while I
am going another steps down before me." ⁸ Jesus said to him, "Get
up, take up your bed, and walk." ⁹ And at once the man was
healed, and he took up his bed and walked. Now that day was
the Sabbath. ¹⁰ So the Jews said to the man who had been healed,
"It is the Sabbath, and it is not lawful for you to take up your
bed." ¹¹ But he answered them, "The man who healed me, that
man said to me, 'Take up your bed, and walk.'" ¹² They asked
him, "Who is the man who said to you, 'Take up your bed and
walk'?" ¹³ Now the man who had been healed did not know who
it was, for Jesus had withdrawn, as there was a crowd in the place.
¹⁴ Afterward Jesus found him in the temple and said to him, "See,
you are well! Sin no more, that nothing worse may happen to
you." ¹⁵ The man went away and told the Jews that it was Jesus
who had healed him (John 5:1–15).

Calvinism – that understanding of biblical teaching that hinges on the sovereignty of God – is a curious animal. It can become highly dangerous, spiritually, when it loses its biblical balance. Just as a high-quality musical instrument sounds superb when finely tuned but produces discord when out of tune, so also is the Calvinistic approach to theology. The most common distortion of Calvin's thought is the tendency so to emphasize God's sovereignty as to play down the equally biblical emphasis on human responsibility.

An unbalanced Calvinist might come to this passage and instinctively focus on Jesus' sovereign intervention in this situation (5:8–9). In so doing he would be overlooking the other details of this incident that are obviously included for a reason. The sovereign role of Christ is beyond question, but the way he exercises his sovereignty is full of significance, not just for the man who was healed but for everyone.

In many ways, the entire incident turns on the question that Jesus puts to the man when he asks, 'Do you want to be healed?' (5:6). It is a question that probes more deeply than first impressions might suggest. In confronting the lame man in this way Jesus is doing two things. Firstly, he is making him face the truth about himself in a way that he may well not have done for many years (given the length of time that he had been disabled). Secondly, he is leading him to discover the life-transforming truth about Jesus, the Christ.

It is this question also that underlines the universal importance of what happened that day by the Pool of Bethesda. Just as the crippled man needed to reach a turning point in life where his deepest needs and longings of soul were exposed, so also do all men and women, crippled as they are by their own sin and rebellion against God. This occurs crucially when people are brought to face their need of responding personally to Christ and to the call of the gospel. It occurs also however throughout the entire journey of the Christian life. On a daily basis Christians are being challenged to bring their deepest desires in life into line with God's perfect desires for them. The more we wrestle with these issues, the more we learn the profoundest truths about ourselves and about our Lord.

There is a sense, therefore, in which the question that Jesus puts to this man is like a spiritual cluster-bomb – one of those pieces of ordnance that is released as a single device, but which on impact explodes into many pieces. Jesus' one question, and the impact it makes, raises at least four major issues for this man, and for all men.

THE TRUTH ABOUT OUR LIFE

When Jesus asks, 'Do you want to be healed?', it seems almost too ridiculous for words. Surely the state of this man's life is so obviously tragic that it is almost an insult to ask the question. How could there be anything else that he would want more in life? But as we consider these disabled people in the colonnades we might well react rather like a group of first-year medical students being taken into an acute hospital ward by a teaching consultant. The group is immediately appalled by what they see, while the veteran takes things in his stride knowing that there is always more than meets the eye in these situations.

For those people who were sitting round that pool in Jerusalem, the shock element of their situation had long since dissipated. This was their normality. For the man that Jesus meets, this had been his normality for thirty-eight years! He had been disabled for almost a lifetime. He had grown used to his condition and might possibly have overcome his initial frustrations. He might even have become quite accustomed to his daily company, surrounded as he was with people with similar needs. It had become, quite simply, his way of life. Indeed, it is quite possible that such a state of existence had its own peculiar perks. Despite the absence of any kind of state welfare system, the generosity of worshippers visiting Jerusalem, the spiritual capital of the land, could make for quite a comfortable income for those having to beg for a living. In this context Jesus' question was a perfectly valid enquiry as to whether or not the man really wanted things to change.

The same is true for the great majority of able-bodied people in the world. They have settled into the rut of a particular lifestyle – knowing full well that it is not perfect – but accepting it as their own little norm. When quizzed about themselves and the life they lead, they shrug their shoulders and say, 'It's the way I am!' Such are the lame excuses that are often invoked as a brush-off for the gospel and its challenge to change. Sadly, the same mentality is found all too often in professing Christians who have settled into a less than satisfactory expression of the Christian life. They slide into a kind of Calvinistic fatalism and abdicate any responsibility for moving on from where they are. When Jesus confronts us and cross-questions us through his Word – whether we claim to be Christians or not – the first thing that happens is that we are made to face the truth about ourselves and our deepest longings.

THE FACT OF OUR OWN HELPLESSNESS

The man's answer to Jesus' question is perfectly straightforward and may well have been rehearsed on numerous previous occasions when he was asked about his condition and aspirations. Yet, even as he again spoke these words, he found himself being sharply confronted with the sheer depth of his personal need. He was paralysed!

As we listen to those pitiful words, 'Sir, I have no one to put me into the pool' (5:7), we are actually listening to our own personal testimony in life! It is not just that we have some awareness of our needs in life – however vague and confused that awareness – but we are also painfully aware of our helplessness in life. Every one of us suffers from a spiritual paralysis that renders us powerless in the face of those things that matter most. This man's physical condition becomes a painfully graphic picture of the spiritual condition of every fallen human being.

As the crippled man answers Jesus, there is a dismal note of resignation in his voice. The bald truth about his condition was that he was powerless to do anything about it. This was life as far as he was concerned. His helpless condition is again a mirror to us all. No matter how fit and healthy we might feel ourselves to be, the truth is we are weak and helpless when it comes to changing those things that need to be changed in our lives. It is not just the wrecks of humanity in their drunken or drug-induced addictions who are so enslaved, but even the most respectable of individuals lie in the grip of a dark power they cannot overcome. Jesus showed how true this is even for the respectable religious leaders of his day when he said, 'Everyone who commits sin is a slave to sin' (8:34). No-one can turn their life around on their own.

The man to whom Jesus was talking must have been utterly flabbergasted by what happened next. He became the object of an unsolicited miracle! He, who had no quality of life, no power to change and no real expectations for his future, is simply told to get up, to pick up his mat and to walk. In that very instant of the command being given to him, he was cured (5:8–9)! There can be no more powerful illustration of a person being confronted by the gospel and by the command to believe in the Lord Jesus to be saved. Countless lives have been miraculously turned around in an instant upon hearing and responding to that call. The natural helplessness that is ours is overcome by the invincible and irresistible power that is Christ's, and our lives are changed forever.

The Cause of All Our Trouble

There follows a most extraordinary encounter between the former cripple and the Jews (5:10–15). John tells us that the miracle had been performed on the Sabbath – the Jewish day of rest – and the Jews were none too pleased at what had happened. It was as though they were more concerned about their rules being infringed than about God's power being displayed. (The 'law' that forbade the carrying of mats on the Sabbath was not part of God's law, but was a Jewish addition to that law.)

The verbal fracas that took place and the somewhat ridiculous spectacle of supposedly religious people being more concerned about rules than about healing, emphasizes the question that follows: 'Who is the man . . . ?' (5:12). The healed man honestly did not know! He had been the recipient of miraculous healing, but he did not know who had performed the miracle.

Again, there is nothing accidental about this. Jesus acted quite deliberately in what he did. He allowed the event and the exchange to sink into the man's consciousness before putting the last piece of the jigsaw in place in his understanding. Jesus sought out the man later in the temple and said to him, 'See, you are well! Sin no more, that nothing worse may happen to you' (5:14).

Jesus was not necessarily implying that this man's condition was the result of some particular sin in his life. That may have been the case, but we are not required to see it in that way. Rather, Jesus is making the connection between sickness in general and sin in particular. We live in a world where things go wrong and suffering abounds because it is a world in which there is sin. He was making it clear to the man (and to all who read the account of what happened) that the greatest need in life is not merely to have bodies that are hale and healthy, but souls that are at peace with God. The 'something worse' of which Jesus spoke was the eternal consequence of sin: the irreversible judgement of God.

The point is simple, yet so easily missed. In a world in which we spend so much of our lives running around frantically trying to patch up all the little things that are going wrong, as well as the big things that might crush us, we manage to miss the root and cause of all our ills: sin. Only when sin has been dealt with by the miracle of Christ's saving grace can we truly and lastingly experience the 'healing' we need most of all – the healing of our souls.

The Hope That Is Found in Jesus

There is a beautiful and almost naïve simplicity in the footnote to this incident. The man who had been made well by Jesus, only to be bombarded by the Jews' questions, goes back to those who had vilified him and tells them who it was who had healed him (5:15). There were many things that he still did not understand, but one thing he knew: it was Jesus who had made him well!

The power of such testimony is indisputable. The man who had been forced to lie as an invalid by a pool for decades was now free for the first time in his life. He wants everyone to know who is responsible. His own words explain the significance of the 'sign' that Jesus has performed. He has been made 'well'. The deepest need of his life has been met through one Person: Jesus of Nazareth. That is the gospel!

14

Jesus' Credentials

And this was why the Jews were persecuting Jesus, because he was doing these things on the Sabbath. [17] *But Jesus answered them, "My Father is working until now, and I am working."*

[18] *This was why the Jews were seeking all the more to kill him, because not only was he breaking the Sabbath, but he was even calling God his own Father, making himself equal with God.* [19] *So Jesus said to them, "Truly, truly, I say to you, the Son can do nothing of his own accord, but only what he sees the Father doing. For whatever the Father does, that the Son does likewise.* [20] *For the Father loves the Son and shows him all that he himself is doing. And greater works than these will he show him, so that you may marvel.* [21] *For as the Father raises the dead and gives them life, so also the Son gives life to whom he will.* [22] *The Father judges no one, but has given all judgement to the Son,* [23] *that all may honour the Son, just as they honour the Father. Whoever does not honour the Son does not honour the Father who sent him.* [24] *Truly, truly, I say to you, whoever hears my word and believes him who sent me has eternal life. He does not come into judgement, but has passed from death to life.*

[25] *"Truly, truly, I say to you, an hour is coming, and is now here, when the dead will hear the voice of the Son of God, and those who hear will live.* [26] *For as the Father has life in himself, so he has granted the Son also to have life in himself.* [27] *And he has given him authority to execute judgement, because he is the Son of Man.* [28] *Do not marvel at this, for an hour is coming when all who are in the tombs will hear his voice* [29] *and come out, those who have done good to the resurrection of life, and those who have done evil to the resurrection of judgement.*

³⁰ *"I can do nothing on my own. As I hear, I judge, and my judgement is just, because I seek not my own will but the will of him who sent me. ³¹ If I alone bear witness about myself, my testimony is not deemed true. ³² There is another who bears witness about me, and I know that the testimony that he bears about me is true. ³³ You sent to John, and he has borne witness to the truth. ³⁴ Not that the testimony that I receive is from man, but I say these things so that you may be saved. ³⁵ He was a burning and shining lamp, and you were willing to rejoice for a while in his light. ³⁶ But the testimony that I have is greater than that of John. For the works that the Father has given me to accomplish, the very works that I am doing, bear witness about me that the Father has sent me. ³⁷ And the Father who sent me has himself borne witness about me. His voice you have never heard, his form you have never seen, ³⁸ and you do not have his word abiding in you, for you do not believe the one whom he has sent. ³⁹ You search the Scriptures because you think that in them you have eternal life; and it is they that bear witness about me, ⁴⁰ yet you refuse to come to me that you may have life. ⁴¹ I do not receive glory from people. ⁴² But I know that you do not have the love of God within you. ⁴³ I have come in my Father's name, and you do not receive me. If another comes in his own name, you will receive him. ⁴⁴ How can you believe, when you receive glory from one another and do not seek the glory that comes from the only God? ⁴⁵ Do not think that I will accuse you to the Father. There is one who accuses you: Moses, on whom you have set your hope. ⁴⁶ If you believed Moses, you would believe me; for he wrote of me. ⁴⁷ But if you do not believe his writings, how will you believe my words?"* (John 5:16–47).

Controversy is not always a bad thing! Very often it is necessary in order to cut through confusion and clear up understanding. The process of challenge, denial and affirmation sharpens knowledge. The proof of that in terms of understanding Christian truth can be seen throughout the history of the church. More often than not, clear formulation of biblical teaching has had to be hammered out on the anvil of debate and controversy, with every doctrine having to be brought back to the touchstone of Scripture for its final verification.

It is hardly surprising therefore that controversy features prominently in the life and ministry of Jesus as he reveals the truth about himself. The intriguing thing about the controversy that surrounded Jesus during his public ministry on earth is that it is not so much his teaching and ideas that were in dispute, but the claims that he made about himself. It was this fact that led C. S. Lewis to make his much-quoted remark:

> Either this man was, and is, the Son of God, or else a madman, or something worse. You can shut him up for a fool, you can spit at him or kill him as a demon; or you can fall at his feet and call him Lord and God. But let us not come to him with any patronising nonsense about him being a great human teacher. He has not left that option open to us. He did not intend to.
>
> *Mere Christianity*, New York, Macmillan: 1943, pp. 55–6.

Throughout history this is how people have responded to Jesus: there is no room for neutrality.

This next section discusses what is perhaps the most significant area of controversy concerning Jesus. It has to do with the staggering claim that Jesus made about himself – the claims that stirred up such fury within his Jewish hearers. Yet this is the claim that brings us to the very pivot of the gospel – the truth upon which its message stands or falls – Jesus' claim that he is God. What begins as a debate over the relationship between Jesus and the Sabbath becomes a sermon on the relationship between Jesus and God.

John is here building up the case for Jesus' being the Christ. He is establishing Jesus' unique credentials as the One on whom 'the Father set his seal' (6:27). As he does so, he leaves us with the challenge of what to believe about Jesus, and how to respond to him. Four things become clear during this next exchange between Jesus and the Jews.

THE CLAIMS THAT JESUS MAKES

In the previous incident of the lame man being healed, the miracle was overshadowed as far as the Jews were concerned, by Jesus' command on the Sabbath day for the man to pick up his mat. This led to an outbreak of persecution against Jesus (5:16).

Jesus' response is complex, but the thrust of his comments could hardly have been lost on his Jewish listeners. He speaks about God 'working until now' (5:17). The Sabbath rest, modelled on God's rest after his work of creation (*Gen.* 2:2–3), is immediately cast in a different light from that of the traditional Jewish perception of it. But what piques his audience more than anything is his reference to God as, 'My Father' (5:17). The Jews knew exactly what was implied in this turn of phrase. They saw that he was 'making himself equal with God' (5:18) and they were infuriated to the point of attempting murder.

Jesus does not back off when he sees their response. Far from denying their suspicions, he proceeds to reinforce and clarify his meaning, so that there might be no doubt in their minds. He does so by affirming his claim to be equal with the Father, not as some rival deity, but by virtue of the mystical oneness between the Father and the Son (5:19–20). This was pure blasphemy to the listening Jews. They had been nurtured throughout their history on the axiomatic truth that 'the Lord is one' (*Deut.* 6:4). In one sense they were quite right to react to Jesus' claims in the way they did. But Jesus was opening a window on God and his nature in a way that hitherto had not been known. What was revealed in a somewhat shadowy form in the Old Testament about the three-in-oneness of God, was now being presented in the flesh in the revelation of Jesus Christ as God incarnate.

It is one thing to make such claims (the mental institutions of the world are homes to many who do so), but a very different matter to prove them. Yet proof is precisely what Jesus goes on to offer. He publicly lays claim to two prerogatives that belong exclusively to God: the ability to raise the dead (5:21, see also *Deut.* 32:39) and the authority to judge (5:22, see also *Gen.* 18:25). In other words, Jesus is putting his own claims to the test. He is inviting a sceptical watching world to wait and see whether his claims will be fulfilled. He throws down the gauntlet by issuing a public manifesto that will ultimately either make him or break him.

The evidence supporting those claims has been provided not merely in the teaching and miracles of Jesus – great as they are –

but uniquely in his death, resurrection and ascension. His claims have been vindicated beyond all expectation.

THE RESPONSE THAT JESUS REQUIRES

It follows that such great claims call for a great response. Unlike the pundits of the modern world, Jesus does not leave his listeners to draw their own conclusions and frame their own responses, he tells them what is expected of them. (This in itself is consistent with his claim to be God, as it is God alone who has the right to make such bold demands of people.)

The supreme response that Jesus calls for is that of worship: 'that all may honour the Son, just as they honour the Father' (5:23). Since they share the same divine nature, both Father and Son deserve the same adoration – that adoration which is the preserve of deity. We can imagine the disciples shifting uncomfortably at this point. They were not yet ready to cope with such an amazing demand from their Master. Yet, eventually, this is precisely the response towards Jesus that we find in them – even in Thomas the sceptic (20:28). This same response is also shown by all those who have been brought face to face with Jesus. Scepticism gives way to wonder, and wonder to worship.

The second response that Jesus requires is that people truly listen to him. If they are to receive the benefits of the salvation he brings, then they must hear and accept the words that he speaks (5:24). It may seem a rather pedantic point, but it needs to be made. We must not respond to a Christ of our own imagination, but only to the Christ of history; the One who speaks authentic-ally in his Word. This is the core of the issue at stake in this exchange. The Jews have indeed listened to Jesus, they know just what he is saying, but they refuse to accept his words about himself. This explains the intensity of the hatred that fuels their persecution.

This second response is bound up inextricably with the third: the call for faith. Interestingly, it is not only faith in himself that Jesus demands, but faith also in 'him who sent me' (5:24). If the Jews responded to Jesus by believing and accepting the truth of his words, they would not be betraying their allegiance to the God of their fathers. However, not to believe in what Jesus was saying would not only be exactly that betrayal but would also exclude them from the blessings of God's salvation.

The need for this threefold response to Jesus has not changed. We cannot have God without Jesus and we cannot have Jesus apart from his words.

THE PROMISES JESUS GIVES

It is only when we consider the promises that Jesus proceeds to make that we begin to realize why his claims are so vitally important. If Jesus is not God, he cannot deliver the kind of salvation about which he speaks. In his promises to those who believe in him, two wonderful elements are found.

First of all there is the promise of blessings in the present. Jesus says, 'truly, truly, I say to you, whoever hears my word and believes him who sent me has eternal life. He does not come into judgement, but has passed from death to life' (5:24). In this statement, together with the previous comment on God's unique ability to give life to the dead (5:22), Jesus emphasizes that this can become the experience of those who are spiritually dead and cut off from God in their sin. He promises new life and new standing with God. He speaks of a salvation that deals not only with sin and its judicial consequences but also with the reign of death in the souls of the living. Whether we receive these blessings or not depends on our hearing and responding to the words of Jesus, and to hearing and responding to him not only as the one who speaks for God, but also as the One who *is* God.

A new era was dawning in which the voice of Jesus, the Son of God, would be heard and all who hear and respond would receive the blessing of new life in him (5:25–26). That in turn would pave the way for the other great facet of his divine responsibility: his authority to act as judge (5:27).

Secondly, Jesus holds out an extraordinary promise for the future. As he speaks of a future day when he will judge, he also emphasizes the future destiny of those who will be judged. He points forward to the day when all the dead of history will be raised to life, some to everlasting life and others to never-ending condemnation. All this will occur when the voice of the 'Son of Man' is heard (5:28–29).

Those words are intended to make us tremble. More than that, they are intended to make us realize that human destiny depends ultimately on Jesus and on the way people respond to him. Jesus drives these comments home by stating again that they are not the ravings of a deluded religious maniac, but the words of the One who sent him – the words of God himself (5:30).

THE PROOF THAT JESUS SUPPLIES

After listening to these great assertions made by Jesus in his discourse to the Jews, we can almost hear them screaming, 'Prove it! Prove it!' Jesus responds to this unspoken demand by offering a six-stranded testimony endorsing all that he has been saying about himself and about the work he is authorized by God to perform.

The first strand is that of his own personal testimony (5:31–32). Given what he has already said about himself and his true identity as God in human flesh, Jesus would be quite entitled simply to declare the truth of who he was and require his hearers to acknowledge it. He foregoes that entitlement.

Even though one day he will indeed command universal acknowledgement (*Phil.* 2:9–11), he chooses to waive this right in the present circumstances. He opts instead to play by the rules of earth and not those of heaven! He bows to the fact that, in God-given Jewish law, an individual's testimony was not sufficient to prove a point at issue. Two independent witnesses were required (*Deut.* 17:6, *Matt.* 18:16). Jesus notes in passing that he could provide his own testimony, but chooses not to.

The second witness Jesus calls is John the Baptist (5:33–35). He has already hinted at there being another testimony that is unassailable (5:32) and the crowd's instinct may well have made them think immediately of John. So Jesus first turns to John. He makes it abundantly clear that the testimony of a mere man is not to be the decisive factor in establishing his divine credentials, but he nevertheless highlights the major significance of John's witness. He says, 'I say these things so that you may be saved.' The manner in which the crowds responded to the preaching of the Baptist would have eternal consequences. That solemn truth has been relevant throughout history whenever and wherever a faithful preaching ministry has borne witness to Jesus as the Christ.

Jesus piles on the evidence. He points next to the testimony borne by the miracles he performs (5:36). These go beyond the words that John had spoken about him. The function of miracles, signs and wonders throughout Scripture is to attest the truth of God's revelation of himself and, in the New Testament particularly, to bear witness to Jesus as the Christ (*Heb.* 2:4). The fact that Jesus performed mighty works in the presence of the Jews was of enormous significance to those people who could read God's sign language as well as appreciate his spoken word. Then Jesus takes this form of evidence to a higher level again. He speaks of 'the works that the Father has given me to accomplish'. This was loaded language! There was one miracle that he was in the process of performing at the Father's behest that superseded all others: the miracle of redemption. When Jesus cried out in his final moments on the cross, 'It is finished!' (19:30), he was signalling the greatest proof of all that he truly was who he had claimed to be: the Saviour of the world.

Jesus continues by pointing to yet another strand of evidence: the testimony of God himself (5:37–38). This may well be a reference to the verbal testimony the Father gave from heaven when Jesus was baptized (*Matt.* 3:17), or it could possibly be the personal assurances that the Son received from the Father in the course of his earthly ministry. Either way, though the Jews would not acknowledge God's testimony, its legal force as testimony to Jesus' claims remained.

With deft choice of words, Jesus moves from the Jews' failure to recognize God's audible voice and testimony to their failure to recognize it in written form in their Hebrew Bible (5:39–40). Like a master defence counsel who turns the tables on the prosecution by using their own evidence against them, Jesus uses the testimony of Scripture to expose the guilt and failure of the Jews. Their rejection of Jesus stemmed ultimately from their refusal to embrace the truth and testimony of God's written word: 'You do not have his word abiding in you!' A true understanding of the Scripture will lead us into the arms of Jesus.

The sixth and final component in Christ's case lies in one key element of the testimony of Old Testament Scripture: the testimony of Moses (5:45–47). Jewish refusal to acknowledge Jesus as the Christ only demonstrated their refusal to acknowledge Moses. On the last day he would become their accuser. He would add his testimony that their rejection of Jesus was the cause of their downfall.

The most painful element of what Jesus says in this exchange is the way he exposes the hearts of those who oppose him. He tells them, 'You do not have the love of God within you' (5:42). The reasons for rejecting Jesus do not in the end have to do with external evidence, but with the internal hardness of our hearts. This is the sad truth about unbelief throughout the ages.

15

Give Us This Day Our Daily Bread

After this Jesus went away to the other side of the Sea of Galilee, which is the Sea of Tiberias. ² And a large crowd was following him, because they saw the signs that he was doing on the sick. ³ Jesus went up on the mountain, and there he sat down with his disciples. ⁴ Now the Passover, the feast of the Jews, was at hand. ⁵ Lifting up his eyes, then, and seeing that a large crowd was coming towards him, Jesus said to Philip, "Where are we to buy bread, so that these people may eat?" ⁶ He said this to test him, for he himself knew what he would do. ⁷ Philip answered him, "Two hundred denarii would not buy enough bread for each of them to get a little." ⁸ One of his disciples, Andrew, Simon Peter's brother, said to him, ⁹ "There is a boy here who has five barley loaves and two fish, but what are they for so many?" ¹⁰ Jesus said, "Have the people sit down." Now there was much grass in the place. So the men sat down, about five thousand in number. ¹¹ Jesus then took the loaves, and when he had given thanks, he distributed them to those who were seated. So also the fish, as much as they wanted. ¹² And when they had eaten their fill, he told his disciples, "Gather up the leftover fragments, that nothing may be lost." ¹³ So they gathered them up and filled twelve baskets with fragments from the five barley loaves, left by those who had eaten. ¹⁴ When the people saw the sign that he had done, they said, "This is indeed the Prophet who is to come into the world!" ¹⁵ Perceiving then that they were about to come and take him by force to make him king, Jesus withdrew again to the mountain by himself.

[16] *When evening came, his disciples went down to the sea,* [17] *got into a boat, and started across the sea to Capernaum. It was now dark, and Jesus had not yet come to them.* [18] *The sea became rough because a strong wind was blowing.* [19] *When they had rowed about three or four miles, they saw Jesus walking on the sea and coming near the boat, and they were frightened.* [20] *But he said to them, "It is I; do not be afraid."* [21] *Then they were glad to take him into the boat, and immediately the boat was at the land to which they were going.*

[22] *On the next day the crowd that remained on the other side of the sea saw that there had been only one boat there, and that Jesus had not entered the boat with his disciples, but that his disciples had gone away alone.* [23] *Other boats from Tiberias came near the place where they had eaten the bread after the Lord had given thanks.* [24] *So when the crowd saw that Jesus was not there, nor his disciples, they themselves got into the boats and went to Capernaum, seeking Jesus* (John 6:1–24).

The miracle of Jesus' feeding of the five thousand is one of the best known of all his miracles – not least because all four Gospel writers record it. Their emphasis upon it indicates to us its vital importance to our understanding of who Jesus is and what he came to do. At the same time it is also one of the most misunderstood of Jesus' miracles. One of the more outlandish explanations proffered by those who dislike the supernatural element of the Bible is that the crowd was so engrossed in Jesus' teaching that they became oblivious of their hunger. It was only when one small boy took out the picnic lunch his mother had packed for him that everyone else suddenly remembered they too had lunches with them and all began to dine!

Such 'explanations' not only insult the text, they also insult the intelligence of the reader. Mere common sense is sufficient to tell us that there are deeper threads to be found in this episode - threads which, in turn, will tie in with the overall tapestry of truth that John is weaving throughout his Gospel.

We must not overlook the wider connections that override the chapter divisions in the text. John did not insert the chapter and verse divisions; they were later additions inserted during the Mediaeval period as a kind of navigation aid for Bible students. The previous chapter ends with Jesus pointing to Moses as the one whose testimony on Judgement Day would condemn the Jews for their unbelief (5:45–47). John now proceeds to this major incident in the ministry of Jesus which, even though it occurred 'some time later' (6:1), ties in perfectly with the testimony of Moses concerning Jesus as God's promised Messiah.

The whole chapter is full of links with Moses, not least the fact that these things happened when 'the Passover, the feast of the Jews, was at hand' (6:4). The miraculous provision of food clearly connects with the daily provision of manna in the wilderness. Indeed the similarities were so striking that the crowd immediately thinks that Moses' prophecy about the coming of an ultimate Prophet (*Deut.* 18:15, 18) is being fulfilled before their eyes (6:15). These connections will become clearer in the second half of chapter 6 as Jesus explains the significance of this miracle-sign in the 'Bread of Life' discourse (6:26–59). The point is this: just as Moses and the Exodus were the focus of Old Testament understanding and expectation of deliverance for God's people, so the fulfilment of that expectation unfolds in the New Testament through the revelation of Jesus as the Christ.

If we keep this background material in mind as we work through this passage, our understanding of many aspects of the salvation that God has promised in his Son will become clearer.

HOW GOD PROVIDES FOR HIS PEOPLE

A massive crowd was following Jesus because of the miracles he was performing (6:1–2). He had gone (as was his custom) up on to a mountainside with his disciples for peace and quiet and for the opportunity to teach. The Passover feast was approaching and Jesus presumably wanted to make use of the occasion in order to lead these men into a fuller understanding of its real meaning (6:3–4). The tranquil scene is interrupted by the arrival of hordes of people looking for Jesus and eager for another miracle. Jesus' response is designed to bring home the truth both to the crowd and to his own close followers.

Jesus raises the question as to the provider of life's basic essentials. This was a burning issue for the Israelites during their years in the wilderness: who could supply bread for some two million people? Jesus brings the issue up to date for the disciples by looking at the crowd, and saying to Philip, 'Where are we to buy bread, so that these people may eat?' (6:5). John makes it clear that the question was deliberately designed to test the disciples because Jesus knew perfectly well how he was going to supply the crowd's needs (6:6). Philip's response in the next verse reveals their inadequacies: 'Two hundred denarii would not buy enough bread for each of them to get a little.' (Two hundred denarii was about eight months' wages for the common people at the time.) Even the suggestion made by Andrew about a small boy's small lunch is only offered in a half-hearted way (6:8–9). The resources that these men have in and of themselves are meagre. Then Jesus steps in, and not only is the crowd well fed, but there are baskets of food to spare (6:10–13).

There are at least three lessons that Jesus is teaching here. The first is the fact that God provides for his people in a way that defies reason. There was no feasible, natural solution to the problem of a hungry crowd; the answer had to be supernatural. This relates, not only to our need of bread but also to our need of salvation. Benjamin Franklin's fabled adage, 'God helps those who help themselves', does not hold! The salvation promised in the gospel is every bit as miraculous as the miracle of feeding the five thousand.

A second dimension to this miracle is the fact that God provides in a way that requires faith in the recipient. The crowds had faith as they waited to be fed. The disciples needed faith as they received from Jesus in order to distribute to the people. Jesus himself expressed his faith as he prefaced the miracle with a prayer (6:11). However weak and tenuous the faith of the people and of the disciples may have been, it was still honoured as God supplied the need.

The third element of instruction is perhaps the most significant of all. When the people had eaten their fill, so much was left over that the surplus filled twelve baskets (6:12–13). Paul's doxology at the half-way point in his Letter to the Ephesians resonates with that same truth: 'Now unto him who is able to do exceeding abundantly, above all that we ask or think . . .' (*Eph.* 3:20–21, AV). God provides for his people – both in their physical and in their spiritual needs – in a way that is supernatural, a way that involves faith and a way that exceeds all human expectations. All of this throws the spotlight on Jesus as the agent of God's provision. And this work of providing occurred not only on a grassy mountainside by the shore of the Sea of Galilee, but pre-eminently on a barren hill outside Jerusalem.

How God Leads His People

Not surprisingly, a miracle that directly touched the lives of five thousand men and, possibly, a further fifteen thousand women and children, provoked an overwhelming reaction from the crowds. As John describes the result, we can almost see the minds of these people turning over as they put two and two together and begin to connect Jesus with the Prophet whom Moses had told them to expect (6:14). However, even though they were quite right in their perceptions – Jesus was indeed the Great Prophet promised by God – they were quite wrong in what they made of the fact. They were intending to take Jesus by force and make him king. He, however, pre-empted them by quietly withdrawing (6:15).

The reason for Jesus' withdrawal was that the people had wrong ideas about the way that God leads. In their minds they foresaw a popular leader who would raise a military or political force, but this was quite contrary to the purpose God had for his Son. They failed to realize that God leads not by force, coercion, or even popular consensus, but by his Word. Moses had led the wilderness generation by the prophetic Word of God. God had led his people through the Old Testament ages by his Word.

Now the true and ultimate Leader and Deliverer that God had promised the world had arrived. He would indeed lead, but he would do so as the embodiment of God's Word in all its fullness. It was a Word to be trusted and not to be twisted or manipulated for political ends. This great truth has been the key to the gospel's ability to cut through ethnic and cultural barriers and to be the message for all nations. God's Word does not reveal Jesus as serving any particular earthly nation or power-base. Instead it draws all peoples to Jesus and by him it brings them to salvation.

How God Delivers His People

It is all too easy to come to the next section in this chapter and find it jarring. It seems even more of an interruption in the context of John's record than it does in the parallel accounts in the other Gospels. Clearly this episode was the next thing that happened after the performing of the miracle, but it is evident from the exchange that then takes place (6:25–59) that the significance of the miraculous meal was far from exhausted. The question, therefore, is, 'What is the connection that caused John to include the episode on the lake in the middle of his discussion about God's provisions?'

The answer has again to do with the reference to the Passover (6:4). With that high-point of the Jewish year approaching, all thoughts were gravitating quite naturally to the events surrounding the Exodus from Egypt. The memorial meal that the Jews would soon be eating was a powerful reminder of that miraculous deliverance, which significantly incorporated two occasions of crossing water - the passing through the Red Sea (*Exod.* 13:17–14.31), and the crossing of the river Jordan (*Josh.* 3:1–4:14).

God used Moses to take his people through the water. God used his Son to walk upon the water and bring his little band of followers safely to the other side. The link is both profound and powerful. God delivers his people from that which would otherwise destroy them by means of a mighty figure appointed by himself. Moses and Joshua were mighty men in their own right, but they were only men. Both died and neither was able to provide deliverance for Israel in the deepest sense of that word. Jesus was different. He was not merely a man; he was both God and man. Therefore when on the cross he was swallowed up by the waters of death, he was not overwhelmed by them but could rise above them in the triumph of his resurrection.

That momentous event and that far-reaching achievement on behalf of God's people and in fulfilment of God's plan of redemption were foreshadowed during the darkness of this night on the Sea of Galilee (6:16–21). Just as the disciples from now on were to view Jesus as the Agent of this deliverance upon the sea, so they were being prepared to see him as the Agent of an infinitely greater and more wonderful deliverance – one that would bring to fulfilment the plan of the ages. This is what God wants us all to grasp: salvation is found in Jesus and in him alone.

16

The Bread of Life

When they found him on the other side of the sea, they said to him, "Rabbi, when did you come here?" ²⁶ *Jesus answered them, "Truly, truly, I say to you, you are seeking me, not because you saw signs, but because you ate your fill of the loaves.* ²⁷ *Do not labour for the food that perishes, but for the food that endures to eternal life, which the Son of Man will give to you. For on him God the Father has set his seal."* ²⁸ *Then they said to him, "What must we do, to be doing the works of God?"* ²⁹ *Jesus answered them, "This is the work of God, that you believe in him whom he has sent."* ³⁰ *So they said to him, "Then what sign do you do, that we may see and believe you? What work do you perform?* ³¹ *Our fathers ate the manna in the wilderness; as it is written, 'He gave them bread from heaven to eat.'"* ³² *Jesus then said to them, "Truly, truly, I say to you, it was not Moses who gave you the bread from heaven, but my Father gives you the true bread from heaven.* ³³ *For the bread of God is he who comes down from heaven and gives life to the world."* ³⁴ *They said to him, "Sir, give us this bread always."*

³⁵ *Jesus said to them, "I am the bread of life; whoever comes to me shall not hunger, and whoever believes in me shall never thirst.* ³⁶ *But I said to you that you have seen me and yet do not believe.* ³⁷ *All that the Father gives me will come to me, and whoever comes to me I will never cast out.* ³⁸ *For I have come down from heaven, not to do my own will but the will of him who sent me.* ³⁹ *And this is the will of him who sent me, that I should lose nothing of all that he has given me, but raise it up on the last day.* ⁴⁰ *For this is the will of my Father, that everyone*

who looks on the Son and believes in him should have eternal life, and I will raise him up on the last day" (John 6:25–40).

The memorable miracle that revolved around bread gives way to one of the most memorable sermons that Jesus ever preached. It too was about bread. In both cases the 'bread' stood as a symbol of Jesus himself and of all that he had come to do. The power of such symbolism is universal. For a person to be 'reduced to the bread line' is for them to be left almost destitute. The 'bread and butter' of life is a metaphor of the basic essentials of life. Jesus taps into that imagery and takes it into spiritual realms, touching the deepest depths of human need.

It must have been a remarkable sight! The vast crowd that Jesus had fed and from which he had deftly escaped when they tried to make him king, had now tracked him down. They immediately began to question him about how he had got to the other side of the lake (6:25). Jesus responded by ignoring their question and instead challenged them about their real needs. The miracle they had seen (and enjoyed) became the occasion for a sermon which contains some of the most pointed application found in the whole of Jesus' ministry.

The heart of its message lies in a statement beginning with the words, 'I am'. This is the first of seven such statements made by Jesus, all beginning with, 'I am', and recorded only in John's Gospel. He says, 'I am the bread of life' (6:35). The full force of this, and of all the other 'I am' sayings, lies in the similarity between this seemingly innocuous verb and the special divine name by which God revealed himself to Moses at the burning bush - 'I AM WHO I AM' (*Exod.* 3:14). It was not long before the Jews began to appreciate the allusion that Jesus was making in these sayings – a thinly veiled claim to deity – and they would soon use it to further their own claims for his death. In this passage Jesus makes use of this phrase, 'I am the bread of life', as a powerful tool for exposing human need and for demonstrating that he alone can meet it.

THE DEEPEST HUMAN NEED

At the heart of his discourse Jesus uses the language of hunger and thirst (6:35). It is the language of longing. It ties in with the fact that all human beings are creatures with longings of one sort or another. Whether it is the desire for food, our inbuilt sexual instincts, the longing for achievement, or simply the need to be entertained, everyone has cravings that need to be satisfied.

Jesus, however, looks beyond the kind of appetites that are merely physical or emotional. He concentrates on the deepest need and the greatest longing that any human being can have, and that all human beings share: the deep-seated desire for spiritual fulfilment and peace. This need is so deep and so complex that many people fail to understand it in themselves and become side-tracked into thinking that by meeting other needs they will find the satisfaction that their soul desires. Almost by a process of elimination, Jesus exposes the superficial cravings that were preoccupying many people in the crowd, but which were a million miles away from satisfying their real needs.

He first rebukes those who simply look for immediate satisfaction in the present – those who followed him because they ate the loaves and had their fill (6:26). To them he says, 'Do not labour for the food that perishes, but for the food that endures to eternal life' (6:27). The word 'food' is used here as an image for whatever satisfies a need. Many things in life – the pleasures derived from money, from sex, or from succeeding at work – provide a temporary satisfaction, just like food with its limited shelf-life. Jesus' counsel is simple: do not expect more from these things than they are able to give.

The crowd acknowledges what he is saying and continues with what seems a very commendable question: 'What must we do, to be doing the works of God?' (6:28). The 'work' (in the sense of 'necessary action') that Jesus points to is to 'believe in him whom he has sent' (6:29). The one who comes complete with God-given credentials (6:27). He wants us to realize that our need is deeper than we think and the only one who can truly meet that need is far greater than we could ever imagine.

GOD'S GREATEST PROVISION

By now, the crowd's interest is assured. The people realize that Jesus has been describing himself as the One whom God has sent and, in keeping with true Jewish concern, they want to know what 'sign' he will give to authenticate his claim (6:30–31). Jesus answers by saying that the Jews had failed to grasp the significance of the manna their forefathers had received in the desert. That 'bread' was not the true 'bread from heaven' that God in his eternal purpose planned to give to his people. Jesus is rebuking them for being more taken up with the sign than with what it signified. The significance of the manna lay ultimately in the fact that God would make a perfect and never-ending provision for his people's need. This provision would be found in the one 'who comes down from heaven and gives life to the world' (6:33).

Just as the woman at the well in Sychar had been captivated by the thought of living water in chapter 4, so here the Jews are taken up with the thought of bread from heaven. So they say, 'Sir, give us this bread always' (6:34). It is in answer to this question that Jesus says, 'I am the bread of life . . . ' (6:35). In other words, God's answer to our need is not ultimately a matter of what we might possess or of the degree of effort we might make, it is rather a matter of who we know. The deepest human need is not met by a something, but by a Someone, and that Someone is Jesus.

Jesus had stated that the 'food that endures to eternal life' is that 'which the Son of Man will give to you' (6:27) and that the provision made in him will be sufficient for the whole world (6:33). How could a carpenter's son from Nazareth justify such extravagant claims? The answer is simple: 'On him God the Father has set his seal' (6:27). He had been supplied with God-given credentials – demonstrated, not by some single, one-off sign but by a life-long series of divine approbations. From his unique conception and the unusual events of his birth, through to the incidents surrounding his baptism at the start of his ministry and to the signs that attested his words, all circumstances had pointed to his being the One promised by God.

In our security-conscious world, no one in their right mind would allow a stranger into his home without first checking the stranger's credentials. How immeasurably more important to do this before allowing someone into the sacred depths of one's soul. In his mercy God has provided a Saviour who has been publicly authenticated throughout his time on earth. As a result, not only the people of his day and age but all peoples throughout history may see him for who he really is. In the two thousand years that have passed, that hallmark of divine approval has not worn away.

THE SIMPLEST RESPONSE

As the Jews recognize the importance of what Jesus is saying and ask him to give them the bread of which he speaks, he answers by spelling out the response they need to make and the obstacle that stands in their way.

In words that reflect the extravagance of the gospel, Jesus says, 'Whoever comes to me shall not hunger, and whoever believes in me shall never thirst' (6:35). The invitation is an open one – it is the offer of a truly free gift with no strings attached. Such an offer went completely against the grain of the religious system of the Jews. It had become a religion of merit and the very language with which they had spoken of 'the works of God' (6:28) was loaded with the assumption that they needed somehow to ingratiate themselves before God. The problem however was much deeper than these people could imagine. After Jesus had spelled out the simplicity of the solution, he still adds, 'But I said to you that you have seen me and yet do not believe' (6:36). Jesus was laying bare the true depth of spiritual need, not just in his Jewish audience, but throughout the entire human race. Even when people are confronted head-on with God's truth and the offer of God's grace they neither recognise it, nor are they able in themselves to respond to it. This is Nicodemus' problem all over again (3:3, 5).

This negative comment is not a cynical gesture on Jesus' part. By it he is emphasizing that God's love is even greater than at first appears. God not only provides the answer to our deepest need, he also provides the necessary enabling for people to respond to that answer. Jesus assures his hearers that all who the Father gives to him will come to him and none who truly come to him will ever be turned away (6:37-40). God not only comes to sinners through his Son offering them salvation, he comes to them also by his Spirit in order to bring them to his Son! All who hear the words of Jesus in the gospel and begin to appreciate the depth of their need, can reach out by faith to him and be assured that he will give them what they ask, because his promise is true.

[97]

FAR-REACHING CONTENTMENT

It is worth noting in passing that Jesus is also emphasizing the extent of the blessing that will come to those who take him at his word. Theirs will be a satisfaction that is eternal in the fullest sense of that word – not just never-ending, but complete.

By using the language of hunger and thirst as a spiritual metaphor he assures all who believe in him that regardless of their physical circumstances in life, they will enjoy a peace and contentment that will penetrate to the depths of their being. That truth is marvellously demonstrated by the quality of spiritual life that is often found even in the poorest places on earth. Christians in such extreme conditions often possess a contentment that money could never buy. They enjoy a communion with God uncluttered by the many other things that can obstruct our relationship with him.

All true believers have also the peace of knowing they will never be driven away (6:37). They will never be rejected by God for the simple reason that they are accepted in Christ. God gives cast-iron promises to this effect in the gospel, and he is bound to honour all such promises.

Perhaps the most amazing thing stated here is that those who trust Jesus will never be abandoned to the grave. Death itself will not rob them of what is theirs in Christ. None of those that God the Father gives to Christ the Son will be lost; all who die as believers will be raised up by the Son on the last day (6:39–40).

Jesus, the bread of life, is for us a spiritual nourishment that will sustain for eternity. Nothing else can compare with him!

17

Turning Points

So the Jews grumbled about him, because he said, "I am the bread that came down from heaven." [42] *They said, "Is not this Jesus, the son of Joseph, whose father and mother we know? How does he now say, 'I have come down from heaven'?"* [43] *Jesus answered them, "Do not grumble among yourselves.* [44] *No one can come to me unless the Father who sent me draws him. And I will raise him up on the last day.* [45] *It is written in the Prophets, 'And they will all be taught by God.' Everyone who has heard and learned from the Father comes to me –* [46] *not that anyone has seen the Father except him who is from God; he has seen the Father.* [47] *Truly, truly, I say to you, whoever believes has eternal life.* [48] *I am the bread of life.* [49] *Your fathers ate the manna in the wilderness, and they died.* [50] *This is the bread that comes down from heaven, so that one may eat of it and not die.* [51] *I am the living bread that came down from heaven. If anyone eats of this bread, he will live forever. And the bread that I will give for the life of the world is my flesh."*

[52] *The Jews then disputed among themselves, saying, "How can this man give us his flesh to eat?"* [53] *So Jesus said to them, "Truly, truly, I say to you, unless you eat the flesh of the Son of Man and drink his blood, you have no life in you.* [54] *Whoever feeds on my flesh and drinks my blood has eternal life, and I will raise him up on the last day.* [55] *For my flesh is true food, and my blood is true drink.* [56] *Whoever feeds on my flesh and drinks my blood abides in me, and I in him.* [57] *As the living Father sent me, and I live because of the Father, so whoever feeds on me, he also will live because of me.* [58] *This is the bread that came down from*

heaven, not as the fathers ate and died. Whoever feeds on this bread will live forever." ⁵⁹ Jesus said these things in the synagogue, as he taught at Capernaum.

⁶⁰ When many of his disciples heard it, they said, "This is a hard saying; who can listen to it?" ⁶¹ But Jesus, knowing in himself that his disciples were grumbling about this, said to them, "Do you take offence at this? ⁶² Then what if you were to see the Son of Man ascending to where he was before? ⁶³ It is the Spirit who gives life; the flesh is of no avail. The words that I have spoken to you are spirit and life. ⁶⁴ But there are some of you who do not believe." (For Jesus knew from the beginning who those were who did not believe, and who it was who would betray him.) ⁶⁵ And he said, "This is why I told you that no one can come to me unless it is granted him by the Father."

⁶⁶ After this many of his disciples turned back and no longer walked with him. ⁶⁷ So Jesus said to the Twelve, "Do you want to go away as well?" ⁶⁸ Simon Peter answered him, "Lord, to whom shall we go? You have the words of eternal life, ⁶⁹ and we have believed, and have come to know, that you are the Holy One of God." ⁷⁰ Jesus answered them, "Did I not choose you, the Twelve? And yet one of you is a devil." ⁷¹ He spoke of Judas the son of Simon Iscariot, for he, one of the Twelve, was going to betray him (John 6:41–71).

In life generally, relationships are never static, they are always on the move and developing, for better or for worse. From friendships in the playground to a courtship that might end in marriage, they lead inexorably on either to commitment or to collapse. The same is true for our relationship with God. Everyone has some relationship with God and there will be some times when he is closer than at others (*Isa.* 55:6–7). But there comes a point when a person must respond in some way to God and his gospel. To use the language of Joshua in the Old Testament, 'Choose this day whom you will serve . . .' (*Josh.* 24:15). It is towards that watershed in their relationship to God that Jesus directs his hearers in these verses.

The passage contains the remainder of the 'Bread of Life' discourse that we began considering in the previous chapter. John mentions that it took place in the synagogue at Capernaum (6:59) and he shows how the whole episode became a defining moment in the relationship between Jesus and the vast majority of those that were following him. There is a striking contrast between the beginning of the chapter, when Jesus had around him a crowd that may have numbered in excess of twenty thousand, and the chapter's end, where he is alone with the twelve – and of that twelve, one is exposed as a traitor.

The critical question, which can reveal a person's true response to Jesus, is found in this passage. 'Do you take offence at this?' (6:61). John's account in these verses therefore is not just an historical record of a key incident that occurred two years into Jesus' public ministry, but a paradigm for all spiritual experience. Ultimately everyone must be brought to this defining moment and their answer to the question will determine where they stand before God.

The Claims

Up until this point in his ministry, Jesus had gone to unusual lengths to veil his identity. He had made no bold, startling claims about himself or about his reason for coming into the world. This is hardly surprising, because to have done so would have been quite out of character. But he certainly knew that the truth concerning himself could not be concealed; it would inevitably manifest itself in due course before the world.

By now, however, he had completed some two-thirds of his public ministry - the work that God had given him to do. There had been sufficient revelation of his identity – both by word and deed – to allow him to speak of it more openly and directly. What is striking is that his claims now become a major irritant to many of his would-be followers!

We find here the Jews 'grumbling' about his claims to be 'from heaven' (6:41). They were so sure that they knew exactly who he was: merely the son of Joseph and Mary from Nazareth (6:42). They were quite content to accept and respect him as a gifted young rabbi from Galilee, but anything beyond that was verging on blasphemy. The oblique claims to deity that Jesus was making were a source of embarrassment and offence to them.

It is at precisely this same point that many others, both in the past and right down to the present, have baulked at trusting in Jesus. In so many of the religions of the world, in so many so-called 'Christian' sects, in the private religious views of so many individuals, it is perfectly acceptable for Jesus to be a great teacher or example, but not for him to be God!

But there is no escaping the thrust and force of Jesus' claims. Far from retreating when he sees that he has upset his listeners, he repeats his message that the way that people respond towards himself is the supreme indicator of whether or not God has worked in their lives (6:44–46). A genuine experience of God is evidenced by a heartfelt response to Jesus. This statement not only caused problems for the Jewish audience of that day – it has been the focus of controversy for all kinds of people ever since. The problem lies almost invariably in the fact that they become tangled up with the issue of the secret workings of God's plan and purpose - the issues of election and predestination. The instinct of most when they come to these things is to reduce them to pure determinism: in seeing God as a detached, cosmic chess-player.

Jesus does not allow us to handle these truths in such a blinkered fashion. The quotation from Isaiah that he refers to: 'They will all be taught by God' (*Isa.* 6:45), demonstrates the mechanism by which God's electing purposes are worked out in people's lives. 'God compels belief . . . not by savage constraint, but by the wonderful wooing of a lover' (Don Carson).

Repeatedly in John's record, Jesus weaves together an emphasis on the necessity of God's sovereign saving activity (how else can the spiritually dead hear, see and enter the kingdom, [3:3,5]?), and an emphasis on the necessity of the response of faith (3:16). He never dilutes one in favour of the other – as we tend to do (see 10:26; 12:37-41).

The offence caused by these statements is further compounded by three more claims from Jesus. In the first, alluding openly to himself, he says, 'Not that anyone has seen the Father except him who is from God; he has seen the Father' (6:46). The second is the assertion that 'whoever believes [in Jesus and in what he says] has eternal life' (6:47). The third is, 'The bread that I will give for the life of the world is my flesh' (6:51). In all of these he is extending his claims about himself far beyond the borders of the Palestine of his day, beyond even the confines of this world and its history.

This last claim had also a particular edge to it that would not have been lost on the Jews gathered in the synagogue. By saying that his flesh would be given 'for the life of the world' (6:51) he was using the language of sacrifice. In so doing he was setting himself over against that entire system of Temple sacrifice, which lay at the heart of Jewish understanding of redemption and deliverance. The scandal of this claim was to intensify continually for the Jews until it reached its climax when Jesus revealed that the culmination of the sacrifice would be his death on the cross. This was to be the ultimate stumbling block for the Jews (*1 Cor.* 1:23) and continues to be so for the many who recoil at the idea of trusting their spiritual salvation to someone who was crucified as a criminal.

Despite the shock element in all that Jesus says, his gospel emphasizes that if we want to know where we stand with God, we need to be sure we understand the claims of Christ.

THE CHALLENGE

The nature of Jesus' claims is such that they cannot be left dangling in mid-air as it were. He presses them home to the hearts of his hearers in a way that leaves those hearers in no doubt as to the challenge of the gospel. The Bible never allows people to remain neutral before God; it provides no fence for agnostics to sit on! The challenge Jesus issues is this: 'Truly, truly, I say to you, unless you eat the flesh of the Son of Man and drink his blood, you have no life in you' (6:53).

At face value the statement seems barbaric. Little wonder that this and similar phrases used in conjunction with the celebration of the Lord's Supper led some genteel Romans in later years to accuse the early Christian Church of cannibalism. The language that Jesus uses is enigmatic in the extreme.

There are strong similarities between the words employed here and those Jesus uses at the institution of the sacrament of communion in the upper room a year later (*Matt.* 26:26–28). This has led some, notably those in the Roman Catholic and High Anglican traditions, to argue for the idea of transubstantiation in their understanding of the sacrament. This is the belief that the bread and the wine are actually transformed into the body and blood of Christ after they are consecrated. Pressing that reasoning and the language of this passage even further, some arrive at a sacramentalist understanding of salvation: that is, saving grace is conveyed literally through the elements of bread and wine.

Even though Jesus uses powerful language in this passage, there is no need to force such a grotesque interpretation on to his words. We need only understand that Jesus is using language that points to intimate communion. Just as the shared life of the persons of the Godhead is bound up with the intimate and eternal communion they enjoy, so the new life of the believer is bound up with the profound union and communion he or she has with Christ (6:57).

The life of faith then is the life of conscious recognition of what Christ is as Son of God and as Saviour of the world, and conscious dependence upon him for a new life in fellowship with God. The gospel does not allow us to come to God without first coming to Christ and to his death on the cross.

THE RESPONSE

We started this chapter by saying that as relationships develop and evolve, sooner or later they reach a turning point that will either make them or break them. John now turns our attention to one such major turning point in the relationship between Jesus and those who professed to be his followers. He makes a contrast between 'disciples' in general (6:60) and the Twelve in particular (6:67).

There were clearly many in Jesus' wider entourage who were disturbed by what they were hearing, particularly because of its implications for them and for their ideas of discipleship. They grumbled and complained about 'hard sayings' that were difficult to accept (6:60–61). It was not so much that it was hard to understand (though there was undoubtedly an element of this involved), but rather that it was hard to embrace.

This is confirmed when we find Jesus adding, 'It is the Spirit who gives life; the flesh is of no avail' (6:63). To an audience that placed a high premium on one's natural ability to contribute to salvation, such a remark was devastating and left them with nothing to offer to God. This is precisely what Jesus intended to do. He strips us of all misplaced notions that we can contribute anything that will count towards our own deliverance.

Such a message was too much for a significant number of those who had set out to follow Jesus (6:66). They had begun to follow him on their own terms and within the limits of their own understanding. So when he confronted them with the truth about himself and about what it truly meant to follow him, they chose to leave him. Jesus then turns to the little band of men he had called originally. To them he says, not for his own benefit, but for theirs, 'Do you want to go away as well?' (6:67). Simon Peter, ever the spokesman for his fellow disciples, replies, 'Lord, to whom shall we go? You have the words of eternal life, and we have believed, and have come to know that you are the Holy One of God' (6:68–69).

There could hardly be a more eloquent or exquisite expression of true saving faith, of that child-like devotion that will not waver in its confidence or commitment, regardless of what others are doing all around. In realizing the dire seriousness of the truth about ourselves and the glorious uniqueness of the Christ of the gospel, we refuse to look to anything or anyone else for our peace with God and for our assurance of life eternal.

The chapter ends, however, on a tragic note. Despite the beauty of Peter's confession, Jesus says, 'Did I not choose you, the Twelve? And yet one of you is a devil' (6:70). From among that inner circle, one was exposed and put to shame. Why? The answer, as someone has said, is because he was trying to hide in church! No matter who we are, or where we are, no one can evade the responsibility to face up to who Jesus is and to respond to his claims. We must all reach that turning point - even as Judas did - and then take our stand either for Jesus or against him.

18

Who on Earth Is Jesus?

After this Jesus went about in Galilee. He would not go about in Judea, because the Jews were seeking to kill him. ² Now the Jews' Feast of Booths was at hand. ³ So his brothers said to him, "Leave here and go to Judea, that your disciples also may see the works you are doing. ⁴ For no one works in secret if he seeks to be known openly. If you do these things, show yourself to the world." ⁵ For not even his brothers believed in him. ⁶ Jesus said to them, "My time has not yet come, but your time is always here. ⁷ The world cannot hate you, but it hates me because I testify about it that its works are evil. ⁸ You go up to the feast. I am not going up to this feast, for my time has not yet fully come." ⁹ After saying this, he remained in Galilee.

¹⁰ But after his brothers had gone up to the feast, then he also went up, not publicly but in private. ¹¹ The Jews were looking for him at the feast, and saying, "Where is he?" ¹² And there was much muttering about him among the people. While some said, "He is a good man," others said, "No, he is leading the people astray." ¹³ Yet for fear of the Jews no one spoke openly of him.

¹⁴ About the middle of the feast Jesus went up into the temple and began teaching. ¹⁵ The Jews therefore marvelled, saying, "How is it that this man has learning, when he has never studied?" ¹⁶ So Jesus answered them, "My teaching is not mine, but his who sent me. ¹⁷ If anyone's will is to do God's will, he will know whether the teaching is from God or whether I am speaking on my own authority. ¹⁸ The one who speaks on his own authority seeks his own glory, but the one who seeks the glory of him who sent him is true, and in him there is no falsehood. ¹⁹ Has not Moses given you the law? Yet none of you keeps the law. Why do you seek to kill me?" [20] *The crowd answered, "You have a demon! Who is seeking to kill you?"* [21] *Jesus answered them, "I did one deed, and you all marvel at it.* [22] *Moses gave you circumcision (not that it is from Moses, but from the fathers), and you circumcise a man on the Sabbath.* [23] *If on the Sabbath a man receives circumcision, so that the law of Moses may not be broken, are you angry with me because on the Sabbath I made a man's whole body well?* [24] *Do not judge by appearances, but judge with right judgement"* (John 7:1–24).

'Who on earth is Jesus?' That is the kind of question that vast numbers of people might ask – not only those who have never heard his name, but even those who have heard, but do not have the slightest idea as to who he was or what he did. As we look at this next section of John's Gospel, we see immediately that his contemporaries were asking the same kind of questions. Although we might think that the problem of understanding Jesus lies in the historical and cultural distance between his day and ours, it really lies elsewhere. Confusion about Jesus arises out of the human heart. Some years later the apostle Paul put his finger on the problem when he said, 'The natural person does not accept the things of the Spirit of God . . . because they are spiritually discerned' (*1 Cor.* 2:14).

This is the issue to which John now turns. As we read through the passage, from the conversation between Jesus and his natural brothers concerning his visit to the Feast of Tabernacles (7:1–5), up to the description of the views about him that were being expressed about Jerusalem (7:11–14), we are struck by the wide variety of opinions. Some saw him as a 'good man'; others as a deceiver (7:13). A number even went so far as to label him as 'demon-possessed' (7:20). Most were openly agnostic (7:13).

The crowds were particularly struggling in their understanding of Jesus because his teaching and his claims were so closely bound up with himself. Unlike any other teacher, there was no neat way of separating who he was and what he did from all that he taught. It was impossible to accept his message without accepting him. This is where the problem lay for them, and that is exactly where the problem continues to lie today. Jesus himself makes it clear that no one can receive the benefits of his teaching apart from receiving his person and his work. John elaborates on this point by highlighting three truths concerning Jesus and his ministry.

(i) HIS MOTIVATION

Documentaries and biographies that give an insight into what makes famous people 'tick' are commonplace. Very often the impact such people make is closely bound up with the kind of people they are. Onlookers are eager to discover what lies behind the public face! This was especially true of Jesus. John uses the many misconceptions about him as a foil for emphasizing his true nature. He shows how Jesus reacts to different people and to the various opinions they represent.

He begins with Jesus' own brothers and their thinly veiled cynicism. As this episode occurs straight after the record of widespread desertion in the previous chapter and at the same time as the death threats mentioned at the start of this chapter (7:1), it shows the degree of opposition that Jesus had to face from so many different quarters. The annual Feast of Tabernacles was drawing near (7:2) and Jews from all over the country were making their pilgrimage to the city. Jesus' brothers were intending to go and they urged him to go too. Their reason for encouraging him to do so was tinged with more than a little irony: 'No one works in secret if he seeks to be known openly. If you do these things, show yourself to the world' (7:4). Their assessment of their older brother could not have been wider of the mark.

They failed to see that Jesus had no intention of 'starting a movement'. He was not just another charismatic figure ready to jump on the bandwagon of popular appeal, and to try his hand at 'starting something'. The opposite was true. Jesus quite deliberately shunned that kind of public adulation. His mission went far deeper than simply appealing to natural human instincts and affections. Instead, he came as the one conscious that he was sent to fulfil a God-mission. He was not operating therefore according to his own agenda and timetable (let alone that of others), but according to God's.

This is seen in the comment he makes in response to his brothers' suggestion: 'My time has not yet come' (7:6). He uses the same word for 'time' that he used in a remark during the wedding at Cana (2:4). It is the word that is often linked to the timing of his crucifixion. Here, however, it simply refers to the day-to-day ordering of his life. Every moment, every word, every action unfolds in keeping with an unseen plan. Just as God had a special time for Jesus' birth (*Gal.* 4:4) and a set time for his death (*John* 17:1), so also God had a specific timetable for his life as a whole. Jesus made it clear to his brothers that even if he was to go to the feast, it would not be at their instigation and on their terms but according to God's schedule (7:8).

The deepest motivation therefore at the heart of Jesus' ministry lay not in men, nor even within himself alone, but in his profound sense of the eternal purpose of God the Father. This has huge implications for our understanding of Jesus and of the means by which we benefit from his work. It is not for us to fit him neatly into our lives and agendas on our terms. The reality is quite the reverse. He has come so that we might be caught up and fitted into God's life and purpose.

(II) HIS TEACHING

John stresses again the teaching of Jesus and the way it is to be received. All that Jesus says leaves no room for neutrality. This becomes clear in the passage as John allows us to mingle as it were with the crowds in Jerusalem and to eavesdrop on what they are saying about Jesus and his teaching (7:10–13). When Jesus eventually emerges from the shadows during the feast and begins to teach publicly in the temple courts, his ministry has a profound effect on everyone (7:14–15).

The Jews were particularly amazed that Jesus was such an able teacher, despite the fact that he never received any formal training. Just because he had not come through their 'system' and had not passed through their schools of training he was outside their area of control. In their frustration they were similar to others who try to reduce Jesus to manageable proportions. Whether by viewing him as just a teacher or as an impressive role model, they would like to define him in their own terms. Jesus' teaching – both in its content and in the manner of its presentation – does not permit such a response. It is teaching that claims openly to be from another world and from an altogether different sphere.

Jesus does not leave us guessing as to which world or sphere. He states plainly, 'My teaching is not mine, but his who sent me' (7:16). In case that might appear to be a somewhat cryptic comment, he clarifies it immediately, 'If anyone's will is to do God's will, he will know whether the teaching is from God or whether I am speaking on my own authority' (7:17). There are only two possibilities concerning the authority underlying Jesus' words. Either his words depend on his authority alone, or they derive from God. The implications are stark. If his ministry rests only on his authority, it can conceivably be dismissed as one might dismiss the teaching of any other religious figure. If it comes from God, that cannot be the case.

Jesus develops this contrast by highlighting the different motives that might lie behind these alternatives. Someone whose teaching is 'his own' is simply seeking his own honour, but the man who genuinely works for the honour of the one who sent him 'is true' (7:18). Jesus stakes his integrity on the fact that there should be a recognizable consistency between everything that he says and everything that God has said. Such a declaration must either authenticate his ministry or disqualify it.

The double edge in all of these words lies in the fact that Jesus is not only providing a fixed point of reference to validate his own ministry, but also using that same point to expose the duplicity within the ministry of the Jewish teachers. He refers next to Moses (and his God-inspired teaching) so as to reveal the inconsistency between their professed adherence to Moses and their secret plans to murder Jesus (7:19). Despite their defensive protests, Jesus presses home his argument by contrasting their willingness to circumcise a child on the Sabbath according (as they thought) to Moses' teaching, with their objection to his healing a lame man on the Sabbath (7:20–24). They were the hypocrites, not Jesus; they were the ones who were denying God's message!

Who on earth is Jesus? On comparing the teaching of God in the Old Testament with the teaching of Christ in the Gospels, we find perfect harmony and consistency. The only right judgement is that Jesus is God's messenger and must be believed.

(III) HIS STANDARDS

All this is confirmed further by a closer look at the terse exchange recorded in the final verses. Jesus reveals the double standards of the Jewish leaders. He knew perfectly well the secret intentions of their hearts, that they were bent on murder. He also knew their attempts at covering their tracks. As he refers them again to the Mosaic law, which they claimed they followed so faithfully, he shows how inconsistent they really are. The punch-line comes at the end: 'Do not judge by appearances, but judge with right judgement' (7:24). Jesus' standards and theirs, when set side by side, are worlds apart. He alone reflects, not merely the outward demands of God's Law, but its true inward reality.

Jewish obsession with outward behaviour and the appearance of righteousness leads to one thing: an uneasy conscience before God! Only in Jesus do we find the perfect unity of a heart for God, together with a message from God. This is not only because he is a messenger from heaven, but primarily because he is the Word of God come down from heaven. This qualifies him to accomplish what neither Jewish teachers nor any other religious teachers can accomplish: our reconciliation to God. He stands alone, he is unique. No other has brought the salvation planned in heaven down into the world of men.

19

Reacting to Jesus

Some of the people of Jerusalem therefore said, "Is not this the man whom they seek to kill? *26* And here he is, speaking openly, and they say nothing to him! Can it be that the authorities really know that this is the Christ? *27* But we know where this man comes from, and when the Christ appears, no one will know where he comes from." *28* So Jesus proclaimed, as he taught in the temple, "You know me, and you know where I come from? But I have not come of my own accord. He who sent me is true, and him you do not know. *29* I know him, for I come from him, and he sent me." *30* So they were seeking to arrest him, but no one laid a hand on him, because his hour had not yet come. *31* Yet many of the people believed in him. They said, "When the Christ appears, will he do more signs than this man has done?"

32 The Pharisees heard the crowd muttering these things about him, and the chief priests and Pharisees sent officers to arrest him. *33* Jesus then said, "I will be with you a little longer, and then I am going to him who sent me. *34* You will seek me and you will not find me. Where I am you cannot come." *35* The Jews said to one another, "Where does this man intend to go that we will not find him? Does he intend to go to the Dispersion among the Greeks and teach the Greeks? *36* What does he mean by saying, 'You will seek me and you will not find me,' and, 'Where I am you cannot come'?"

37 On the last day of the feast, the great day, Jesus stood up and cried out, "If anyone thirsts, let him come to me and drink. *38* Whoever believes in me, as the Scripture has said, 'Out of his heart will flow rivers of living water.'" *39* Now this he said about *the Spirit, whom those who believed in him were to receive, for as yet the Spirit had not been given, because Jesus was not yet glorified.*

⁴⁰ When they heard these words, some of the people said, "This really is the Prophet." ⁴¹ Others said, "This is the Christ." But some said, "Is the Christ to come from Galilee? ⁴² Has not the Scripture said that the Christ comes from the offspring of David, and comes from Bethlehem, the village where David was?" ⁴³ So there was a division among the people over him. ⁴⁴ Some of them wanted to arrest him, but no one laid hands on him.

⁴⁵ The officers then came to the chief priests and Pharisees, who said to them, "Why did you not bring him?" ⁴⁶ The officers answered, "No one ever spoke like this man!" ⁴⁷ The Pharisees answered them, "Have you also been deceived? ⁴⁸ Have any of the authorities or the Pharisees believed in him? ⁴⁹ But this crowd that does not know the law is accursed." ⁵⁰ Nicodemus, who had gone to him before, and who was one of them, said to them, ⁵¹ "Does our law judge a man without first giving him a hearing and learning what he does?" ⁵² They replied, "Are you from Galilee too? Search and see that no prophet arises from Galilee."

⁵³ They went each to his own house (John 7:25–53).

All through this portion of his Gospel, John is not only demonstrating the increasingly polarised reactions to Jesus during his earthly ministry, but also highlighting the reasons that lay behind these reactions. This all confirms what Jesus himself said elsewhere, 'Do not think that I have come to bring peace to the earth. I have not come to bring peace, but a sword' (*Matt.* 10:34).

Once again there is an abiding relevance in all of this. These truths about Jesus accentuated by John demolish those saccharine notions of a Christ with whom anyone can be comfortable and who is happy to tolerate each and every alternative religion. Such notions are simply untenable.

John highlights four different aspects of Jesus' character and ministry, each of which produces different responses.

(1) The Authority of His Teaching

Again and again throughout his public ministry we find Jesus startling people with the authority of his teaching. This is clearly seen, for example, in the astonished reaction of his followers to the Sermon on the Mount (*Matt.* 7:28–29). The underlying authority of Jesus' words could not be dismissed or denied.

As Jesus steps into public view towards the end of the Feast, John first contrasts the reaction of the crowd, 'Is not this the man whom they seek to kill?' (7:25), with the previous denials of the religious leaders (7:20). Christ's authoritative knowledge of the latter's plans shows his superiority over both groups.

But there is more in view here. In an extremely apt choice of words, the people ask, 'Can it be that the authorities really know that this is the Christ?' (7:26). Have the appointed guardians of official Jewish teaching finally given a definitive ruling on the identity of Jesus? Even though the crowds recognized the authority of Jesus' teaching, they instinctively deferred to the official organ of the Jewish faith. At face value, the refusal of the Jewish leaders to take decisive action against Jesus seemed to speak in his favour. Nevertheless, a degree of reservation is expressed on the grounds that no one would know from where the Messiah had come, but everyone knew where Jesus was from (7:27).

Jesus answers their doubts and uncertainties with a bold public statement. He 'proclaimed' in the temple courts, 'You know me, and you know where I come from? But I have not come of my own accord, He who sent me is true, and him you do not know. I know him, for I come from him, and he sent me' (7:28–29). He declared who he was, where he was from, and why he had come, with a calm and confident conviction. There could be no mistaking his authority. It was so obvious to all, that when the temple guards – the very men who were there to uphold the authority of the temple regime – were questioned about their failure to arrest him, they replied, 'No one ever spoke like this man' (7:46). The sheer authority of Jesus' words, both here in the Gospels and throughout the Bible, comes home with a force that cannot be ignored.

(II) The Power of His Presence

The impression of authority is hardly surprising. Jesus possessed a commanding presence to an unique degree.

This is evident, most dramatically, in the failed attempt of the temple guard to arrest him (7:30) and again in the failure of some in the crowd to seize him. It would appear from the wider context that more is going on here than a mere clash of strong personalities. The fact that the failure to lay hold of Jesus is linked directly to the idea that 'his hour had not yet come' (7:30) seems to indicate a clash between the wishes of men and the will of God. The power of God's purpose was being displayed in the presence of his Son. His simple humanity robed the power of deity.

This was a striking feature of his incarnate life on earth, but it continues to be so after his ascension, in his ongoing ministry by his Spirit and through his Word. We see its dramatic effect in what Paul says to the Christians in Ephesus concerning the way God's work was established among them. He speaks of the time Christ 'came and preached peace to you who were far off and peace to those who were near' (*Eph.* 2:17). Even though Christ's physical presence never graced the city of Ephesus, nevertheless his real presence was felt as his Word was proclaimed and his Spirit was at work. In the same way that his presence had a powerful impact on all who heard him in Jerusalem, Judea and Galilee, so also, as his gospel has been heard throughout the world and across all ages, the power of his presence has never lost its impact.

(III) The Beauty of His Offer

Those who opposed Jesus drew back from his presence because of the power and authority that were so obviously his. To those however who looked to him in faith, Jesus extended an exquisitely beautiful offer. In the most dramatic manner, Jesus chose the last day of the Feast of Tabernacles for his proclamation, 'If anyone thirsts, let him come to me and drink. Whoever believes in me, as the Scripture has said, "Out of his heart will flow rivers of living waters"' (7:37–38). God's provision is declared alongside man's need. Christ's attributes of grace and mercy are as evident as his power and authority!

On the one hand he speaks of the never-ending ache of the human soul – that longing which wealth, learning, friends or family, can never adequately ease. To all afflicted by that longing, Jesus says, 'Come to me and I will quench your thirst forever!' Not only was he promising to satisfy the deepest longings of an individual soul, he was promising to do it in such a way that the blessing poured into that soul would overflow and touch the lives of many others.

The drama of the situation lies in the association between the words and imagery that Jesus uses, and one of the daily rituals associated with this feast. This most significant of rituals involved the ceremonial filling of a flagon, carrying it in procession and then pouring it out as an offering before God. This symbolized both the outpouring by God of water in the desert and his outpouring of his Spirit in the last days. Jesus adds a third element to the picture by predicting the outpouring of his Spirit in salvation (7:39).

There is no need for people to fear before this Christ, though all power and authority in heaven and on earth are his. For all those who hear and respond to his gracious invitation in the gospel, he holds out the promise of full and satisfying salvation.

(IV) The Penetration of His Truth

The chapter ends with the identification of those shadowy figures who have been lurking behind all the opposition to Jesus. Even though the temple guards had been in the forefront of the various attempts to thwart Jesus' influence, it was their masters – the chief priests and Pharisees – who were responsible. To them the guards returned (7:45). These leading figures of the religious establishment made no effort to conceal their vitriolic hatred of Jesus (7:45–49). The truth of John's comment on the meeting between Jesus and Nicodemus was becoming disturbingly apparent: 'Light has come into the world, and people loved the darkness rather than the light because their deeds were evil' (3:19). The truth of Jesus' claims was beginning to penetrate the hypocritical cloak of religiosity covering these most respected Jews. Their animosity towards him goes far beyond reason. It was the result of sin in the depths of the soul, driving from within.

Then, on a totally different note, the focus falls on Nicodemus. He is not now a lone figure under the cover of darkness, but a lone voice in the midst of a clamour of opposition. He intervenes from a true concern for natural justice, stating that Jesus deserved a proper hearing at least before being convicted (7:50–51). Was this the moment when this prominent Pharisee went public and declared his faith in Jesus? Certainly from this point on he appears as a follower of Jesus, preparing to distance himself from the Sanhedrin.

For him the truth of Christ had penetrated to such an extent that he could no longer fight against it. He no longer tried to hide. He bowed before the truth and acknowledged Christ in public. Thus it is that true and saving faith always reveals itself.

20

Light and Truth

But Jesus went to the Mount of Olives. ² Early in the morning he came again to the temple. All the people came to him, and he sat down and taught them. ³ The scribes and the Pharisees brought a woman who had been caught in adultery, and placing her in the midst ⁴ they said to him, "Teacher, this woman has been caught in the act of adultery. ⁵ Now in the Law Moses commanded us to stone such women. So what do you say?" ⁶ This they said to test him, that they might have some charge to bring against him. Jesus bent down and wrote with his finger on the ground. ⁷ And as they continued to ask him, he stood up and said to them, "Let him who is without sin among you be the first to throw a stone at her." ⁸ And once more he bent down and wrote on the ground. ⁹ But when they heard it, they went away one by one, beginning with the older ones, and Jesus was left alone with the woman standing before him. ¹⁰ Jesus stood up and said to her, "Woman, where are they? Has no one condemned you?" ¹¹ She said, "No one, Lord." And Jesus said, "Neither do I condemn you; go, and from now on sin no more."

¹² Again Jesus spoke to them, saying, "I am the light of the world. Whoever follows me will not walk in darkness, but will have the light of life." ¹³ So the Pharisees said to him, "You are bearing witness about yourself; your testimony is not true." ¹⁴ Jesus answered, "Even if I do bear witness about myself, my testimony is true, for I know where I came from and where I am going, but you do not know where I come from or where I am going. ¹⁵ You judge according to the flesh; I judge no one. ¹⁶ Yet even if I do judge, my judgement is true, for it is not I alone who judge, but I and the Father who sent me. ¹⁷ In your Law it is

written that the testimony of two men is true. [18] *I am the one who bears witness about myself, and the Father who sent me bears witness about me."* [19] *They said to him therefore, "Where is your Father?" Jesus answered, "You know neither me nor my Father. If you knew me, you would know my Father also."* [20] *These words he spoke in the treasury, as he taught in the temple; but no one arrested him, because his hour had not yet come.*

[21] *So he said to them again, "I am going away, and you will seek me, and you will die in your sin. Where I am going, you cannot come."* [22] *So the Jews said, "Will he kill himself, since he says, 'Where I am going, you cannot come'?"* [23] *He said to them, "You are from below; I am from above. You are of this world; I am not of this world.* [24] *I told you that you would die in your sins, for unless you believe that I am he you will die in your sins."* [25] *So they said to him, "Who are you?" Jesus said to them, "Just what I have been telling you from the beginning.* [26] *I have much to say about you and much to judge, but he who sent me is true, and I declare to the world what I have heard from him."* [27] *They did not understand that he had been speaking to them about the Father.* [28] *So Jesus said to them, "When you have lifted up the Son of Man, then you will know that I am he, and that I do nothing on my own authority, but speak just as the Father taught me.* [29] *And he who sent me is with me. He has not left me alone, for I always do the things that are pleasing to him."* [30] *As he was saying these things, many believed in him* (John 8:1–30).

Many Bible versions mark off this next section of John's Gospel (7:53–8:11) in some way and include a note to indicate that the passage does not appear in the early manuscripts of the New Testament. Discussion of this point is more appropriate in commentaries that are more technical than this one. The passage certainly has a long tradition of acceptance within the Christian Church, and as we examine it we can appreciate why. It provides a helpful bridge between Jesus' exposure of the hypocrisy of the Pharisees (7:45–53) and the further expression of the integrity of his person and claims (8:12–30).

As we follow the flow of events, we observe on the one hand the insidious depths of human sin, and on the other the absolute perfection of God's Saviour from sin. A number of significant facts come to light.

The Ugliness of Human Sin

If we were to ask, with respect to this history of the woman caught in adultery, 'What is the ugliest expression of sin in these verses?' the answer in response might well be, 'The woman's sexual behaviour'. Certainly this was the judgement of the Jewish onlookers. Here was an offence that carried a capital sentence according to Old Testament law. However, as events unfold, Jesus provides a completely different perspective of the situation. It is not the woman's behaviour that is exposed as being most reprehensible, but rather that of the Jewish leaders. They were not interested in justice for the woman, nor in upholding the honour of God among his people. They were only interested in trying to trap Jesus (8:6).

James Montgomery Boice, in his exposition of John, argues convincingly that this whole incident was a deliberate set-up designed to ensnare Jesus and discredit him. He points to a series of details that look very suspicious. For example, the man who must also have been 'caught in the act' (8:4) is strangely absent from proceedings, even though under Jewish law he would have been equally guilty. Again, that same law required the presence of at least two eyewitnesses if a prosecution was to succeed. This was highly unlikely, given the nature of the crime. If indeed the episode was a set-up, the perverse hypocrisy of these so-called spiritual leaders is far more distasteful than the actions of the woman.

All sin is evil and offensive in God's sight, but some sins are more so than others. The worst sins are not those of debauchery, but of wilful hypocrisy (*Matt.* 11:20–24).

The Beauty of Divine Wisdom

What kind of trap were the Pharisees trying to set for Jesus? It is clear that, in part, it was to see if he would stand by the requirements of the law of Moses. (From other sources we find that had he done so his verdict would have been somewhat unusual for first-century Palestine, where the full penal sanction was rarely enacted in such cases.) There may well have been another strand to it as well. Given the tension between the requirements of the Jewish law and those of the Roman Empire, if Jesus were to press for the death penalty he would very likely have fallen foul of the Roman authorities. We can well imagine these men folding their arms and standing back smugly, as if they were some kind of religious chess players, waiting to see the consequences of their moves!

The reality of the problem was far worse than they had imagined. It was not merely that Jesus was cornered between the demands of Jewish law and the impositions laid upon it by the Roman system, but he needed additionally to demonstrate the demands of divine justice together with the constraint of divine love. His was that dilemma of unimaginable proportions that Paul put his finger on in his Letter to the Romans: how can God justify sinners and yet maintain his own integrity? (*Rom.* 3:26). Upon the answer to that question hangs the fate, not just of this woman, but of every human being.

Jesus turns the tables on his devious opponents by means of a simple ultimatum: 'Let him who is without sin among you be the first to throw a stone at her' (8:7). The perversity and guile of human 'wisdom' is laid bare by the simple beauty of divine wisdom, embodied in Christ (*1 Cor.* 1:30). It highlights the emptiness of man's solutions to the problem of evil, while at the same time displaying the perfect answer that God provides in Jesus.

THE WONDER OF INCARNATE LOVE

The wonder of that answer is demonstrated by Jesus' treatment of the woman after all the men have slunk away, afraid to compound their own hypocrisy. It is seen in the way that the one who is the very incarnation of truth, holiness, righteousness and justice can stand before a sinner, whose guilt is beyond question, and say, 'Neither do I condemn you' (8:11). For the first time in her life this woman began to realize that divine perfection and justice cannot be fully understood in isolation from divine mercy and love. For the first time in her life she could hear someone say, 'sin no more' and actually want to comply.

Obviously there were many things that the woman would not have grasped at this time, not least the legal basis upon which God could deal with her in this way. However, the events in the life of Jesus that would unfold over the coming months would make that clear. Not long after this incident Jesus himself would be in the dock. He would there face accusations that would be false rather than true. The court would be given contrived and perjured evidence. The accused would be condemned and killed, rather than being spared. God's own Son would take the place of guilty sinners, such as this woman. He therefore has every right to set them free!

THE LIGHT OF GOSPEL TRUTH

The darkness that hangs over the first eleven verses of this chapter because of the moral failure of this woman and of the lies of those who were meant to bring spiritual light to God's people, is broken by Jesus' next public utterance. Speaking to the people (presumably still those who had come to Jerusalem for the Feast of Tabernacles), he says, 'I am the light of the world' (8:12). Into the pall of spiritual darkness that so obviously hung over this supposedly spiritually enlightened nation, Jesus shone the light of his own person and teaching.

This is the second of the seven great 'I am' sayings that John records. They constitute what might be regarded as a kind of *Pocket Guide to Understanding Jesus*. In a sequence of pithy statements, we are brought face to face with the monumental truths concerning him. Again, the fact that Jesus made this statement at or just after the Feast of Tabernacles is highly significant. The feast had strong associations with joy for the Jewish people and was marked also by four huge lampstands used to illuminate the temple court by night. So for Jesus to describe himself as a light could hardly have been more dramatic. He was proclaiming himself to be the good and joyful news from God, not just for the Jews, but for the whole world.

As the darkness of despair was settling on a people who were beginning to realize that they could not trust their own spiritual leaders, Jesus comes as the true light that will banish their darkness forever.

THE PERFECTION OF GOD'S ANSWER

Another heated exchange between Jesus and the Pharisees follows (8:13–26). The Jewish leaders again question Jesus' credentials, calling for witnesses to corroborate his claims (8:13). Jesus responds by asserting boldly that were his testimony to stand alone, his claims would still be valid. (He is clearly referring to his absolute uniqueness). Nevertheless, he points to that other supporting testimony which was his, namely, that supplied by his Father (8:14–18). The Jews press him further, asking where his Father was, but Jesus answers by emphasizing the damning truth that they do not know his Father. Such an answer, of course, carried the implication that they did not know God (8:19).

The bottom line in what Jesus says to them is this: 'You are from below; I am from above. You are from this world; I am not of this world' (8:23). In the starkest possible terms, he goes on to warn them, 'I told you that you would die in your sins, for unless you believe that I am he, you will die in your sins' (8:24). The original is even more pointed here. Jesus does not say, 'unless you believe that I am he,' but 'unless you believe that I am'. He is again taking God's special name – his 'calling card' as it were, 'I AM' (*Exod.* 3:14) – and identifying himself not merely with God, but as God! In other words, the perfect salvation that God promised in the gospel would come from above, and it would come in the person of Jesus Christ – who is God himself.

Such claims are easily made, but not so easily verified. Jesus however addresses that issue also. Pointing forward to the cross and using highly charged language, he says, 'When you have lifted up the Son of Man, then you will know that I am he' (8:28). In the darkness that would engulf the world on that day of crucifixion, the light of God's perfect salvation would shine in all its brilliance.

21

Starting All Over Again

So Jesus said to the Jews who had believed in him, "If you abide in my word, you are truly my disciples, ³² and you will know the truth, and the truth will set you free." ³³ They answered him, "We are offspring of Abraham and have never been enslaved to anyone. How is it that you say, 'You will become free'?"

³⁴ Jesus answered them, "Truly, truly, I say to you, everyone who commits sin is a slave to sin. ³⁵ The slave does not remain in the house forever; the son remains forever. ³⁶ So if the Son sets you free, you will be free indeed. ³⁷ I know that you are offspring of Abraham; yet you seek to kill me because my word finds no place in you. ³⁸ I speak of what I have seen with my Father, and you do what you have heard from your father."

³⁹ They answered him, "Abraham is our father." Jesus said to them, "If you were Abraham's children, you would be doing what Abraham did, ⁴⁰ but now you seek to kill me, a man who has told you the truth that I heard from God. This is not what Abraham did. ⁴¹ You are doing what your father did." They said to him, "We were not born of sexual immorality. We have one Father— even God." ⁴² Jesus said to them, "If God were your Father, you would love me, for I came from God and I am here. I came not of my own accord, but he sent me. ⁴³ Why do you not understand what I say? It is because you cannot bear to hear my word. ⁴⁴ You are of your father the devil, and your will is to do your father's desires. He was a murderer from the beginning, and has nothing to do with the truth, because there is no truth in him. When he lies, he speaks out of his own character, for he is a liar and the father of lies. ⁴⁵ But because I tell the truth, you do not believe me. ⁴⁶ Which one of you convicts me of sin? If I tell the

truth, why do you not believe me? ⁴⁷ Whoever is of God hears the words of God. The reason why you do not hear them is that you are not of God."

⁴⁸ *The Jews answered him, "Are we not right in saying that you are a Samaritan and have a demon?" ⁴⁹ Jesus answered, "I do not have a demon, but I honour my Father, and you dishonour me. ⁵⁰ Yet I do not seek my own glory; there is One who seeks it, and he is the judge. ⁵¹ Truly, truly, I say to you, if anyone keeps my word, he will never see death." ⁵² The Jews said to him, "Now we know that you have a demon! Abraham died, as did the prophets, yet you say, 'If anyone keeps my word, he will never taste death.' ⁵³ Are you greater than our father Abraham, who died? And the prophets died! Who do you make yourself out to be?" ⁵⁴ Jesus answered, "If I glorify myself, my glory is nothing. It is my Father who glorifies me, of whom you say, 'He is our God.'*

⁵⁵ *But you have not known him. I know him. If I were to say that I do not know him, I would be a liar like you, but I do know him and I keep his word. ⁵⁶ Your father Abraham rejoiced that he would see my day. He saw it and was glad." ⁵⁷ So the Jews said to him, "You are not yet fifty years old, and have you seen Abraham?" ⁵⁸ Jesus said to them, "Truly, truly, I say to you, before Abraham was, I am." ⁵⁹ So they picked up stones to throw at him, but Jesus hid himself and went out of the temple* (John 8:31–59).

The exchange between Jesus and the Pharisees recorded in the first half of this chapter and played out apparently in full public view seemed to have one encouraging effect. John tells us, 'As he was saying these things, many believed in him' (8:30). It is to these new 'believers' that Jesus now turns his attention, with startling consequences.

I remember once observing a building development in an old church hall. One of the engineers involved at an early stage of the work had proposed some structural solutions to a wall that was causing problems. However, when the builders moved in they discovered that the problem was more serious than had appeared.

They found that old layers of cladding which the engineer had failed to notice were covering up a more deep-seated problem in the structure.

So here, as Jesus begins to probe the faith of the Jews who had turned to him, he too uncovers a problem that went far deeper than these people had imagined. He says, quite innocuously, 'If you abide in my word, you are truly my disciples, and you will know the truth, and the truth will set you free' (8:31–32). Almost immediately their hackles begin to rise, and by the end of the chapter these very people who had professed to believe in Jesus were ready to stone him (8:59). Though a sad episode, this was a necessary step in exposing the depth of human need and highlighting the true nature of God's deliverance. Salvation means nothing less than starting all over again.

THE TERRIFYING POWER OF SIN

As Jesus begins to probe the hidden thoughts of these Jews who had believed in him, some disturbing things start to emerge. The upshot of it all is that Jesus describes them to their faces as children of the devil (8:44). Either Jesus was being unnecessarily provocative, or else the problem of sin is significantly more serious than is often realized.

What irked these followers was the suggestion that they needed to be made free, and that this could only happen when they came to know the truth (8:32). Their indignant reaction was to claim that they had never been enslaved to anyone, so how could they need to be set free? (8:33). Jesus' answer is blunt and to the point. He says that everyone who sins is a slave to sin and, even worse, that if they are slaves then (according to ancient law) they have no place in the family (8:34–35). Only someone from within the family – 'the Son' – is actually able to liberate them (8:36). He presses this home by acknowledging their relationship to Abraham by virtue of nationality, but stressing that their attitude to himself reveals a different story. Their readiness to kill Jesus points to an altogether different paternity (8:37–38).

Again the Jews protest and reassert their bond with Abraham. Again Jesus declares that their actions are a denial of such a claim (8:39). The acid test is found in their response to the words of truth: they are determined to kill the One who speaks them (8:40). Such conduct is not at all consistent with the attitude of the nation's father, Abraham, but very consistent with that of a very different father (8:41). To that the Jews reply, 'We have one Father, even God' (8:42).

What Jesus is doing is exposing the frightening grip that sin has on people's lives. It is not merely that life is muddied by 'sins' here and there, but that human life is literally under the control of an alien power, namely, the devil himself. The full horror of this is seen in the way that people under the domination of sin react to Jesus and his message – they seek to murder him. Paul says precisely the same thing when he talks about mankind in its natural condition. Men 'by their unrighteousness suppress the truth' (*Rom.* 1:18). Before they can be set free, men and women need first to realize that they are enslaved.

THE IRREPRESSIBLE FORCE OF TRUTH

It is striking that the Jews find themselves in head-on collision with truth, not as an abstract concept, but as embodied in the person of Jesus. He has already made it clear that there is a vital connection between the truth that liberates and the Son who liberates (8:32, 36). As he presses home his argument in this encounter, he will not allow his hearers to wriggle off the hook and avoid the question as to their personal response to him.

Those who genuinely know God as their Father will prove it through their love for Jesus, God's Son (8:42). The relationship between the two is such that to truly relate to one will inevitably mean a corresponding relationship with the other. The fact that the Jews are baulking at this point, in not wholeheartedly accepting Jesus and his Word, only indicates that the deepest bond in their lives is with a father from hell and not the true Father from heaven. The devil's imprint on the lives of men leaves them deceived about God and his truth. Just as Satan's deception marked the beginning of the Fall in Eden (*Gen.* 3:1–5), so it becomes the shackle that has kept people from God throughout the ages (*Rom.* 1:25).

Jesus is God's irrepressible answer to that deception. Even though he is neither recognized, nor acknowledged, he is still God's truth in human flesh. Jesus touches the raw nerve of conscience in his hearers by saying, 'because I tell the truth, you do not believe me'

(8:45). Indeed, the truth in Christ which they deliberately oppose at this stage of his ministry would ultimately be vindicated at the climax of his ministry, when he would be put on trial formally and his innocence and integrity shown to be beyond dispute.

Here then is the acid test of how we stand with God. Those who belong to him hear what Jesus says. Those who listen to what God says listen to his Son.

THE LIBERATING POWER OF GRACE

There are two threads running through these verses: one negative, the other positive. The negative thread is tragically clear: stubborn resistance to Jesus and his truth. Such an underlying attitude always fails ultimately to maintain the respectable neutrality or religious veneer behind which it so often takes refuge. The more it is confronted with the truth of Christ in the gospel, the more antagonistic it becomes. In this case the Jews, reaching the depths of unreason, dismiss Jesus as a demoniac (8:48) and would murder him if allowed to do so (8:59). Such an attitude does not belong only to this particular group of Jews confronted by Jesus, it is the shared reaction of millions through the ages. It is the ultimate proof of a parentage from hell.

By contrast, the positive thrust in these verses is seen, not just in Jesus' promise to set people free by the truth of his Word, but in the reason why he is able to make such an extravagant claim. He can do so because he is God (8:58).

The more the Jews tried to demonize Jesus, the more he laid out his defence. If the Jews had only looked more closely they would have seen that Jesus, far from exhibiting demonic traits in his life and ministry, was supremely concerned for God's glory (8:49–50). Jesus then takes matters a step further by saying that those who keep his Word (and so acknowledge its truth) 'will never see death' (8:51). This is the crux of God's answer to man's deepest problem. Just as sin separates man from God in this life and will lead to eternal exclusion from his presence in the next, so God's grace in Christ provides eternal release from that alienation.

Hearing this sends the Jews into a fiercer frenzy still. They point to the fact that Abraham and all the prophets died, so that Jesus must be out of his mind in making such a claim (8:52–53). Jesus answers that he will not glorify himself, but that the Father will glorify him (8:54). Using language that recurs throughout this Gospel and which points in a singular fashion to the cross (17:1), Jesus is content to say, in effect, 'The truth will out.' He adds, 'Your father Abraham rejoiced that he would see my day. He saw it and was glad' (8:56). The venerable patriarch to whom these people claimed allegiance had greater insight into these truths than they had and demonstrated as much by the life of faith he lived, and the confidence in God's Word he displayed.

The crowd was incensed by this statement and ridiculed him (8:57). Jesus responds, 'Before Abraham was, I am' (8:58). There was no mistaking what Jesus was saying. More clearly than ever before he was taking the divine Name and using it for himself. The reason for this is obvious. The only way that the Son through the truth could truly liberate those deceived by the devil and under the tyranny of sin, was because he, uniquely, was the truth of God incarnate - the Son of God in human flesh. God's purpose was to undo through him the eternity of damage that had been done through Adam.

This was surely the greatest news a sin-cursed world could ever hear. It was the very news for which the Jewish people had been waiting throughout their history. Yet, as John has already indicated in his Prologue, 'He came to his own, and his own people did not receive him' (1:11). Their rejection could not have been stronger: 'They picked up stones to throw at him' (8:59), but Jesus slipped away!

22

I Once Was Blind,
But Now I See!

As he passed by, he saw a man blind from birth. [2] And his disciples asked him, "Rabbi, who sinned, this man or his parents, that he was born blind?" [3] Jesus answered, "It was not that this man sinned, or his parents, but that the works of God might be displayed in him. [4] We must work the works of him who sent me while it is day; night is coming, when no one can work. [5] As long as I am in the world, I am the light of the world." [6] Having said these things, he spat on the ground and made mud with the saliva. Then he anointed the man's eyes with the mud [7] and said to him, "Go, wash in the pool of Siloam" (which means Sent). So he went and washed and came back seeing.

[8] The neighbours and those who had seen him before as a beggar were saying, "Is this not the man who used to sit and beg?" [9] Some said, "It is he." Others said, "No, but he is like him." He kept saying, "I am the man." [10] So they said to him, "Then how were your eyes opened?" [11] He answered, "The man called Jesus made mud and anointed my eyes and said to me, 'Go to Siloam and wash.' So I went and washed and received my sight." [12] They said to him, "Where is he?" He said, "I do not know" (John 9:1–12).

The tragic irony of the present generation is that it has never been more enlightened, while at the same time it has never been more confused! It has developed theories and technologies that are able to unlock the secrets of outer space and the mysteries of the structure of matter, but is totally at sea when it comes to reality, identity, morality and destiny. The lyrics of so many songs and the content of so many plays and films reflect the emptiness and agony that so many people feel.

This only shows the extent to which people today still find themselves in exactly the same place as the generation of Jesus' day. Despite the outward contrasts with respect to knowledge and technology, the inner similarities are impossible to miss. The essential problems of human nature never change. Although in one way this is tragic – two thousand years of history and still we never learn – in another way it is comforting. If the heart of man's problem has not altered, then the essence of God's solution is still as relevant. The hope of the gospel is truly the hope of the ages.

This next episode recorded by John brings this truth into sharp focus. Repeating his statement of the previous chapter (8:12), Jesus expands upon the truth about himself as 'the light of the world' (9:5). This truth set forth in words is then illustrated by his actions. He comes to a man who has lived in physical darkness all his life and heals him, turning him as it were into a living parable on the need of the world and the provision of God.

The backdrop to this incident is still the Feast of Tabernacles and the festival of lights that was an integral part of that celebration. In a wider context, John reiterates one of his central themes laid out in his Prologue: the fact that the eternal Word was also the eternal light that shone into the darkness of a fallen world (1:4–9). This larger truth lifts this incident on to a timeless plane. It is not only a fascinating and heart-warming miracle that revolutionized the life of a poor man of Jerusalem, it becomes part of God's message of hope to a hopeless world. It speaks eloquently of the world's need in its sin and God's answer through his Son.

A CONGENITAL PROBLEM

One of the many fascinating developments in modern medicine is the ability of specialists to diagnose problems at the earliest stages of life. Indeed, by understanding the genetic make-up of the parents, they know precisely what kind of problems to anticipate in their children - even before these have been conceived! Many medical conditions are therefore classified as 'congenital' – a condition present from birth.

Despite the relatively primitive state of medicine, by comparison, in the days of Jesus, we find his disciples reflecting on this blind man's problems at an even deeper level. They too consider his condition as congenital, but not because of some genetic defect in him or his parents, but rather because of a spiritual defect. They see the problem and they instinctively ask the question, 'Who sinned, this man or his parents, that he was born blind?' (9:2). Jesus answers (just as the Bible does so often in this context) by steering them away from intricate personal connections within a single family unit, to the deeper issues of the wider human family to which all belong. He points to the wider dimension of a world in the grip of suffering on account of sin, and the way that God will be glorified in such a world (9:3). God's work in this one individual will be a paradigm of the work God does throughout the world.

The congenital spiritual problem of sin shared by the entire human race since the fall of Adam is met by the universal answer provided by God in Jesus Christ his Son.

An Urgent Need

As Jesus responds to his disciples' question, he is less interested in discussing the cause of the blind man's problem (and the wider problem of which it is a symptom) than in stressing the urgency of finding and applying God's solution. He places the particular work he is about to perform in this instance in the context of the infinitely larger work that he is performing for the world (9:3–5). He wants the disciples to see the bigger picture and the part they have to play in it.

In a subtle, but breathtaking way, Jesus shows how God has chosen to propagate his work in the world through the involvement of ordinary people. He says, '*We* must work the works of him who sent *me* while it is day' (9:4). (Some other translations opt for a variant reading of this verse that restricts the statement to Jesus himself and render it, 'I must work . . .'). It would have been a most extraordinary revelation for these ordinary disciples to think that they were to be involved in God's incredible work, but this was precisely the case. As Paul was to put it much later, 'We are God's fellow workers' (*1 Cor.* 3:9).

The urgency involved in the work is emphasized by Jesus' contrast between night and day. In an age when there was no such thing as 'round-the-clock production', he was pressing home the need to make full use of every opportunity provided by God. Therefore, being presented by a blind man in this situation was not so much a problem to be discussed and analysed, as an opportunity to be seized for the glory of God. Jesus was setting forth an enduring principle that Christians have all too often managed to overlook: that there is an urgency to the gospel that is commensurate with the seriousness of the world's condition. Amy Carmichael, the quiet, but greatly used missionary to India, was impelled into service by a disturbing dream. In the dream she saw hundreds of unreached people plunging over a cliff to their deaths, while Christians sat and made daisy chains!

Jesus wants the Church in all ages to grasp the urgency of the need. As he has indicated already, there is a great harvest to be reaped and there is an urgent need for workers to do the reaping (4:35).

A UNIQUE SOLUTION

The bane of all high quality products in the world is the cheap (and often dangerous) imitations that try to copy and usurp them. Nowhere is this more prevalent and more insidious in life than in the area of spiritual need. In the verses that follow, Jesus goes to great lengths to demonstrate his uniqueness as an answer to that need.

Having restated his claim, not just to be *a* light in the world, but '*the* light of the world' (9:5), he immediately proves that these are no empty words. He backs up what he says by what he does. He performs another miracle-sign that restores sight and light to blinded eyes (9:6–7). The significance of this sign lies not so much in the method employed, as in the instructions issued. The emphasis falls on the name of the pool where the man was to wash the mud off his eyes: 'Siloam'. (John translates so as to make sure that the meaning of the Aramaic name is not lost on his Greek readers.) It is impossible to miss the link with what Jesus has already said about himself and his own coming into the world. He has been 'sent [by God]' to bring light into the world (9:4), and so he in turn sends this man to the miracle that will bring light back into his life.

As with all Jesus' miracles, the supernatural power displayed is a pointer to the supernatural uniqueness of the One who performs it. It is designed to point beyond the joy of the individual to the offer of spiritual healing that Jesus holds out to all. All his claims are endorsed by his unique power and authority.

A Dramatic Change

The outcome of this incident could hardly have been more dramatic. It is pinpointed by the sequence of verbs that John uses: 'So he went . . . washed . . . came back seeing' (9:7). As the man took Jesus at his word and followed his instructions fully, his sight was restored and a seemingly bizarre ritual became the vehicle of God's healing power.

It illustrates for us the way that the instruction of the gospel to come to Jesus Christ by faith for our salvation (which to many may seem just as bizarre as the instruction Jesus gave to the blind man) will also become the vehicle for restoration of life. The gospel requires a response to the command of Christ, just as the healing in this instance required obedience to his words. The gospel tells us to go to Christ for our salvation, and so to Christ we must go!

The glory of this greater miracle of grace is beautifully expressed in the words of John Newton, once so far away from God as a slave-trading sea captain, but dramatically converted and led into the Christian ministry:

> *Amazing grace, how sweet the sound,*
> *That saved a wretch like me;*
> *I once was lost, but now am found,*
> *Was blind, but now I see.*

When God works in a person's life the effect will be plain to see. Just as it was beyond dispute that the man born blind had been given sight (9:8–12) – even though some could hardly believe it – so it is with every true convert. The power of God that saves is a power that will begin to show itself in a transformed life.

23

The Moment of Truth

They brought to the Pharisees the man who had formerly been blind. [14] Now it was a Sabbath day when Jesus made the mud and opened his eyes. [15] So the Pharisees again asked him how he had received his sight. And he said to them, "He put mud on my eyes, and I washed, and I see." [16] Some of the Pharisees said, "This man is not from God, for he does not keep the Sabbath." But others said, "How can a man who is a sinner do such signs?" And there was a division among them. [17] So they said again to the blind man, "What do you say about him, since he has opened your eyes?" He said, "He is a prophet."

[18] The Jews did not believe that he had been blind and had received his sight, until they called the parents of the man who had received his sight [19] and asked them, "Is this your son, who you say was born blind? How then does he now see?" [20] His parents answered, "We know that this is our son and that he was born blind. [21] But how he now sees we do not know, nor do we know who opened his eyes. Ask him; he is of age. He will speak for himself." [22] (His parents said these things because they feared the Jews, for the Jews had already agreed that if anyone should confess Jesus to be Christ, he was to be put out of the synagogue.) [23] Therefore his parents said, "He is of age; ask him."

[24] So for the second time they called the man who had been blind and said to him, "Give glory to God. We know that this man is a sinner." [25] He answered, "Whether he is a sinner I do not know. One thing I do know, that though I was blind, now I see." [26] They said to him, "What did he do to you? How did he open your eyes?" [27] He answered them, "I have told you already, and you

would not listen. Why do you want to hear it again? Do you also want to become his disciples?" [28] *And they reviled him, saying, "You are his disciple, but we are disciples of Moses.* [29] *We know that God has spoken to Moses, but as for this man, we do not know where he comes from."* [30] *The man answered, "Why, this is an amazing thing! You do not know where he comes from, and yet he opened my eyes.* [31] *We know that God does not listen to sinners, but if anyone is a worshipper of God and does his will, God listens to him.* [32] *Never since the world began has it been heard that anyone opened the eyes of a man born blind.* [33] *If this man were not from God, he could do nothing."* [34] *They answered him, "You were born in utter sin, and would you teach us?" And they cast him out.*

[35] *Jesus heard that they had cast him out, and having found him he said, "Do you believe in the Son of Man?"* [36] *He answered, "And who is he, sir, that I may believe in him?"* [37] *Jesus said to him, "You have seen him, and it is he who is speaking to you."* [38] *He said, "Lord, I believe," and he worshipped him.* [39] *Jesus said, "For judgement I came into this world, that those who do not see may see, and those who see may become blind."* [40] *Some of the Pharisees near him heard these things, and said to him, "Are we also blind?"* [41] *Jesus said to them, "If you were blind, you would have no guilt; but now that you say, 'We see,' your guilt remains* (John 9:13–41).

The truth has a nasty habit of coming into the open and making itself felt. It cannot be concealed or suppressed; sooner or later it becomes plain for all to see. So it is with the truth about Jesus. As his public ministry progresses and the exchanges between him and his opponents intensify, the truth about who he is begins to crystallise and people are forced to react. Their reaction becomes based less and less on ignorance and more and more on inescapable fact.

The miracle of the blind man's healing, combined with Jesus' repeated remarks about being 'the light of the world', make a powerful declaration concerning the identity of Jesus. It is a declaration pushing people towards that moment of truth when they must make their personal response. The unfolding revelation of Jesus in the gospel has precisely the same effect on all those exposed to it, regardless of their historical or cultural context. The mists of ignorance are swept away and the truth becomes plain to see. Then comes the real moment of truth: how will they respond to the one who is set before them? No matter how much a person may wish to sit on the fence, there is no room for neutrality, they must respond in one way or another.

As the news spreads about the incredible healing of a man who had been blind from birth, so does the pressure on people to respond to the One who had performed the miracle. There are in effect three different reactions to Jesus in the exchanges that follow, but when we look more closely they reduce to two: the only two possible options – faith or rejection.

THE REACTION OF UNBELIEF

The most bitter reaction against Jesus in these verses comes from the most surprising quarter: the religious community. The religious leaders are antagonistic in the extreme. Even though the evidence that points to Jesus' being the Messiah is growing, their stance against him is hardening all the time and their hatred is becoming plain. In a frightening way we see the ugliness of the human heart being exposed. Even where human nature is carefully concealed beneath the most plausible veneer of piety and devotion to God, the horrible truth of what we are in our sin will sooner or later be seen.

The prejudice of heart in these men is revealed in their irrational attitude and unreasonable abuse: they try to deny the obvious and heap insults upon Jesus. They first latch on to the fact that Jesus performed this miracle on the Sabbath day and see it as a reason for discrediting him (9:13–16). Even though Jesus had already engaged them on this subject and left them speechless (7:20–24), in the blindness of their rage they invoke the same defeated argument again. Yet their objection is so hollow that even onlookers in the crowd expose its lack of logic: 'How can a man who is a sinner do such signs?' (9:16).

Turning to the man who had been healed, the Pharisees then ask for his opinion of the One who had healed him. The man, clearly not the most religious of individuals by nature, simply says, 'He is a prophet' (9:17). The Pharisees will not even countenance this possibility and start to question whether or not the man had been blind in the first place (9:18–23). They call for his parents and put them under pressure to explain what had happened, but they are terrified of the Jewish authorities. It had already been made clear that anyone acknowledging Jesus as Messiah would be put out of the synagogue (9:22).

The Pharisees return to the man who had been healed. They start to intimidate him as well, asserting that they 'know this man is a sinner' (9:24) – the unspoken threat against anyone daring to question the received wisdom of the Jewish authorities is only thinly veiled! The man, however, refrains from expressing opinions in ignorance, he simply states the facts (9:25). When the Jews persist in their questioning, the man – either in naïvety, or with sarcasm – says, 'Do you also want to become his disciples?' (9:26). This was too much for the already frustrated rulers. Seeing that their attempts to intimidate their witness had failed, they resort to verbal abuse and he is summarily excommunicated from the synagogue (9:27–34).

This whole exchange in fact revealed far more about the Jews than it did about Jesus. The weakness of their case and the underhand nature of their tactics serve only to strengthen the evidence supporting the messianic credentials of Jesus. Such blind and bitter hostility becomes a hallmark of that unbelief which has manifested itself, not only throughout the rest of the New Testament, but again and again through history. The truth about Jesus serves to stir up the fiercest opposition and resentment of the human heart.

THE REACTION OF THE UNDECIDED

There was, however, another shade of unbelief in the crowd that day: that of the polite agnostics. They were aware of the force of evidence that was staring them in the face concerning the healing of the man born blind. But even though their 'undecided' stance was a source of obvious annoyance to the Pharisees and Jewish leaders (9:16), their position was in reality no different from those who opposed Jesus outright.

This becomes evident in the expression of indecision over Jesus that we see in the man's parents. When they were subjected to cross-examination by the authorities they baulked at telling 'the truth, the whole truth and nothing but the truth'. Instead, they thrust the focus of attention back on to their son (9:20–23). The reason for their reluctance to make a stand for what was so obviously true is plain: they were afraid of what others might say or do (9:22–23). They were more concerned about where they stood with their neighbours than about where they stood with God.

The story of these parents is the sad story of all too many people. They are quiet, polite and respectable people. They simply want to get on with their own lives. They wish to interfere with other people's business as little as they wish other people to interfere with theirs. The tragedy is that though such people get to 'stay in the synagogue', they are ultimately excluded from the kingdom of God. Their reaction to Jesus may be more genteel than that of the Pharisees, but at the end of the day it is no different. Agnostics are nothing more than polite atheists.

THE REACTION OF FAITH

It is interesting to notice that for the man at the centre of this episode, his physical experience of Christ did not coincide with his spiritual experience of Christ. His physical healing and his spiritual healing were two separate events. His encounter with the power of God led to his later and further experience of that power in a deeper and more lasting way. That is not at all unusual with respect to the way that God chooses to work in people's lives. Often there will be something that happens which awakens spiritual questions that otherwise might never have crossed their minds. This leads to further divine intervention that eventually leads to saving faith.

As we trace the progress of this man's response to Jesus, we can identify three distinct and significant stages. At first Jesus is just 'the man' (9:11), as far as he is concerned. After some time to reflect and to listen to the subsequent arguments, Jesus became 'a prophet' (9:17). Finally, after the perplexing events that followed and the treatment he received from the Pharisees and from his parents, Jesus became to him an object of worship (9:38). The moment of truth for this man was when Jesus revealed to him the truth about himself (9:35–37). Whether or not the man fully appreciated that the term

'Son of Man' was an Old Testament designation for the Messiah (and the phrase that Jesus used most frequently with reference to himself) is a moot point. What is clear is that he came to realize that in Jesus he was face to face with God, and he worshipped him as such. That is the ultimate turning point for anyone: realizing that Jesus is the God who saves and makes us whole.

The two stark and painful extremes of the events of this chapter are drawn together in the closing comment of Jesus: 'For judgement I came into this world, that those who do not see may see, and those who see may become blind' (9:39). He is of course playing on the double meaning of the word 'see'. It is not just physical sight that counts – spiritual perception counts even more. Those who realize that they are spiritually blind and in their helplessness hang on to Jesus will have their sight restored. Those who refuse to admit spiritual blindness (like the Pharisees) and think they see will find themselves plunged into a darkness that will never end.

The Pharisees catch a glimpse of what Jesus is saying and feel its sting in their own consciences. Jesus, knowing their hearts, confirms their suspicions (9:40–41).

24

A New Life in a New Relationship

Truly, truly, I say to you, he who does not enter the sheepfold by the door but climbs in by another way, that man is a thief and a robber. ² But he who enters by the door is the shepherd of the sheep. ³ To him the gatekeeper opens. The sheep hear his voice, and he calls his own sheep by name and leads them out. ⁴ When he has brought out all his own, he goes before them, and the sheep follow him, for they know his voice. ⁵ A stranger they will not follow, but they will flee from him, for they do not know the voice of strangers." ⁶ This figure of speech Jesus used with them, but they did not understand what he was saying to them.

⁷ So Jesus again said to them, "Truly, truly, I say to you, I am the door of the sheep. ⁸ All who came before me are thieves and robbers, but the sheep did not listen to them. ⁹ I am the door. If anyone enters by me, he will be saved and will go in and out and find pasture. ¹⁰ The thief comes only to steal and kill and destroy. I came that they may have life and have it abundantly. ¹¹ I am the good shepherd. The good shepherd lays down his life for the sheep. ¹² He who is a hired hand and not a shepherd, who does not own the sheep, sees the wolf coming and leaves the sheep and flees, and the wolf snatches them and scatters them. ¹³ He flees because he is a hired hand and cares nothing for the sheep. ¹⁴ I am the good shepherd. I know my own and my own know me, ¹⁵ just as the Father knows me and I know the Father; and I lay down my life for the sheep. ¹⁶ And I have other sheep that are not of this fold. I must bring them also, and they will listen to my voice. So there will be one flock, one shepherd. ¹⁷ For this reason the Father loves me, because I lay down my life that I may take it up again. ¹⁸ *No one takes it from me, but I lay it down of my own accord. I have authority to lay it down, and I have authority to take it up again. This charge I have received from my Father."*

¹⁹ *There was again a division among the Jews because of these words.* ²⁰ *Many of them said, "He has a demon, and is insane; why listen to him?"* ²¹ *Others said, "These are not the words of one who is oppressed by a demon. Can a demon open the eyes of the blind?"* (John 10:1–21).

As we move into the tenth chapter of this Gospel, the connection with what has gone before is not immediately obvious. This has led some commentators to argue that there is a radical break between the material in the previous chapter and the new material in this one. However, there is really no need to opt for such a disruptive suggestion. John is obviously a careful writer and the threads that tie his gospel record together are skilfully woven.

The link between the healing of the man born blind and Jesus' discourse on the Good Shepherd lies in the closing verses of chapter 9. There, Jesus had exposed the Pharisees – the spiritual shepherds of Israel – as being spiritually blind. They were disqualified from the task they were supposed to perform on God's behalf. In contrast, Jesus presents himself as the One who is the true Shepherd of his people and the One who will do all that is necessary to guarantee their eternal security.

In all of this there is a strong echo of Ezekiel's ministry to the exiles of Judah in Babylon. He had preached there against the false shepherds of Israel: those who had abused their spiritual privileges and abdicated their spiritual responsibilities over God's people. God's answer is not only to castigate those men for their failure, but to assure his people that he himself would be their perfect Shepherd (*Ezek.* 34:1–31). That great prophecy was now being fulfilled in God's own Son.

The timeless beauty of this discourse lies in the way that it portrays Jesus as the true Shepherd-King of our souls. Drawing on wider Old Testament and ancient Near Eastern imagery of the king as shepherd of his people, it shows how Jesus provides, in the lives of those who trust him, the loving leadership that will bring them into eternal joy and peace. Given the betrayal that we are bound to experience when we commit ourselves to the other leaders of our society – whether in the form of politicians, success gurus, or whatever – here is One who is worthy of our deepest confidence. We would do well to reflect deeply on this portrait of Christ, to appreciate what it is he promises, and to realize why he is worthy of our trust.

TRUE DIRECTION

The thrust of Jesus' message in the opening paragraph of this discourse relates back to two things: the failure of the spiritual leaders of the Jews and the fact that the people are beginning to question their integrity. The previous incident had revealed the coolness of the Pharisees towards the needy of their flock and the evident doubts arising in people's minds as they listened to the debate between Jesus and their leaders. In response to both aspects, Jesus paints a word-picture that would have been more than familiar to his listeners: a sheep-pen, some shepherds and their flocks.

With reference to the failing shepherds of Israel, Jesus speaks of men entrusted with the care of God's sheep who try to enter the pen by some way other than the gate and who are nothing more than thieves and robbers (10:1). They themselves are misguided in both motive and method and therefore cannot provide the care and direction needed by the flock. Only the one who enters by the gate of the sheep-pen is a genuine shepherd who truly cares for the sheep. In this way the gate becomes the means for identifying a genuine shepherd. The sheep instinctively look for the one who enters by the way they know and look to him to lead and provide. For the Jews, God had marked out the true way in his Word, the Old Testament. They were beginning to realize that those who were their current spiritual leaders were not leading them in the paths mapped out in the Scriptures, but they saw in Jesus One who was. God's way of life and salvation is set out permanently in the Bible and provides the necessary touchstone by which to test the claims of all who profess to be spiritual leaders of the church.

With regard to the needy sheep of Israel, Jesus describes a scene that was common in the pasturelands of Palestine: that of a shepherd leading his flock (10:2–6). Instead of driving his flock, the shepherd would gently lead them simply by the sound of his voice – a voice that they knew and trusted. Clearly Jesus was alluding to himself and to the sound of his own voice; not in a literal sense, but as a voice bearing a ring of truth in that it echoed the voice of God that had been heard in Israel through the ages.

Throughout Israel's history, everything about the voice of God had been gentle and reassuring for those who were prepared to trust him. And now, that voice and its reassurance was being heard again in the ministry of Jesus. In the midst of the many needs and broken lives that surround us today, there has never been a time when people so desperately need to hear a voice upon which they can rely. Jesus stands alone as the One who perfectly follows God's way. He can therefore be trusted to lead his followers in that everlasting way.

REAL SECURITY

The image, it seems, was lost on the people in the audience (10:6); Jesus therefore elaborates. He concentrates on the fact that, more than anything else, the sheep need safety and security (10:7–9). He makes the picture a more explicit portrayal of himself and spells out in starker terms the contrast between the true and the false shepherd.

Using vivid imagery, he says, 'I am the door' (10:9). In terms of ancient Middle Eastern pastoral practice the shepherd was literally the human gate to the sheep-pen. He lay across the opening at night and was the key to protection and provision. Jesus takes these two concepts and uses them in the context of salvation. Our spiritual protection and provision are ensured only through him. Two points stand out in this passage. The first is the unrestricted offer Jesus makes. The other is the restricted route he maps out. The promise of salvation and security is for 'anyone' who 'enters', but the experience of salvation and security is only for those who enter 'by me' (10:9). Such exclusivism is not popular in this age of openness, but there never has been an age when that message in its truest sense was popular. Yet it is a message that makes perfect sense. When a ship is sinking, there is only one place where people can be secure and that is in the lifeboats. So it is in a world that is sinking ever deeper into sin and guilt and into the experience of God's judgement. The only safe place for sinners is in the Saviour, Jesus, whom God has provided and approved.

Unique Freedom

The beauty of what Jesus offers to all that trust him is seen in the promise of a new and unique quality of life. He expresses it in two different ways in two consecutive verses: 'He will come in and go out and find pasture' (10:9), and, 'I have come that they may have life and have it to the full' (10:10). The picture of sheep finding pasture says it all! A flock being led to a meadow where there is perfect provision and where they are free to roam and graze. The extravagance of what God gives us in Christ must never be underestimated. Paul describes it in terms of being blessed in Christ with all spiritual blessings in heavenly places (*Eph.* 1:3). There is nothing more and nothing better that God could give!

This thought is continued in the second statement about 'life to the full' or 'abundant life', as an older translation puts it. J. C. Ryle explains this in terms of a life for true believers that was qualitatively better than that experienced by their Old Testament counterparts. That is certainly the case. The fulfilment of God's saving purpose in Jesus Christ and the dawning of the new covenant era is not different, but it is better, than what was true under the old covenant. However, Jesus is also highlighting the fact that the life that he offers is different from the kind of life on offer in the world. It is a life that belongs to a totally different order because it revolves around a restored fellowship with God.

Genuine Certainty

Extravagant promises and fulfilled promises are two very different things. Where is the guarantee that Jesus will really be the kind of shepherd and provide the kind of care of which he speaks? The answer is found in the next verse: 'I am the good shepherd. The good shepherd lays down his life for the sheep' (10:11). He is the 'good', or genuine shepherd who stands in contrast with all the spiritual impostors that abound (10:12–13). He proves himself ultimately in the lengths to which he is prepared to go for the eternal welfare of his sheep. He will ultimately lay down his life for them.

The wording of that last statement would almost certainly have raised a few eyebrows amongst his Jewish hearers. This was the language of sacrifice and substitution – of a shepherd who literally takes the place of his sheep in the face of danger. In one sense the shepherd metaphor seemed to break down at this point. What kind of shepherd would be prepared to die for his sheep? Jesus, of course, was pointing forward to something that would only be clear at the climax of his ministry. It would be through his substitutionary death on the cross – where, as sacrificial lamb, he would take the place of his sinful people – that Jesus would finally secure their redemption. There could be no greater guarantee for any promise. The promise of the gospel is sealed with the blood of the Saviour-Shepherd, Jesus Christ.

NEW IDENTITY

There is one final detail in this section that would have taken the Jewish audience of that day into new territory. It was not new in terms of what God had planned and revealed through the Old Testament, but it was new in terms of its fulfilment in the experience of Israel. It was the fact that Jesus looked forward to the day when there would be 'one flock, one shepherd' (10:16). The 'other sheep' that did not belong to 'this fold' (10:15) was a reference to future converts from among the Gentiles. God through Christ would fulfil his covenant promise to Abraham and make him and his Jewish descendants a blessing to the nations (*Gen.* 12:3). The Gentiles would be gathered into the fold of God.

The new identity that was to be found in Jesus Christ would, for his original listeners, transcend their Jewishness. It would be more than a national or ethnic identity that would mark them out; something far richer and deeper; something found only in Jesus. This has a bearing on all who look to Christ for their salvation.

They also will receive a new identity: one that comes from being brought into God's new creation (2 Cor. 5:17).

God's good news is all about a brand new life in an utterly new relationship with him through fellowship with Jesus Christ his Son.

25

Spurning God's Greatest Offer

At that time the Feast of Dedication took place at Jerusalem. It was winter, [23] *and Jesus was walking in the temple, in the colonnade of Solomon.* [24] *So the Jews gathered around him and said to him, "How long will you keep us in suspense? If you are the Christ, tell us plainly."* [25] *Jesus answered them, "I told you, and you do not believe. The works that I do in my Father's name bear witness about me,* [26] *but you do not believe because you are not part of my flock.* [27] *My sheep hear my voice, and I know them, and they follow me.* [28] *I give them eternal life, and they will never perish, and no one will snatch them out of my hand.* [29] *My Father, who has given them to me, is greater than all, and no one is able to snatch them out of the Father's hand.* [30] *I and the Father are one."*

[31] *The Jews picked up stones again to stone him.* [32] *Jesus answered them, "I have shown you many good works from the Father; for which of them are you going to stone me?"* [33] *The Jews answered him, "It is not for a good work that we are going to stone you but for blasphemy, because you, being a man, make yourself God."* [34] *Jesus answered them, "Is it not written in your Law, 'I said, you are gods'?* [35] *If he called them gods to whom the word of God came – and Scripture cannot be broken –* [36] *do you say of him whom the Father consecrated and sent into the world, 'You are blaspheming,' because I said, 'I am the Son of God'?* [37] *If I am not doing the works of my Father, then do not believe me;* [38] *but if I do them, even though you do not believe me, believe the works, that you may know and understand that*

*the Father is in me and I am in the Father." ³⁹ Again they sought
to arrest him, but he escaped from their hands.*

*⁴⁰ He went away again across the Jordan to the place where
John had been baptizing at first, and there he remained. ⁴¹ And
many came to him. And they said, "John did no sign, but
everything that John said about this man was true." ⁴² And many
believed in him there* (John 10:22–42).

In the second half of chapter 10 the scene changes but the
connecting thought is carried through – the theme of widespread
rejection of Jesus by the Jews, especially by the Jewish leaders. Here
John focuses on the reason for their rejection: the fact that they refuse
to listen to Jesus' voice as the Shepherd of Israel (10:27) and so prove
their own disqualification for a place among God's chosen people.

This incident took place during the Feast of Dedication in
Jerusalem and John adds, almost as a passing comment, that 'it was
winter' (10:22). This may well have simply been a statement of fact,
but it is more likely that it was one of those pregnant remarks often
used by John with an intended double edge to it. It was not merely
the frostiness of the season that was so striking, but the increasingly
frosty reception Jesus was receiving from his own people.

Although there is a once-and-for-all dimension to the events that
unfold in these verses, relating uniquely to God's dealings with his
ancient people, there is in them also something of a universal
paradigm. The rejection Jesus experiences at the hands of the Jews
bears the marks of the rejection he experiences at the hand of all who
spurn the gospel offer made by God through him. It has at least three
sad characteristics.

BLINDNESS

As the Jewish crowd in the temple courts gathers yet again around
Jesus, their opening question seems, on the surface, both promising
and plausible: 'If you are the Christ, tell us plainly' (10:24). Surely
a simple answer to what seemed a simple question would have settled
the matter once and for all! But the question was loaded as is seen in
the way it was expressed. The Jews are not merely complaining that

Jesus is keeping them in suspense, they are really saying, 'How long will you annoy us?' They had their own ideas about the kind of Messiah they were waiting for and, to date, Jesus had not lived up to their expectations. Their preconceived ideas had surfaced briefly after the feeding of the five thousand, when the crowd had attempted to take Jesus by force and make him their king (6:15). By now they had closed their minds and hearts to him because they were looking for a Messiah on their own terms.

Jesus' answer is intriguing. He says, 'I told you, and you do not believe' (10:25). True, at least in John's record, Jesus had not spelled this out in words. But the message was clear enough to the eyes and ears of faith. For the reason that has been stated already in this Gospel, Jesus did not want people responding to him merely on the basis of a title that he had taken to himself. He wanted them rather to see and grasp the truth of who he was. Mistaken perceptions of Christ would only lead to mistaken responses to him.

So Jesus goes on to explain what he meant. He says, 'The works that I do in my Father's name bear witness about me.' The miracles were mighty acts with a mighty message. As we have seen, John, in his record of this aspect of Jesus' ministry, emphasizes that they were 'signs' laden with significance. They were a visible and tangible revelation of the truth about Jesus. If these Jews had really known their Hebrew Bible, they would have seen the identikit picture of the Messiah – what he would be like and what kind of works he would perform – seen in its fullness in Jesus and his miracles! But they did not believe because they were not truly part of God's flock (10:28). They claimed to see, but in reality, as they stood around Jesus, they were blind to what was staring them in the face.

How striking and how disturbing it is that the amazing truths about Jesus set before us in the gospel can thrill the hearts of many, yet leave others, because they are blind to who he is, completely unaffected.

Arrogance

Jesus adds a further fundamental reason why they do not believe in him. It is because 'you are not part of my flock' (10:26). Even though outwardly they belonged to God's flock by virtue of their nationality, in reality they were not of God's chosen people. Their attitude and response to Jesus proved the point.

Jesus is here underlining the significant truth concerning the God of the Bible, namely that he is a God who chooses, or elects, to save some people but not others. This is one of those Bible doctrines that has often been the source and focus of sharp debate among Christians. This can especially be the case when Christians try to reconcile it with the equally prominent Bible teaching on human responsibility. Difficulties with these teachings arise almost invariably when people try to get inside the secret will and purposes of God, even though the Bible tells us plainly that this is an area which is out of bounds for human minds (*Deut.* 29:29). The key for making sense of these truths is found in what Jesus says next.

How does someone know whether or not they are elect? Jesus answers, 'My sheep hear my voice, and I know them, and they follow me' (10:27). Those who are 'known' by Christ, that is, loved from before time, will be brought into the open by the sound of his voice. Whether it be through his preaching in person while on earth, or through hearing his voice in the gospel as his message goes forth, those whom God has chosen will answer his call. Those who are of his flock will 'follow'; they will not only recognize, but will also respond in faith and obedience to the voice of Jesus. There will be an initial response in conversion and an ongoing response through a life of discipleship. Those who react to him in this way will know the everlasting security that only Christ can guarantee (10:28).

All of this calls for humility before Christ. And it was exactly that humility which the Jews were not prepared to embrace. In their arrogance they rejected not only Jesus, they rejected God.

Hollowness

The Jews immediately latch on to the fact that Jesus had again claimed that he and his Father were one (10:30). For this, they 'picked up stones again to stone him' (10:31). Jesus challenged their action, saying, 'I have shown you many good works from the Father; for which of them are you going to stone me?' (10:32). The Jews responded by stating that it was because he was guilty of blasphemy (10:33).

Jesus' reply is interesting. He could have appealed again to the hard evidence of his performance of his Father's work as demonstrated by his miracles – all of which tallied with Old Testament prediction. Instead, he appeals to the Law (meaning the whole of the Old Testament). He cites a reference from the Psalms: 'I said, you are gods' (*Psa.* 82:6), and he proceeds to argue from a lesser truth to a greater. If this verse was true for those to whom God's Word came, would it not be more true for 'him whom the Father consecrated and sent into the world' (10:36)? He exposes the hollowness of their case against him, if they thought to prove it on bare legal grounds.

Like so many since, the Jewish leaders were seeking to dismiss Jesus for the flimsiest of reasons. In reality they were no different from those who reject Christ because 'He is not my kind of God' or 'Not my idea of a saviour'.

The twist in the tale comes at the very end, when Jesus says to those gathered round him: 'If I am not doing the works of my Father, then do not believe me' (10:37–38). He points supremely to the complete consistency between the revelation of God and his work in the Old Testament, and what was presently being seen in himself. The miraculous power displayed by God in the Old Testament was now being seen again in the miracles of Jesus. The sheer weight of evidence, plain for all to see, was sufficient to crush the hollow objections being raised by Jesus' opponents.

After this exchange Jesus withdrew from Jerusalem, the centre of the Jewish religious world, and went instead to the quiet country area beyond the Jordan river that had been strongly affected by the ministry of John the Baptist. There 'many came to him' (10:41). These were ordinary, unsophisticated people. They believed in Jesus simply because all that John had said about him was true (10:41–42). Those who genuinely are the chosen of the Lord do not need spectacular displays to lead them to the Saviour. The simple truth will win them.

26

Afraid of Death No More

Now a certain man was ill, Lazarus of Bethany, the village of Mary and her sister Martha. ² *It was Mary who anointed the Lord with ointment and wiped his feet with her hair, whose brother Lazarus was ill.* ³ *So the sisters sent to him, saying, "Lord, he whom you love is ill."* ⁴ *But when Jesus heard it he said, "This illness does not lead to death. It is for the glory of God, so that the Son of God may be glorified through it."*

⁵ *Now Jesus loved Martha and her sister and Lazarus.* ⁶ *So, when he heard that Lazarus was ill, he stayed two days longer in the place where he was.* ⁷ *Then after this he said to the disciples, "Let us go to Judea again."* ⁸ *The disciples said to him, "Rabbi, the Jews were just now seeking to stone you, and are you going there again?"* ⁹ *Jesus answered, "Are there not twelve hours in the day? If anyone walks in the day, he does not stumble, because he sees the light of this world.* ¹⁰ *But if anyone walks in the night, he stumbles, because the light is not in him."* ¹¹ *After saying these things, he said to them, "Our friend Lazarus has fallen asleep, but I go to awaken him."* ¹² *The disciples said to him, "Lord, if he has fallen asleep, he will recover."* ¹³ *Now Jesus had spoken of his death, but they thought that he meant taking rest in sleep.* ¹⁴ *Then Jesus told them plainly, "Lazarus has died,* ¹⁵ *and for your sake I am glad that I was not there, so that you may believe. But let us go to him."* ¹⁶ *So Thomas, called the Twin, said to his fellow disciples, "Let us also go, that we may die with him."*

¹⁷ *Now when Jesus came, he found that Lazarus had already been in the tomb four days.* ¹⁸ *Bethany was near Jerusalem, about two miles off,* ¹⁹ *and many of the Jews had come to Martha and Mary to console them concerning their brother.* ²⁰ *So when*

Martha heard that Jesus was coming, she went and met him, but Mary remained seated in the house. [21] Martha said to Jesus, "Lord, if you had been here, my brother would not have died. [22] But even now I know that whatever you ask from God, God will give you." [23] Jesus said to her, "Your brother will rise again." [24] Martha said to him, "I know that he will rise again in the resurrection on the last day." [25] Jesus said to her, "I am the resurrection and the life. Whoever believes in me, though he die, yet shall he live, [26] and everyone who lives and believes in me shall never die. Do you believe this?" [27] She said to him, "Yes, Lord; I believe that you are the Christ, the Son of God, who is coming into the world."

[28] When she had said this, she went and called her sister Mary, saying in private, "The Teacher is here and is calling for you." [29] And when she heard it, she rose quickly and went to him. [30] Now Jesus had not yet come into the village, but was still in the place where Martha had met him. [31] When the Jews who were with her in the house, consoling her, saw Mary rise quickly and go out, they followed her, supposing that she was going to the tomb to weep there. [32] Now when Mary came to where Jesus was and saw him, she fell at his feet, saying to him, "Lord, if you had been here, my brother would not have died." [33] When Jesus saw her weeping, and the Jews who had come with her also weeping, he was deeply moved in his spirit and greatly troubled. [34] And he said, "Where have you laid him?" They said to him, "Lord, come and see." [35] Jesus wept. [36] So the Jews said, "See how he loved him!" [37] But some of them said, "Could not he who opened the eyes of the blind man also have kept this man from dying?"

[38] Then Jesus, deeply moved again, came to the tomb. It was a cave, and a stone lay against it. [39] Jesus said, "Take away the stone." Martha, the sister of the dead man, said to him, "Lord, by this time there will be an odour, for he has been dead four days." [40] Jesus said to her, "Did I not tell you that if you believed you would see the glory of God?" [41] So they took away the stone. And Jesus lifted up his eyes and said, "Father, I thank you that you have heard me. [42] I knew that you always hear me, but I said this on account of the people standing around, that they may believe that you sent me." [43] When he had said these things, he

*cried out with a loud voice, "Lazarus, come out." ⁴⁴ The man
who had died came out, his hands and feet bound with linen strips,
and his face wrapped with a cloth. Jesus said to them, "Unbind
him, and let him go"* (John 11:1–44).

The movement of John's narrative takes us inexorably forward
towards the climactic moment in Christ's work in this world.
The full extent of Christ's power and the full measure of what he
came to do for sinners is becoming clearer, but so too is the depth of
opposition that he faces. The unfolding drama of the gospel is
propelling us towards the horror and the glory of the cross.

With the paradox of the previous chapter behind us in which the
gentle Shepherd-King is met, not with an enthusiastic welcome, but
with an attempt at lynching him, this next chapter presents an even
greater paradox. The one who so dramatically proves his power over
death is not hailed universally as the greatest deliverer this world
has ever seen, but is despised and rejected. In this way, the final pieces
that will lead eventually to his own death, slot into place.

In one of the most graphic pastoral encounters witnessed in the
ministry of Jesus (one that is recorded in considerable detail), we find
him confronting what the Bible describes as the 'last enemy' (*1 Cor.*
15:26). The narrative provides a moving and personal insight of
Jesus' treatment of that fear which holds every human being hostage
(*Heb.* 2:15). It makes use of this one incident, where Jesus deals with
death within the confines of a single family, to pave the way for that
supreme moment when he deals with death once and for all on a
global scale. It is the last of the seven signs that John records, and
involves also the greatest of the 'I am' sayings spoken by Jesus. The
significance of the passage becomes apparent very quickly as events
unfold.

DESPAIR AT THE PROSPECT OF DEATH

Death lurks like an ominous shadow above all that is said and done
in the first part of this chapter. Though we are not brought face to
face with it around a deathbed or in the ceremonies of burial, yet
from the very outset, death is in the air. It is the evident fear gripping
the hearts of the two sisters (11:3). Their urgent message sent to Jesus

is not merely fired by the thought that their brother was ill and they wanted him healed, but that he was so ill they were afraid he would die. These two women found themselves held by that same paralysing fear that has frozen so many hearts, as they watched their dear brother being dragged into the jaws of death and they were powerless to save him. It is the sense of utter despair known both by the dying and by those they love. Death is a powerful and ominous adversary.

Jesus' response to the sisters' request is enigmatic, but reassuring: 'This illness does not lead to death' (11:4). It is enigmatic because Jesus makes no immediate move to go to Bethany. It is reassuring because, whatever lay ahead, death would not be the final outcome. Nevertheless, when Jesus finally announces to his disciples that he is ready to go to his friend, they start to object. Together they remind him that it is not that long since the Jews of Judea had made an attempt on his life (11:8). They were also, in the politest possible way, expressing their fears for their own safety. Then, when Jesus fails to be deterred, Thomas speaks out with typical cynicism and says, 'Let us also go, that we may die with him' (11:16). These men also are afraid of death and are in no rush to hasten their departure from this life.

In many ways these reactions are perfectly understandable and reasonable. The Old Testament had revealed relatively little about the way that God would deal with death. Even though it shows clearly that death is not the end and that there is the hope of heaven for those who die believing, it is fairly sketchy as to what people were to expect with regard to the end. That to some extent explains the rather cryptic comment Jesus makes about walking in daylight and stumbling in the dark (11:9–10). He highlights the urgent need to seize the opportunity that this situation was providing in order to gain more light on this dark and sombre issue.

This opening scene confronts not only the disciples, but ourselves also, the readers, with the stark reminder that in the midst of life we are in death.

DEFEAT IN THE FACE OF DEATH

By the time Jesus arrived in Bethany, Lazarus had been in the tomb for four days (11:17). The family and the village community were still very much in mourning. The defeat inflicted by death on those still living was plain to see. When the sisters met with Jesus, they too had an air of defeat about them. Despite their faith in God and Jesus and despite their conviction that there would be a resurrection at the end of time, they were clearly in the grip of a profound sense of loss.

As Martha and Mary meet Jesus in turn, the first immediate greeting from both is the words, 'If only you had been here . . .' (11:21, 23). It was as though they had come so close to defeating this awful enemy, but had ultimately lost. They had yet to grasp the fact that their dearest friend not only had power to heal the sick, he had power also to raise the dead. At that moment they felt that death had had the last word.

Even when Jesus tried to reason with Martha with words that have been an enormous source of comfort to many ever since (11:25–26), they proved of little consolation to her in her bereavement. Indeed, even though she was able to confess Jesus as both Messiah and Son of God (11:27), the power of death still loomed so largely on her horizons that it seemed to eclipse even the power of Jesus.

Only those who have felt the chill intrusion of death into life and the ominous power it wields, can appreciate something of what Martha felt. The immediacy and the seeming finality of death are such that comfort of a unique order is needed to begin to banish its shadow.

DISGUST AT THE UGLINESS OF DEATH

Comfort begins to dawn as we witness Jesus' own reaction to the death of Lazarus. John tells us that when he met with Mary and saw her grief and that of the townsfolk he was 'deeply moved' (11:33). The word is much stronger in the original and is closer to being 'outraged in spirit' or 'indignant and angry'. It is Jesus' instinctive reaction to the presence of death in the world that he made.

As a race, and even as Christians, we have become too accustomed to death and are too ready to regard it as 'normal'. We see it as simply the final step in the sequence of life. For Jesus nothing could be further from the truth. For him, death was an ugly intruder in his beautiful world. It was a curse: the very antithesis of the life that is cradled in creation. He displays all the disgust of the Creator whose good creation has been marred and scarred by the presence of an evil intrusion.

It is not all that uncommon for there to be angry outbursts from mourners during a funeral service or at a graveside – especially when the deceased, like Lazarus, was not old. These are the passionate outcries of sorrow and helplessness. But that is not the explanation for Jesus' reaction. He made heaven and earth, and created human beings to function uniquely in fellowship with their Maker. When death entered the world, through Adam's disobedience, and severed that bond between the creature and his Creator, the whole universe felt the consequences. Jesus perceives that truth in microcosm in this graveyard, and he displays his anger at all that it signifies.

In a thrilling way, his strength of feeling reflects his determination to overcome death once and for all.

DELIVERANCE FROM THE POWER OF DEATH

If it is true to say that death broods like the darkest night over these verses, then it is just as true that the words of Jesus here shine like stars. Yet they are words that could have sounded like pious platitudes had they not been backed up by action. It is possible to say the most wonderful things at funerals and yet fail to impart true comfort and fail, most certainly, to bring back the dead. As Jesus stands with the mourners at the graveside, however, he leads them into an experience beyond anything they could have ever imagined (11:38–44).

He orders the removal of the large stone that sealed the entrance to the tomb – producing great fears in the sisters' hearts. He prays, and his prayer is then acknowledged from heaven in a most startling way. He issues the boldest of commands into the cold darkness of the grave, 'Lazarus, come out!' (11:43), and the man who had been buried four days previously emerges, very much alive.

This final sign that Jesus performed demonstrated climactically and beyond a shadow of a doubt that he alone has power over death. It paves the way for his own death and resurrection just a few short months later, which in turn would lay the foundation for the spiritual and, ultimately, the physical resurrection of all who trust in him.

Here is the hope and comfort that the gospel gives to all who believe in Jesus. Just as the glory of God was displayed locally in the resurrection of Lazarus (11:40) and supremely in the resurrection of Jesus, so it will be displayed and experienced ultimately in the resurrection of all who turn to him for their salvation.

27

Facing Up to Truth

Many of the Jews therefore, who had come with Mary and had seen what he did, believed in him, [46] *but some of them went to the Pharisees and told them what Jesus had done.* [47] *So the chief priests and the Pharisees gathered the Council and said, "What are we to do? For this man performs many signs.* [48] *If we let him go on like this, everyone will believe in him, and the Romans will come and take away both our place and our nation."* [49] *But one of them, Caiaphas, who was high priest that year, said to them, "You know nothing at all.* [50] *Nor do you understand that it is better for you that one man should die for the people, not that the whole nation should perish."* [51] *He did not say this of his own accord, but being high priest that year he prophesied that Jesus would die for the nation,* [52] *and not for the nation only, but also to gather into one the children of God who are scattered abroad.* [53] *So from that day on they made plans to put him to death.*

[54] *Jesus therefore no longer walked openly among the Jews, but went from there to the region near the wilderness, to a town called Ephraim, and there he stayed with the disciples.*

[55] *Now the Passover of the Jews was at hand, and many went up from the country to Jerusalem before the Passover to purify themselves.* [56] *They were looking for Jesus and saying to one another as they stood in the temple, "What do you think? That he will not come to the feast at all?"* [57] *Now the chief priests and the Pharisees had given orders that if anyone knew where he was, he should let them know, so that they might arrest him.*

[1] *Six days before the Passover, Jesus therefore came to Bethany, where Lazarus was, whom Jesus had raised from the dead.* [2] *So they gave a dinner for him there. Martha served, and Lazarus was one of those reclining with him at the table.* [3] *Mary therefore took a pound of expensive ointment made from pure nard, and anointed the feet of Jesus and wiped his feet with her hair. The house was filled with the fragrance of the perfume.* [4] *But Judas Iscariot, one of his disciples (he who was about to betray him), said,* [5] *"Why was this ointment not sold for three hundred denarii and given to the poor?"* [6] *He said this, not because he cared about the poor, but because he was a thief, and having charge of the moneybag he used to help himself to what was put into it.* [7] *Jesus said, "Leave her alone, so that she may keep it for the day of my burial.* [8] *The poor you always have with you, but you do not always have me."*

[9] *When the large crowd of the Jews learned that Jesus was there, they came, not only on account of him but also to see Lazarus, whom he had raised from the dead.* [10] *So the chief priests made plans to put Lazarus to death as well,* [11] *because on account of him many of the Jews were going away and believing in Jesus.*

[12] *The next day the large crowd that had come to the feast heard that Jesus was coming to Jerusalem.* [13] *So they took branches of palm trees and went out to meet him, crying out, "Hosanna! Blessed is he who comes in the name of the Lord, even the King of Israel!"* [14] *And Jesus found a young donkey and sat on it, just as it is written,*

[15] *"Fear not, daughter of Zion;*
 behold, your king is coming,
   sitting on a donkey's colt!"

[16] *His disciples did not understand these things at first, but when Jesus was glorified, then they remembered that these things had been written about him and had been done to him.* [17] *The crowd that had been with him when he called Lazarus out of the tomb and raised him from the dead continued to bear witness.* [18] *The reason why the crowd went to meet him was that they heard he had done this sign.* [19] *So the Pharisees said to one another, "You see that you are gaining nothing. Look, the world has gone after him"* (John 11:45–12:19).

The seed-thoughts planted by John in the Prologue to his Gospel have been growing and spreading throughout his account of the life and work of Christ. One of these key themes is that of Jesus as the embodiment of truth. At the climax of the Prologue, John declared Jesus to be the Word who became flesh and who was 'full of grace and truth' (1:14). The significance of that statement has become clearer as the life and ministry of Jesus has unfolded. What was stated by way of testimony has been systematically demonstrated by way of evidence, and now, as we approach what was to be the final week before the crucifixion, the force of the truth about Jesus makes its final, decisive impact on those who knew him.

As we have already seen on more than one occasion, the recognition of the truth about Jesus forces people into one of two responses: rejection or belief. Now again, in the aftermath of the raising of Lazarus, the impact of this final sign makes a decisive mark upon many lives.

John records three specific incidents of contrasting reactions to Jesus. Those of the crowd and the council (11:45–57); of Mary and Judas (12:1–11); and of the people of Jerusalem and their leaders (12:12–19). The light of Jesus' presence in the world is shining ever more clearly and brightly, and the natural darkness of a fallen world is continuing its desperate efforts to overcome that light but failing completely to do so.

TRUTH OPPOSED

In one sense it is hardly surprising that a miracle as dramatic as raising a man who was dead should lead to the conversion of many people (11:45). If ever there was proof that the one who performed a miracle was no impostor, this was it. What is surprising, on the surface at least, is the callous response of those who should have known better: the Jewish leaders.

Some in the crowd that had witnessed the miracle in Bethany did not believe but went instead to the chief priests and Pharisees and reported what had happened. This led to the calling of a special meeting of the Sanhedrin (11:46–47). Two things are clear: these men recognised that Jesus was performing miraculous signs (11:47), and they were bent on stopping him (11:48). The facts were not in question. The religious leaders no longer considered that the discrediting or exposing of Jesus was a solution to their problem. They were now formalizing and finalizing their plan to kill him.

Their own words reveal the reason for their rejection of Jesus despite all the evidence that endorsed his claims. They were afraid that a mass turning to Jesus would lead to Roman intervention and that they would then lose their place (a reference possibly to the temple) and their nation. They were afraid that Jesus' popularity would result in their losing their comfortable niche in life and they were so obsessed with their own selfish interests that they could not see the larger issues involved. Self-interest is the ultimate obstacle to acknowledging self-evident truth.

What is fascinating is that even in their blind and wilful refusal to acknowledge Jesus, one of their own number, unwittingly, becomes a vehicle for an even greater revelation of the truth concerning him! Caiaphas, who was the high priest for that year, argued, 'It is better for you that one man die for the people, not that the whole nation should perish' (11:50). All he had in mind as he spoke those words was the expediency, as they saw it, of the crime that they all knew they were plotting. John, however, declares that something far deeper was going on. It was not Caiaphas who chose those words, it was God speaking through him in words of prophecy (11:51–52); a prophecy that did not merely speak of Jesus' death but explained its significance in terms of vicarious atonement.

Even while stubbornly refusing to bow to the truth about Jesus, the chief priests and Pharisees could not gain the upper hand over him. His truth was always stronger than their deceit; his light more powerful than the darkness of their souls. The culmination of such conflict, Paul tells us, will occur on that day when, at the name of Jesus, every knee will bow and every tongue will confess him as Lord (*Phil.* 2:10–12). There will always be opposition to Jesus, but that opposition will ultimately be crushed at the final revelation of his glory.

Truth Embraced

The scenes of bitter animosity in dark corners of Jerusalem give way to a very different scene in the home of Mary, Martha and Lazarus, in Bethany. As the Feast of Passover drew near, a celebratory dinner was held in Jesus' honour. During the meal Mary made a gesture of loving recognition of Jesus which was to have far-reaching significance.

She took an appreciable quantity of expensive perfume, poured it over his feet and then wiped them with her hair (12:3). Her action is immediately criticized by Judas Iscariot – the betrayer. He claims that the perfume would have been better sold and the money given to the poor (12:4-5). John comments that Judas' motive was not concern for the poor but personal greed, because, as keeper of the common purse, he was used to helping himself to its contents (12:6).

How different was the impact of the truth of Christ upon the life of Mary. Profoundly moved by Jesus and grateful for all he had taught and done, she expresses her devotion in the most extravagant way that she could think of. And Jesus, with much deeper understanding of what was involved in her action, defends her and indicates that her gesture pointed forward in a more wonderful way than she could realize to what would happen to him in a few days' time (12:7-8). The remark that 'the house was filled with the fragrance of the perfume' (12.3) is more than just a statement of fact – it provides a picture of how a loving response to the truth of Christ touches the lives of many others.

In total contrast to the self-sacrificing love of Mary towards Jesus, we have the self-gratifying love of Judas, who denied the truth about his Master, even though he had lived in such close proximity to him for almost three years. Our genuine response to Jesus is seen not in the words that we offer to him or parade before others, but in the whole orientation of our love and life.

TRUTH ACKNOWLEDGED

Less than a week before his arrest, Jesus made the journey from Bethany over the hills to Jerusalem. The city, already bursting with visitors who had come for Passover, welcomed Jesus with the highest of accolades. Using the language of Messianic praise from the Psalms, the people hailed Jesus as 'he who comes in the name of the Lord' and 'the King of Israel' (12:13). Here was Jesus, at the very climax of his earthly ministry, being hailed as the One for whom Israel was waiting. He was being acknowledged as the fulfilment of the central truth that runs through the whole of Old Testament Scripture.

Although it is undoubtedly true that there were many people in the crowd that day who neither fully appreciated nor meant sincerely the things they were shouting, nevertheless it constituted a major recognition of Jesus as the Christ. It was certainly greeted with serious concern by the religious leaders in their fears of mass conversions to his side (12:18–19).

There is a similarity between the shouts and cries of the crowd and the divine ordering of the words of Caiaphas. The truth about Jesus was being declared and acknowledged to an extent that had not previously been the case. And ever since this time, this has been so throughout history and will be, ultimately, at the close of history – the truth of Jesus will be seen and recognized for what it is. The thrust of the gospel is that it should be acknowledged *now* by faith, while there is opportunity of salvation, rather than on that last day when all opportunity will be past.

28

We Wish to See Jesus

Now among those who went up to worship at the feast were some Greeks. [21] *So these came to Philip, who was from Bethsaida in Galilee, and asked him, "Sir, we wish to see Jesus."* [22] *Philip went and told Andrew; Andrew and Philip went and told Jesus.* [23] *And Jesus answered them, "The hour has come for the Son of Man to be glorified.* [24] *Truly, truly, I say to you, unless a grain of wheat falls into the earth and dies, it remains alone; but if it dies, it bears much fruit.* [25] *Whoever loves his life loses it, and whoever hates his life in this world will keep it for eternal life.* [26] *If anyone serves me, he must follow me; and where I am, there will my servant be also. If anyone serves me, the Father will honour him.*

[27] *"Now is my soul troubled. And what shall I say? 'Father, save me from this hour'? But for this purpose I have come to this hour.* [28] *Father, glorify your name." Then a voice came from heaven: "I have glorified it, and I will glorify it again."* [29] *The crowd that stood there and heard it said that it had thundered. Others said, "An angel has spoken to him."* [30] *Jesus answered, "This voice has come for your sake, not mine.* [31] *Now is the judgement of this world; now will the ruler of this world be cast out.* [32] *And I, when I am lifted up from the earth, will draw all people to myself."* [33] *He said this to show by what kind of death he was going to die.* [34] *So the crowd answered him, "We have heard from the Law that the Christ remains forever. How can you say that the Son of Man must be lifted up? Who is this Son of Man?"* [35] *So Jesus said to them, "The light is among you for a little while longer. Walk while you have the light, lest darkness*

overtake you. The one who walks in the darkness does not know where he is going. [36] *While you have the light, believe in the light, that you may become sons of light."*

When Jesus had said these things, he departed and hid himself from them. [37] *Though he had done so many signs before them, they still did not believe in him,* [38] *so that the word spoken by the prophet Isaiah might be fulfilled:*

> *"Lord, who has believed what he heard from us,*
> *and to whom has the arm of the Lord been revealed?"*

[39] *Therefore they could not believe. For again Isaiah said,*

> [40] *"He has blinded their eyes*
> *and hardened their heart,*
> *lest they see with their eyes,*
> *and understand with their heart, and turn,*
> *and I would heal them."*

[41] *Isaiah said these things because he saw his glory and spoke of him.* [42] *Nevertheless, many even of the authorities believed in him, but for fear of the Pharisees they did not confess it, so that they would not be put out of the synagogue;* [43] *for they loved the glory that comes from man more than the glory that comes from God.*

[44] *And Jesus cried out and said, "Whoever believes in me, believes not in me but in him who sent me.* [45] *And whoever sees me sees him who sent me.* [46] *I have come into the world as light, so that whoever believes in me may not remain in darkness.* [47] *If anyone hears my words and does not keep them, I do not judge him; for I did not come to judge the world but to save the world.* [48] *The one who rejects me and does not receive my words has a judge; the word that I have spoken will judge him on the last day.* [49] *For I have not spoken on my own authority, but the Father who sent me has himself given me a commandment—what to say and what to speak.* [50] *And I know that his commandment is eternal life. What I say, therefore, I say as the Father has told me"* (John 12:20–50).

This mid-point of chapter twelve marks the mid-point of the Gospel in terms of its length. The first half has covered the three years of Jesus' public life and ministry; the second half is devoted almost entirely to just one week. That in itself should make us realize that in order to understand who Jesus is and what he came to do, the main focus of our reflection must be on what happened during that week. We are at the point at which Jesus' public ministry is all but over and the climax of the incarnation is at hand.

The section is introduced with a request from some Greeks, 'Sir, we wish to see Jesus' (12:21). There is far more to their petition than they themselves realized. John emphasizes this point by recording the caustic comment of the Pharisees: 'Look, the whole world has gone after him' just before this incident (12:19). Here, quite literally, a little band of seekers representing 'the rest of the world' came looking for Jesus, and he gladly responds to their request. John is indicating in advance that the fulfilment of Christ's work on earth will have an impact not just upon the Jewish people, but also upon people of all races. He is indeed the Saviour of the world.

It is interesting to note that Jesus responds to these Greeks, not with a private audience, but with a public proclamation. It is highly likely that they had been drawn to the Jewish faith and the God of the Bible and had been made aware of Jesus and the impact of his teaching. However, Jesus' answer is clearly not just for them alone as a particular group of seekers from another land, but for all who seek God and the blessings of his salvation, regardless of nationality or background. What he says crystallises the truth about himself and his work in a way that is universally accessible.

What follows constitutes the essence of who Jesus is, of the reason why he came, and of what he would achieve. And all of these points, most strikingly, find their focus in the cross. Everything in this conversation and all that it points to hinges on the fact, 'The hour has come' (12:23). That moment, which on many occasions throughout his public ministry Jesus said had not yet come, had now finally arrived. This was the crucial time towards which everything else had been leading. Clearly, if we are to understand Jesus, we need to understand the cross and to see it as his time. The question is, 'His time for what?'

TIME FOR GLORY

After thirty-three years during which 'the time had not yet come', Jesus now announces publicly that it has finally arrived. The curtain is about to be drawn aside. God's purpose in Christ's coming is on the verge of being revealed. We can well imagine the sense of anticipation among the disciples as he uttered these words. What was he going to say or do next?

Jesus does not keep them in suspense. He says, 'The hour has come for the Son of Man to be glorified' (12:23). The full weight of his identity and being would now be brought to light. The days of speculation were over and God's true purpose centred in Christ's incarnate life is to be demonstrated. Everything else in the incarnation, life, and ministry of Jesus had paved the way for this unique moment in history. It is as if everything in the Gospel (and indeed in the Bible itself) up to this point is like the first half of a climb up a mountain. Each step along the way was important and valuable, but incomplete in itself. Now, however, the summit and pinnacle of all that God was to reveal is coming into view. This is what his message was all about. If then we are genuinely trying to get to grips with God's message in his Word, here is the point that we must reach. This is the key for making sense of all that he says.

But as Jesus proceeds to spell out the climax of God's purpose, we can almost feel the sense of dismay among his hearers, especially when we consider the charged and excited atmosphere that surrounded Christ's entrance into Jerusalem. Using the image of a single grain of wheat having to die in order to give life to the many seeds that would grow from it, he points to the fact that he too must die if he is to bring life to many (12:24). There has to be death before there can be life. Indeed, Jesus goes on to indicate that the kind of death that lay ahead for him was a death of the most hideous sort: being 'lifted up from the earth' in crucifixion (12:32–33). This was the way in which God's purpose in salvation would be fulfilled.

Jesus takes the imagery further by showing that the same principle applies not only to the way in which salvation would be secured, but also to the way in which it must be received. Although his application of the image to himself and his own death is by way of inference, his application to believers is explicit. 'Whoever loves his life loses it, and whoever hates his life in this world will keep it for eternal life. If anyone serves me, he must follow me . . .' (12:25–26). Confronting, not least, the spirit of self-interest and self-preservation that lay behind the Pharisees' rejection of him (11:48), Jesus shows that salvation and self-exaltation are not compatible.

As he looks forward to this moment of 'glory' Jesus does not hide the fact that the prospect of what it means troubles him deeply (12:27–28). But although he is troubled, he is in no way deterred. He is utterly determined to carry through the mission that the Father had entrusted to him, because only in that way would the glory that God had planned be fulfilled.

TIME FOR JUDGEMENT

We cannot fully understand the cross without understanding its great positive implications for those who respond to it by faith. It is God's instrument of salvation and the gateway to a new life in this world and the next. It is impossible also to understand the cross fully without appreciating its negative implications for those who reject it in their unbelief. Simple logic dictates that if an act of extraordinary generosity and kindness is spurned, there is no excuse for the consequences that follow. So Jesus goes on to spell out what the cross will mean for the world as it spurns God's grace. The cross is not only the time for the glory of God's Son and the salvation of God's people, but also the time for judgement on the world in its present fallen state and upon 'the prince of this world' – the devil – as the cause of the Fall and of all rebellion.

The cross therefore is the pivot upon which the entire history of the world turns. It represents the unique moment in time that determined the very future of history itself. Ironically, the whole world has acknowledged this fact, without ever understanding it, by its acceptance of a global division of time and history according to the date of Christ's coming. The millennium celebrations were not about marking a number on the calendar, but about an event in history! An event and a moment of such significance that no one can afford to ignore it.

Jesus continues his discussion by saying, 'Now will the ruler of this world be cast out' (12:31). That is, Satan would be dealt a deathblow by Christ's work on Calvary. The cross would mark his victory. It would prove to be the decisive battle for the one who thought he could steal the world from its Maker. As Jesus puts it elsewhere, it would be the moment when the 'strong man' of the world would be bound and his domain plundered (*Matt.* 12:29). At the cross he would secure not only the salvation of God's people, but also the destruction of his arch-enemy.

In what way would this constitute 'the judgement of this world' (12:31)? The cross would expose the ugly depths of human depravity and the extent to which mankind is in the grip of the devil. Man would try to kill God! It would also reveal the horror of hell. As Jesus endured the agony and awfulness of being cut off from God, his sufferings may be seen as a warning example of the fate awaiting the devil and all who follow his ways.

This all emphasizes that the cross has to do with the frightening reality of God's judgement and the urgent need of deliverance from it.

TIME TO LISTEN

The remainder of this chapter deals with what it means to listen to God and to respond to his Word by faith. Drawing on the imagery of light and darkness once more and emphasizing the need to make use of every opportunity afforded by light, Jesus shows the urgency not only of appreciating God's message, but also of acting upon it (12:34–36). He highlights the need to trust in him as Saviour before meeting him as Judge. His illustration of making use of the hours of daylight could hardly be more graphic. Use the opportunity to listen to Christ and his message while it is still there! The problem with so many of the Jews and their leaders was that they were too busy listening to themselves.

Jesus spells it out in the clearest of terms: 'While you have the light, believe in the light, that you may become sons of the light' (12:36). It is a simple fact of life: the opportunity to believe will not always be there. It is not only that we have no guarantee that we will live to see tomorrow, but we have no guarantee that true concern for our soul will last beyond today. God makes it clear in Scripture that no one can presume that they may be saved as and when they please. Isaiah says, 'Seek the LORD while he may be found; call upon him while he is near' (*Isa.* 55:6) and Paul says, 'Behold, now is the favourable time; behold, now is the day of salvation' (*2 Cor.* 6:2).

Not only do people need to seize the opportunity afforded by hearing the message of Jesus, they also need to acknowledge the

LET'S STUDY JOHN

evidence that supports it. John now notes that despite all that Jesus had said and done in the presence of the Jews, 'they still did not believe in him' (12:37). It was not that they could not, but rather that they stubbornly refused to do so. They dismissed the facts and flew in the face of the evidence; that evidence which would one day testify against them. In their behaviour may be seen the fulfilling of another of Isaiah's prophecies (*Isa.* 12:38–40) that pointed to the hardness of the human heart, even in the face of the greatest revelation of God's grace. Yet even such blind rebellion and rejection are brought into line with God's purpose.

Despite the reaction of the religious establishment as a group, there were many from within their number who did believe – perhaps influenced by the blatant prejudice of their peers (12:42–43). Even though at this stage these were not willing to profess their faith publicly, nevertheless, in their hearts they had crossed the line from unbelief to faith.

John presses home the need for a positive response to Jesus' words by quoting what would seem to be the last great public statement that Jesus made before withdrawing from public view (12:44–50). He 'cried out' (12:44). He was making the final impassioned plea of his earthly ministry. He reminds everyone that the way people respond to him will ultimately be the way they respond to God (12:44–46); to reject him is to invite judgement (12:47–49) but to obey the command of God in trusting in himself leads to 'eternal life' (12:50). That is the solemn note that is left ringing in the ears of the world as Jesus steps off the stage of public view. That is the urgent message that has reverberated around the world ever since.

The request of that little band of Greek enquirers holds the key to eternity itself, 'Sir, we wish to see Jesus'!

29

The Servant King

Now before the Feast of the Passover, when Jesus knew that his hour had come to depart out of this world to the Father, having loved his own who were in the world, he loved them to the end. *2 During supper, when the devil had already put it into the heart of Judas Iscariot, Simon's son, to betray him, *3 Jesus, knowing that the Father had given all things into his hands, and that he had come from God and was going back to God, *4 rose from supper. He laid aside his outer garments, and taking a towel, tied it around his waist. *5 Then he poured water into a basin and began to wash the disciples' feet and to wipe them with the towel that was wrapped around him. *6 He came to Simon Peter, who said to him, "Lord, do you wash my feet?" *7 Jesus answered him, "What I am doing you do not understand now, but afterwards you will understand." *8 Peter said to him, "You shall never wash my feet." Jesus answered him, "If I do not wash you, you have no share with me." *9 Simon Peter said to him, "Lord, not my feet only but also my hands and my head!" *10 Jesus said to him, "The one who has bathed does not need to wash, except for his feet, but is completely clean. And you are clean, but not every one of you." *11 For he knew who was to betray him; that was why he said, "Not all of you are clean."

*12 When he had washed their feet and put on his outer garments and resumed his place, he said to them, "Do you understand what I have done to you? *13 You call me Teacher and Lord, and you are right, for so I am. *14 If I then, your Lord and Teacher, have washed your feet, you also ought to wash one another's feet. *15 For I have given you an example, that you also should do just *as I have done to you. [16] Truly, truly, I say to you, a servant is not greater than his master, nor is a messenger greater than the one who sent him. [17] If you know these things, blessed are you if you do them* (John 13:1–17).

The time Jesus spent with the twelve disciples during that final week before his death was of enormous significance. Many of the things he had taught them during their three years together were reinforced and reapplied. Many new things were presented to them in preparation for all that lay ahead – teachings that would become clear only after his death and resurrection and after the events of Pentecost. The setting is the upper room; the occasion is the night on which Jesus was betrayed; and the celebration is the Passover meal.

Of the four Gospel writers, John devotes the most space by far to what happened in this intimate gathering that night. He leaves it to the others to record the inauguration of the sacrament of the Lord's Supper, while he himself concentrates on the rich teaching that Jesus passed on to his apostles at that time. The section spans five chapters. It begins with a symbolic act, leads into a lengthy discourse, and concludes with a prayer.

To introduce the occasion and all that it entailed, John says, 'Having loved his own who were in the world, he [Jesus] loved them to the end' (13:1). The theme of love will dominate all that follows, and in order to increase the disciples' understanding of himself Jesus demonstrates what love means in practice before going on to explain its principles.

In both practice and principle, the emphasis is very much on God's love for us, rather than on ours for him. Contrary to a once popular understanding of this episode that suggested that Jesus was teaching by example what we can do for God, he was actually demonstrating through his actions the full extent of God's love for his children. As Jesus makes clear, through the commentary that John here provides, this was the love that was motivating so many of Jesus' actions as his work was nearing completion. In this passage we find examples of four of the goals that were continually before his mind.

(1) To Fulfil God's Purpose

The wonder of Jesus' love in this episode is set against the backdrop of his complete knowledge of the rapidly approaching climax. As he gathered with the disciples in that room, he 'knew that his hour had come to depart out of this world to the Father' (13:1). Even though he could so easily have been preoccupied with the ordeal ahead of him, he was taken up instead with the very people on whose behalf that ordeal was necessary. He saw everything in terms of God's purpose and his own unique role in fulfilling it. So, 'having loved his own who were in the world, he loved them to the end' (12:1).

Even though he was profoundly conscious of the dark shadow of the devil's influence present in the disciple who had been induced to betray his Master (13:2), Jesus was even more determined to focus, not on himself and his needs, but upon his disciples and theirs. His perspective on the scene in that room was completely different from that of the Twelve. He saw it all in terms of the eternal plan and purpose of God. This was the fulfilment on earth of all that had been scripted in heaven (13:3). John focuses on this and, with the benefit of Spirit-inspired hindsight, he reveals that in that room on that night the destiny of the world was gathering. Despite all the factors ranged against him, Jesus was lovingly determined to carry through to completion all that the Father had given him to do.

The love of God in Christ (in contrast to our natural love for ourselves) lifts us on to a higher plane from which to view and understand our world and life. It takes us out of our petty temporal concerns and brings us face to face with the greatest, eternal issues. It makes us realize what really matters.

(2) To Pay God's Price

What happened next did not immediately make sense to the disciples, but later, after the events of that weekend and beyond, they would come to an understanding of it (13:7). The events are to be viewed as an acted-out parable in which Jesus powerfully demonstrates what lay behind his coming into the world and the reason he was willing to go to the cross. The disciples' astonishment at what they were witnessing was only a foretaste of the even greater astonishment produced by the events of the coming days. And that element of astonishment would remain with them throughout their lives as they understood more and more of the full significance of the deeds they had witnessed.

Jesus did for them what they hardly would have dreamed of doing for each other, something that not even a Jewish slave would have been expected to do – he donned a slave's apron and washed their feet. Even though he was none other than the Son of God and the promised Messiah, he stooped to the level of a servant and washed the feet of sinners. He was acting out his own explanation as to why he had come into the world: 'Not to be served, but to serve and to give his life as a ransom for many' (*Matt*. 20:28). For the disciples – certainly for Peter – this was almost too much to take. But the actions pointed to the almost unbelievable self-sacrifice which the gospel required on the part of Jesus: a self-sacrifice that Paul would later express in the words of a hymn (*Phil*. 2:5–11).

It is precisely at this point that many people stumble at the message of the gospel. The thought of Christ having to do so much for them, as opposed to their being able to offer something to him, is too much for them to accept. But the depths to which Jesus had to stoop in order to save us is but a reflection of the depth of the need of our unsaved condition.

(3) TO SAVE GOD'S PEOPLE

From the very outset of his earthly mission, God had revealed the purpose of his Son's coming. The angel who spoke in a dream to Joseph had said, 'You shall call his name Jesus, for he will save his people from their sins' (*Matt*. 1:21). Human sin has created the great obstacle to fellowship with God; an obstacle which no one can remove by themselves. In order to find God and his salvation, someone else therefore must save.

When Jesus came to Peter and prepared to wash his feet, Peter protested. Jesus responded by explaining what lay behind his action, and what it symbolized for all who were truly his followers (13:6–11). Peter could not see the symbolism, but Jesus pressed it home by saying, 'If I do not wash you, you have no share with me' (13:8). When Peter then asks for a complete bath, Jesus declares that he does not need a total cleansing. He has received that already (13:9–11). The fact that this was a symbolic way of speaking about the spiritual cleansing of conversion is clear from the overt reference to Judas who knew no such renewal (13:12).

Jesus was teaching his disciples that there is a once-and-for-all dimension to the pardon they receive on coming to faith in him. In that moment of believing they are forgiven and accepted as righteous in God's sight, all on account of Christ and what he has done. That does not mean they are perfect – every Christian falls into sin – but they do not need a new conversion experience every time that happens. The once-for-all cleansing underpins the daily cleansing they receive each time they come confessing their sin to God.

This is a vivid picture of what happens in conversion. Jesus provides that first complete cleansing of salvation. It is upon the basis of this forgiveness that we receive subsequent washing as we journey through the Christian life. It is this initial forgiveness also that is the foundation for our Christian assurance.

(4) To Restore God's Pattern

Jesus goes on to apply his actions in order to show these men the effect his atoning work must have upon them. It saves, not only in the sense of restoring people to a right relationship with God, but it also transforms them. The self-sacrifice of Christ becomes the life-pattern for God's children. If the picture accompanying a jigsaw is lost, then there is little hope of putting the pieces together in the correct way. But if the picture is rediscovered, then the puzzle may be remade. The same is true in redemption. Ever since man's fall into sin, the pattern of a true humanity has been lost. After Adam's disobedience, human beings ceased to be what they were meant to be, or to function in the way that God intended. Matters changed when Jesus came. He is not only the Saviour of life, he is also the true pattern for life. Here, therefore, he says explicitly, 'I have given you an example . . .' (13:15). He was not only the Redeemer whom they were to trust; he was the model they were to emulate.

Here is the love of God seen in its broadest canvas – a love that stooped in humility to meet the needs of a dirty fallen world. Jesus calls his followers also into a life of service where they too must deny self in order to serve both Christ and the world. If the King has stooped to serve, then it is not unreasonable for his subjects to do so also. And the reward for such behaviour is found in what Jesus says at the end of the passage: 'If you know these things, blessed are you if you do them' (13:17).

30

Preparing for His Passion

I am not speaking of all of you; I know whom I have chosen. But the Scripture will be fulfilled, 'He who ate my bread has lifted his heel against me.' ¹⁹ *I am telling you this now, before it takes place, that when it does take place you may believe that I am he.* ²⁰ *Truly, truly, I say to you, whoever receives the one I send receives me, and whoever receives me receives the one who sent me."*

²¹ *After saying these things, Jesus was troubled in his spirit, and testified, "Truly, truly, I say to you, one of you will betray me."* ²² *The disciples looked at one another, uncertain of whom he spoke.* ²³ *One of his disciples, whom Jesus loved, was reclining at table close to Jesus,* ²⁴ *so Simon Peter motioned to him to ask Jesus of whom he was speaking.* ²⁵ *So that disciple, leaning back against Jesus, said to him, "Lord, who is it?"* ²⁶ *Jesus answered, "It is he to whom I will give this morsel of bread when I have dipped it." So when he had dipped the morsel, he gave it to Judas, the son of Simon Iscariot.* ²⁷ *Then after he had taken the morsel, Satan entered into him. Jesus said to him, "What you are going to do, do quickly."* ²⁸ *Now no one at the table knew why he said this to him.* ²⁹ *Some thought that, because Judas had the moneybag, Jesus was telling him, "Buy what we need for the feast," or that he should give something to the poor.* ³⁰ *So, after receiving the morsel of bread, he immediately went out. And it was night.*

³¹ *When he had gone out, Jesus said, "Now is the Son of Man glorified, and God is glorified in him.* ³² *If God is glorified in him, God will also glorify him in himself, and glorify him at once.* ³³ *Little children, yet a little while I am with you. You will seek*

me, and just as I said to the Jews, so now I also say to you, 'Where I am going you cannot come.' [34] A new commandment I give to you, that you love one another: just as I have loved you, you also are to love one another. [35] By this all people will know that you are my disciples, if you have love for one another."

[36] Simon Peter said to him, "Lord, where are you going?" Jesus answered him, "Where I am going you cannot follow me now, but you will follow afterwards." [37] Peter said to him, "Lord, why can I not follow you now? I will lay down my life for you." [38] Jesus answered, "Will you lay down your life for me? Truly, truly, I say to you, the rooster will not crow till you have denied me three times (John 13:18–38).

It has become common practice in contemporary medicine to prepare patients for what lies ahead of them: observation, surgery, or whatever particular course of treatment is involved. The reason is both simple and sensible: such preparation minimises fear and lessens the shock that might arise. In a sense, Jesus is doing just that in these verses as he prepares his disciples for the ordeal that both he and they would face in the next twenty-four hours. He has gathered them round the table for the Last Supper. He has demonstrated the depth of his devotion to them. Now he gives them a preview of what is soon to happen, and the way it will shape their future life's-work and ministry. We see again the gentleness with which he deals with these men, calling them 'little children' (13:33). Far from being condescending or patronizing towards them, he displays the genuine affection he has for them, and the father-like concern for their welfare. In all of this he wants not only his disciples, but all who read of him in the Gospels, to understand fully what is going on, to appreciate what it means and to respond accordingly. Many things come to a head in the hours Jesus spent with the disciples around the table that night.

An Identity Confirmed

Once again Jesus predicts his betrayal (13:18). He has done so already (6:70), but now the prediction is specific. The reason for identifying his betrayer is not due in any way to spite or vindictiveness towards Judas (we shall see later on in the passage that the opposite was true). It was, rather, in order to reveal exactly the ongoing sequence of circumstances that would result in the horrendous events of the next day.

Jesus is about to be killed. Many people have been killed or assassinated throughout history, but all, in one way or another, have been the victims of the circumstances. If they could have avoided their deaths, they would most certainly have done so. This was not the case with Jesus. He knew that his death – in all its details, manner and circumstances – had been planned from eternity, prophesied of in Scripture, and was now being fulfilled in time. It was foreordained as the culmination and climax of Messiah's ministry. Jesus therefore wanted his disciples to know that the disturbing events they would witness were not the negation of his identity as Messiah, but rather its confirmation.

He makes this clear, partly by explaining that all the circumstances that would befall him were necessary in order for the Scripture to be fulfilled (13:18); but primarily: 'I am telling you this now, before it takes place, that when it does take place you may believe that I am he' (13:19). Once again there is a subtle twist in Jesus' choice of words. His literal meaning is, '. . . that when it does take place you will know that I AM'. He is again taking the divine Name and using it of himself. In other words, as these events unfold and are seen against the backdrop both of Old Testament revelation and of Jesus' own teaching, the disciples will see not only that the Messiah is Jesus, but that Jesus is God!

That is the only way that the events of the betrayal, arrest, trial and crucifixion of Jesus make sense and offer true hope. If the identity of Jesus is anything less than that of God, then the achievement of his suffering, whatever else it may involve, is a great deal less than that necessary for salvation.

A DESTINY DETERMINED

What happens next not only serves to reveal the sovereign plan and purpose of God in these events, but the heart of God as well. They show us that although he is omniscient (he knows all things) and has sovereign control over all events, he is anything but a detached and mechanical manipulator.

We catch another glimpse of the intensity of the pain that lies ahead for Jesus. We are told, 'Jesus was troubled in his spirit' (13:21). He was beginning the final descent into the anguish of the cross. Every step towards its paradoxical heights and depths increased the burden of the pain that was being laid upon him. At the very outset it is made worse because his betrayal will be by the hand of a friend: 'One of you will betray me' (13:21).

The disciples are understandably curious to know who he meant (13:22), so Peter asks the disciple 'whom Jesus loved' to enquire discreetly, since he was reclining beside Jesus (13:23–24). Jesus responds to the enquiry quite openly and publicly and indicates that Judas is the man (13:26). Jesus' words and action serve both as a warning and as a final appeal. He was making it clear to Judas that he knew completely what he was planning. However, the way he expressed it – by dipping a morsel of bread and sharing it with him – was a recognised gesture of love and affection. Judas accepts the piece of bread, but spurns the love that lies behind it.

John chillingly records the deeper dynamics at work in these events. He tells us that it was at that moment that Satan's grip finally closed around Judas' heart (13:27); and that Judas went out, 'And it was night' (13:30). With another double-edged phrase so typical of John, he indicates not only that it was dark outside but that the darkness of hell had closed around this man.

The mystery here is that on the one hand it is clear that the destiny of Judas had been foreordained and foretold, but that on the other hand Judas was being offered a choice, right to the very end – a choice he refused to take. In other words, it was not Jesus who confirmed the destiny of Judas, but Judas himself.

A GLORY DISPLAYED

The spiritual darkness that engulfed Judas at that moment contrasts with the glorious truth described in Jesus' next words. Even though Judas and his collaborators were about to perpetrate the darkest act in human history, in the purpose of God this very act would be the instrument of his brightest glory. Hence Jesus says, 'Now is the Son of Man glorified and God is glorified in him' (13:31). In all that was to be involved in the crucifixion of Jesus, both the Father and the Son would be simultaneously glorified (13:32). It is in that hour that the infinite love, wisdom and justice of God's purpose would reach out beyond the furthermost limits of the sin, guilt and depravity of man and secure salvation.

Jesus tells his disciples in advance so that they are aware of the dynamics of what is taking place. They could so easily view the forthcoming events purely from the dark perspective of the evil that was at work, but he wanted them to recognise the hand of God.

Most of all, he explained these things to them not as if they were mere spectators, but as those who were trusting in him. To those who are onlookers of some terrible disaster, the rescuers who pull people from the rubble are heroes; to the victims whom they rescue, they are saviours! This is how Jesus would have them, and ourselves, see him: not as the greatest hero the world has ever known, but as the greatest Saviour we could ever have.

A Testimony Shaped

Jesus repeats to the disciples what he had already stated to the Jews (7:33–34), that there was an absolute uniqueness in the nature of the work he would fulfil. He says, 'Where I am going, you cannot come' (13:33). He proceeds however, having already referred often to the cross as the supreme demonstration of divine love, to stress how his unique love for them must now of necessity be mirrored also in their love for one another (13:34). The cross would shape their testimony.

When he says that he is giving them 'a new commandment', he is not suggesting that this is something they had never heard of before; rather, here was something they had never seen on this scale before. Their whole understanding of what it meant to love was being taken on to a completely different plane.

Most significantly, this self-sacrificing love is to become the visible hallmark of the Church. 'By this all people will know you are my disciples, if you have love for one another' (13:35). That kind of love is impossible and unknown in this world in natural terms. Its only possible source is Christ and the love that he brought into the world and displayed on the cross – the love that he imparts to his children.

The love of the church therefore becomes a living testimony to the love of the Saviour.

A WEAKNESS EXPOSED

Simon Peter hears what Jesus has to say, but does not hear! He catches hold of Jesus' comment that no one else would be able to go where he is going. Peter wants to know more and concludes that even if Jesus was talking about death, he, Peter, was ready to lay down his life for him (13:36–37). He uses the very words that Jesus had used to describe the sacrifice he was about to make.

Jesus gently takes his friend and follower in hand and says, 'Will you lay down your life for me? Truly, truly, I say to you, the cock will not crow, till you have denied me three times' (13:38). Far from being the strong support who would carry Jesus through his darkest hour, Peter would be a tragic failure who would desert him. Jesus here is not putting Peter on notice, warning him that if he did this he would be banished. What we have in these words is an expression of Jesus' love for his friend, whom he will ultimately use to great effect – weaknesses, failures and all.

Peter was boasting to his Lord and Master, 'You need me!' Jesus was saying to his dear disciple, and to every follower, 'No, my friend, you need me!'

31

No Place Like Home

Let not your hearts be troubled. Believe in God; believe also in me. ² In my Father's house are many rooms. If it were not so, would I have told you that I go to prepare a place for you? ³ And if I go and prepare a place for you, I will come again and will take you to myself, that where I am you may be also. ⁴ And you know the way to where I am going." ⁵ Thomas said to him, "Lord, we do not know where you are going. How can we know the way?" ⁶ Jesus said to him, "I am the way, and the truth, and the life. No one comes to the Father except through me. ⁷ If you had known me, you would have known my Father also. From now on you do know him and have seen him."

⁸ Philip said to him, "Lord, show us the Father, and it is enough for us." ⁹ Jesus said to him, "Have I been with you so long, and you still do not know me, Philip? Whoever has seen me has seen the Father. How can you say, 'Show us the Father'? ¹⁰ Do you not believe that I am in the Father and the Father is in me? The words that I say to you I do not speak on my own authority, but the Father who dwells in me does his works. ¹¹ Believe me that I am in the Father and the Father is in me, or else believe on account of the works themselves.

¹² "Truly, truly, I say to you, whoever believes in me will also do the works that I do; and greater works than these will he do, because I am going to the Father. ¹³ Whatever you ask in my name, this I will do, that the Father may be glorified in the Son. ¹⁴ If you ask me anything in my name, I will do it (John 14:1–14).

Few things in life evoke deeper feelings or have richer associations than the thought of 'Home'. Very often when we find ourselves in the midst of some terrible crisis, our instinctive reaction is, 'I want to go home!' This was presently very true for the disciples. They were on the brink of a crisis of unthinkable proportions. Everything that Jesus was saying round that table had an ominous ring to it. They had just been told that their fellow disciple whom they had always regarded as 'the rock' would crumble in less than ten hours' time. And what does Jesus do? How does he prepare them to meet this crisis? He starts talking about 'home'!

With words which have become some of the most familiar and most comforting that Jesus ever spoke, he begins, 'Let not your hearts be troubled!' (14:1). Even though the disciples had every reason to be troubled (after all, Jesus himself was deeply troubled), Jesus urged them to take a step back and see their situation from a broader perspective.

What he does is to show them that the spiritual 'home' of which they had been a part for the past three years – the home which seemed that night to be on the verge of being blown apart – had far more to it than met the eye. It was part of something that possessed eternal proportions, though it had drawn near and taken hold of them in their world of space and time. Jesus begins to open their eyes to the security that was theirs in that home, and not only theirs, but the security belonging to all those who put their trust in him.

FUTURE HOPE

Jesus begins to comfort his little beleaguered band of followers by pointing them to the future – a future that they were beginning to doubt – and reassuring them. Much of what he had been saying during the last weeks and months of his ministry had to do with his 'going away'. It was vitally important that they understood what that meant.

The immediate reality of this 'going away' was his imminent arrest, crucifixion and ascension, but Jesus had in mind a reality that lay further ahead again. With great emphasis, he was pointing beyond the horizons of the present world to that future horizon of the world to come. He was looking forward to what had already been described in Scripture as 'a new heavens and a new earth' (*Isa.* 65:17). This new world is by its very nature beyond the reach of ordinary human enquiry and investigation, but Jesus momentarily allowed the disciples a glimpse of what it is like. Just as every prospective home-owner is thrilled by a sneak preview of where they will soon be living, so it is also for those looking forward to their eternal home.

Jesus draws attention to many of the wonderful features of this home in heaven. He says it is a large home: 'In my Father's house are many rooms' (14:2). Even though the disciples that night were small in number and could be fitted into a single room, God is preparing a home with vast accommodation for vast numbers of people. This indication of the scale of Christ's work and salvation is a great encouragement.

It will also be a safe home. Whatever the fear and foreboding felt that night by the disciples as they faced the impending crisis, Jesus' presence with them in that room calmed their fears. Similarly, it will be his presence that will give them peace in heaven (14:3). Like a child in the dark who says to its parent, 'Stay with me!', so it is with every spiritual child in the family of God. Heaven will be 'home' because Jesus is there.

This home will also be an open home. Unlike the many palatial residences of every age, homes only to a privileged elite and barred to the masses, the home that Jesus is preparing is open to any one who will come. The way to this home, he says, is completely familiar (14.4).

Jesus wants people to realize that no one has any lasting home in this world. Our ultimate destiny lies in the eternity that is to come. We therefore need a lasting hope in order to face that future.

PRESENT REALITY

It is sometimes said facetiously that gospel ministers are men who make a living in this world out of other people's prospects in the next; the cynical implication being that they are just clever spiritual con men. It is true that there always have been and always will be spiritual charlatans who promise all kinds of things in the future in order to increase their personal gain in the present, but Jesus is not one of these!

Thomas had listened to all that Jesus was saying and now interrupts him, rather pessimistically, 'Lord, we do not know where you are going. How can we know the way?' (14:5). To this Jesus replies, 'I am the way, and the truth, and the life. No one comes to the Father, except through me' (14:6). Of all the 'I am' sayings of Jesus, this is perhaps the most profound. Whether it should be translated as it appears in the ESV, or whether it should be rendered, 'I am the true and living way', is immaterial. The sense of both translations is the same: Jesus is the way to the Father and to heaven.

For someone who is lost, there is a world of difference between a person who says, 'I'll show you the way', and one who says, 'I'll take you there!' Jesus does not merely point the way to heaven, he takes people there. With these words Jesus invites people into a secure relationship with him on earth that will guarantee them the security of an eternal home in heaven.

LIVING RELATIONSHIP

The full extent of this new relationship is revealed as Jesus responds to another question, this time from Philip. 'Lord, show us the Father, and it is enough for us' (14:8). In many ways this is the ultimate question that so many people ask: 'What is God like and how can he be known?' Despite the mystery and mysticism that have characterized the multitude of answers offered by religions and philosophies throughout the ages, Jesus' answer is simple in the extreme. He says, 'Whoever has seen me has seen the Father' (14:9). To know Jesus is to know God.

The life he offers is not one of endless rules, regulations and desperate struggles for achievement, but rather a living, loving relationship with God through himself. He was effectively urging his disciples to look again at the life and the work of the One with whom they had spent the past thirty-six months. He wanted them to realize and recognize that his life was God's life, his words were God's words, and his works were God's works. Through their relationship with him they had been brought into an everlasting relationship with God. That is the timeless message and hope of the gospel. The way to heaven is identical to the way to God, and they are both found through faith in Jesus.

DYNAMIC USEFULNESS

Jesus continues to expand the horizons of these men by showing them the incredible potential of this spiritual family to which they now belong. He makes an amazing statement about those who believe in him, saying that they will do even greater works than he himself has done (14:12–14). There has always been a temptation to read that statement in terms of some kind of ongoing ministry of miracles that would eclipse even the miracle-ministry of Jesus, but such an interpretation does not fit with either the record of the rest of the New Testament nor of church history. Instead, Jesus seems to be pointing to the coming of the Holy Spirit (which he will explain more fully in the verses that follow) and the work that the disciples and the Church would accomplish through him. This is borne out by the opening words of the book of Acts which speak of what Jesus 'began to do' when he was present on earth and, by implication, of what the Holy Spirit continued to do through the apostles after his ascension.

In this way, the 'greater works', as recorded in the book of Acts and throughout church history, constitute the numerical and geographical explosion of the kingdom of God as the gospel spread. This is the most thrilling of works that we as Christians can be part of as we place ourselves at Christ's disposal for the service of his gospel.

CONSCIOUS TRUST

What then is the key to this most unusual of homes and most extraordinary of lives described by Jesus? When our lives are touched by the members of some special family, who are a delight to be with and who are eminently useful, we immediately want to know what their secret is. In the case of God's family, the 'secret' is simple: faith. That is why at the very start of this passage Jesus says, 'Believe in God; believe also in me' (14:1).

This is the fundamental issue of life: who is it we can trust, and who can carry the weight of our confidence? Some people look for the answer in themselves, others look to science, and still others to the safety of the crowd, but can any of these meet the deepest burdens of our soul? As Jesus points us to God and to himself, he is making it clear that the faith he calls for in the gospel is not a spiritual leap in the dark, but a leap into the arms of the God revealed fully in himself. In the events that are about to follow, God proves himself in Christ to be more than worthy of our trust and confidence. A God who goes to such amazing lengths to save, is a God who will be sure to keep, and that forever!

32

Not Left as Orphans

If you love me, you will keep my commandments. [16] *And I will ask the Father, and he will give you another Helper, to be with you forever,* [17] *even the Spirit of truth, whom the world cannot receive, because it neither sees him nor knows him. You know him, for he dwells with you and will be in you.*

[18] *"I will not leave you as orphans; I will come to you.* [19] *Yet a little while and the world will see me no more, but you will see me. Because I live, you also will live.* [20] *In that day you will know that I am in my Father, and you in me, and I in you.* [21] *Whoever has my commandments and keeps them, he it is who loves me. And he who loves me will be loved by my Father, and I will love him and manifest myself to him."* [22] *Judas (not Iscariot) said to him, "Lord, how is it that you will manifest yourself to us, and not to the world?"* [23] *Jesus answered him, "If anyone loves me, he will keep my word, and my Father will love him, and we will come to him and make our home with him.* [24] *Whoever does not love me does not keep my words. And the word that you hear is not mine but the Father's who sent me.*

[25] *"These things I have spoken to you while I am still with you.* [26] *But the Helper, the Holy Spirit, whom the Father will send in my name, he will teach you all things and bring to your remembrance all that I have said to you.* [27] *Peace I leave with you; my peace I give to you. Not as the world gives do I give to you. Let not your hearts be troubled, neither let them be afraid.* [28] *You heard me say to you, 'I am going away, and I will come to you.' If you loved me, you would have rejoiced, because I am going to the Father, for the Father is greater than I.* [29] *And now*

I have told you before it takes place, so that when it does take place you may believe. [30] I will no longer talk much with you, for the ruler of this world is coming. He has no claim on me, [31] but I do as the Father has commanded me, so that the world may know that I love the Father. Rise, let us go from here (John 14:15–31).

It is hard to look at images in the media of orphaned children–whether victims of epidemic or disaster, war-zones or famines – and not be deeply moved by them. They constitute a tragic sight of human need at its worst. In the Old Testament, orphans, together with widows, represented the most vulnerable and helpless people in society, those who needed special help. Similarly, in this next section of the discourse in the upper room, Jesus uses the imagery of orphans in relation to his disciples (14:18) to express not only the depth of their need, but the extent of help that God would supply.

His reassurance hinges on the promise of the coming of the Holy Spirit and the unique aid that the Spirit would provide for God's children. In speaking in this way, Jesus opens his disciples' eyes more fully to understand the mystery of God's being. There is here a further glimpse of the fact that the God who revealed himself in Scripture, whom they worshipped and in whom they trusted, was one, and yet was more than one. Even though they were well aware of the references to the Spirit of God that occurred frequently in the Old Testament, this was the first time they had heard any extended teaching on the Spirit. They would begin to discover that God's Spirit is a distinct person in his own right. He is a person, and not merely a force or a presence. Jesus draws attention in particular to the work of God's Spirit in the lives of God's people.

He highlights the fact that a relationship with the Holy Spirit is absolutely essential for being a Christian; it is the experience of all true believers, not just of some. As he opens up this vital dimension of Christian experience, Jesus maps out the complex, interwoven relationships that are involved in the Spirit's work. These all undergird the fullness of salvation that God provides in his Son. He traces out four key elements in what the Spirit comes to do.

(1) To Forge Fellowship with God

Although this section does not begin with a direct reference to the Holy Spirit, his work is very much in view. Jesus says, 'If you love me, you will keep my commandments' (14:15). The verb he uses for 'obey' is not an imperative but a future tense. The verse is just as much a statement of fact as it is an expression of obligation. In other words, Jesus is not merely saying that true love for him is seen in obedience to him (though that is undoubtedly true), but that true obedience to him is enabled by virtue of a new and loving relationship with him.

Like every follower of Jesus, these first disciples were painfully conscious of the weakness of their love for him and their failure to obey him genuinely (as the recent exchange with Peter had proved). How is it possible to live in a way that even begins to express real love?

The answer lies in what Jesus says next about 'another Helper' (14:16), one who is called, 'the Spirit of truth' (14:17). There are two important details that ought to be noted in these designations of the Holy Spirit. The first is that Jesus promises to send 'another' Helper. The word conveys the notion of 'another of the same kind'. In other words, whatever the Spirit would be and do when he came, would be a continuation of what the disciples had already known and experienced during the past three years with Jesus.

The second significant detail, tied in with the first, is the fact that the Spirit is called 'Helper'. The Greek word underlying this translation can also be rendered, 'Counsellor', 'Comforter', 'Strengthener' or 'Advocate'. Often it was the word used simply for a person's best friend who would stand with them for support when they had to go to law. The Spirit, then, would provide that kind of support to Jesus' followers in the face of all the legal obligations that God laid upon them.

Putting all this together, we find that Jesus was promising these men that the Spirit when given, would so stand with them that they would be enabled to show their love for Christ through obedience rendered to him. The obligation of God's law is not diminished, but the power to fulfil its obligation is provided. The dynamic of this unique relationship becomes clearer as Jesus reveals more of what is involved.

He says that the world does not accept the Spirit because 'it neither sees him nor knows him'; however, the disciples do, 'for he dwells with you and will be in you' (14:17). Jesus is talking about the special relationship between himself and the Spirit which in turn would provide the new dimension of his relationship with his disciples, after he had ascended back into heaven (14:18–19). He shows how the apparent break caused by his going away will, in reality, be no break at all, because his presence will continue through his Spirit. When the Holy Spirit comes – as 'the Spirit of truth' (14:17) – he will bring the disciples into an understanding of the relationships within the Godhead and of the way in which those who believe in Christ are caught up into those relationships in the fullness of salvation (14:20–21).

This leads us full circle back to the question of obedience to Christ. Only when God's Spirit comes to bring us into fellowship with the Father through the Son does the obedience God requires become a reality. This is what will distinguish those who belong to Christ from those who belong to the world.

(2) To Lead into God's Truth

The Spirit is repeatedly described as the 'Spirit of truth' in these chapters. This description emphasizes a key function of the Spirit of God, namely, to reveal the truth of God to the Church and to the world. Given the inter-personal bonds of fellowship within the Godhead, of which Jesus has been speaking, we see the link here between this 'Spirit of truth' and Jesus' own statement, 'I am . . . the truth' (14:6). He is again pointing to the continuity between his work and that of the Spirit. The Holy Spirit would guide the disciples of Jesus into all truth (14:26; see also 16:13).

There is an exclusive focus to what Jesus is saying here. The promise relates to these men specifically, Christ's apostles, and to the unique and foundational role they would play in the formation of the New Testament church. In particular, he is pointing to the way in which these men would be instrumental in bringing God's written revelation to climax and completion in the Scriptures of the New Testament. They would be the agents of God's special revelation.

The importance of this lies in the fact that although the Holy Spirit continues to be the 'Spirit of truth' for all generations, and the one who leads all true believers into truth, he does not do so without reference to the once-for-all revelation of truth in the completed Bible. What he provided for the disciples by means of revelation, he continues to provide to the Church by means of illumination: shedding light on the meaning of Scripture and showing how it is to be applied.

(3) To Establish God's Peace

In the middle of all that Jesus says about the coming of the Holy Spirit, he suddenly interjects, 'Peace I leave with you; my peace I give to you. Not as the world gives do I give to you. Let not your hearts be troubled, neither let them be afraid' (14:27).

'Shalom' was the Hebrew word for 'peace' and it had passed into Jewish culture as the word used for greeting or parting. As with so many expressions in different cultures, the word had become somewhat devalued in its meaning; but here Jesus takes it and reinvests it with fresh significance, binding it up with the hope of the gospel.

He reminds these men of the distinctiveness of God's peace. The peace he leaves is 'My peace' as opposed to that of the world. It is a peace rooted in the sacrifice he would offer on the cross. It depends upon propitiation – God's anger being turned aside – and reconciliation being made. It is a peace that has nothing to do with a person's circumstances or emotional state. It has everything to do with an objective peace established between a holy God in heaven and sinful people on earth. Jesus' sacrifice alone would be the reason for banishing fear and anxiety, and for resting in the security that comes through peace with God.

Given the context of this statement, it is clear that the experience of God's peace through Christ cannot be divorced from the work of God's Spirit in his followers. It is as the Spirit fulfils his task of revealing God's truth and leading into an understanding of God's truth, that peace in Jesus will consequently be found.

(4) To Provide Comfort through God's Purpose

If it is true that John's Gospel is 'shallow enough for a child to paddle, but deep enough for an elephant to swim', then the closing verses of this chapter must constitute the elephant's diving pool! As Jesus draws together the threads of who he is, why he came, and what he was about to do, he points to the comfort that is to be found in the mysterious will and purpose of God.

He does so by explaining how it is he will be present with his people by his 'coming to them' after 'going away' (14:28). There seem to be three events being referred to here: Jesus' resurrection; Pentecost; and his return at the end of time. Each provides its own particular encouragement, and together they provide a triple comfort.

He points to the joy he has promised to impart to those who trust him: 'If you loved me, you would have rejoiced, because I am going to the Father, for the Father is greater than I' (14:28). The reference to the Father's being 'greater' than Jesus is not some suggestion that he is somehow more divine or more powerful than the Son. It rather points to the fact that the Father at that moment is in a higher position than Jesus – he is in heaven. But the fact that Jesus is soon to return to heaven is good news, because it will mark the Father's approval and acceptance of all that he has achieved on earth.

Once again, this comfort is not divorced from the Holy Spirit's work. He does not provide support and encouragement for God's children by simply stirring warm and pleasant thoughts and feelings within them. He comforts them by pointing to the perfect finished work of Christ and the sure foundation it provides for our salvation. There can be no deeper assurance than that which the Spirit provides in this way.

Jesus has been preparing his followers for this very moment, teaching them again and again that the cross would be the climax of his coming (14:29). But the world had yet to see and understand these things (14:30–31). The only way the world would do so would be as the Spirit, through Christ's followers, would take the message of the cross and proclaim it to the very ends of the earth.

33

A Most Productive Life

I am the true vine, and my Father is the vine dresser. ² Every branch of mine that does not bear fruit he takes away, and every branch that does bear fruit he prunes, that it may bear more fruit. ³ Already you are clean because of the word that I have spoken to you. ⁴ Abide in me, and I in you. As the branch cannot bear fruit by itself, unless it abides in the vine, neither can you, unless you abide in me. ⁵ I am the vine; you are the branches. Whoever abides in me and I in him, he it is that bears much fruit, for apart from me you can do nothing. ⁶ If anyone does not abide in me he is thrown away like a branch and withers; and the branches are gathered, thrown into the fire, and burned. ⁷ If you abide in me, and my words abide in you, ask whatever you wish, and it will be done for you. ⁸ By this my Father is glorified, that you bear much fruit and so prove to be my disciples. ⁹ As the Father has loved me, so have I loved you. Abide in my love. ¹⁰ If you keep my commandments, you will abide in my love, just as I have kept my Father's commandments and abide in his love. ¹¹ These things I have spoken to you, that my joy may be in you, and that your joy may be full.

¹² "This is my commandment, that you love one another as I have loved you. ¹³ Greater love has no one than this, that someone lays down his life for his friends. ¹⁴ You are my friends if you do what I command you. ¹⁵ No longer do I call you servants, for the servant does not know what his master is doing; but I have called you friends, for all that I have heard from my Father I have made known to you. ¹⁶ You did not choose me, but I chose you and appointed you that you should go and bear

fruit and that your fruit should abide, so that whatever you ask the Father in my name, he may give it to you. [17] These things I command you, so that you will love one another (John 15:1–17).

Having spoken objectively of the salvation he was about to secure for his people, Jesus now proceeds to speak about the experience of that salvation subjectively, and the difference it will make to their lives in real terms. He takes us into the realm of that 'abundant life' of which he had already spoken (10:10). He brings us into the realm of meaning and purpose in life – that deep-seated longing that burns somewhere within every human being. It is that sense of personal longing that distinguishes humanity from what is merely animal. Jesus wants his disciples to know that the final outcome of the events of the next eighteen hours culminating in his death, will be the potential for a life that had hitherto been unknown.

There is no obvious reason why he should have suddenly chosen the image of a vine for himself and his fellowship with his people (15:1) – perhaps there was a trailing branch visible through the window, or possibly the fruit of the vine set out on the table. Either way, this is the last of his 'I am' sayings and it taps into some of the richest veins of Old Testament expectation and of spiritual experience. Jesus is saying that the true Israel (and the true humanity) is nothing less than God and man in fellowship through Jesus Christ.

Here is the heartbeat of the life of the Church, the very pulse of genuine Christian experience. It is the essence of a truly fulfilled and productive life, and in these verses Jesus spells out all that it involves.

WHAT IT ENTAILS

If we were to ask people at random what they thought life was all about, no doubt there would be a variety of answers. For some, life is all about work; for others, leisure and recreation; still others see it in terms of family, or education, or simply living as long as is possible and making the most of what happens to come their way. The problem with all these views of life is that they end in a cul-de-sac; they have inbuilt limits in themselves and are restricted to life in this world.

However, even a quick scan of this part of Jesus' discourse shows that what Jesus has in mind as he talks about life in the Vine is a life that is both everlasting and eternally worthwhile. It is a life that has to do with fruitfulness (15:2, 4, 5, 8, 16); a fruitfulness that involves living to the maximum of our God-given potential in this world and realizing the fullness of that potential in the world to come.

It is, as we have hinted, tied up with the very essence of what it means to be human. At the very beginning of the Bible when we are told about God making man and then commissioning him to a life of service and blessing, he says to Adam, 'Be fruitful ' (*Gen.* 1:28). That fruitfulness that was lost through the Fall is recovered through Christ and his redemption.

It is not surprising therefore that the recovery of true fruitfulness in life is bound up with recovery of fellowship with God through Jesus Christ. Hence Jesus pointedly connects fruitfulness with fellowship throughout this passage. To bear fruit, he says, requires that you are always 'in me', 'in my love' (15:4–11). In a natural sense it is the relationships we enjoy with other people that make us blossom – whether with a spouse, a parent, child, or friend. How much more fruitful still will we be therefore when in a relationship with God through his own Son? This is the supreme purpose for which we have been created.

This relationship has to do with love in the richest sense of that word; not the self-gratifying kind of love that is so common in a sinful world, but a love which is self-giving (15:9, 10, 12, 13, 16, 17). It is a love that reflects the unique self-sacrificing love of Christ. It is guaranteed to revolutionize our lives and lead us into the kind of joy that this world can never give (15:11). It is the joy of knowing Christ, the joy that fuels all our worship.

Here then is a life that cannot be more fulfilled, cannot know any greater purpose, can experience no greater security and offer no greater service. To quote the title of a book written by Henry Scougal many centuries ago, it is nothing less than *The Life of God in the Soul of Man*.

Who It Involves

When an unskilled amateur looks at a magnificent garden, the obvious question to ask the gardener responsible is, 'How did you do that?' Similarly, as the disciples (and anyone else) look at the end-product of this life described by Jesus, they too must wonder how it is produced. The answer lies not so much in the materials and processes but in the figures and the people involved. Jesus points to three in particular.

He points primarily to himself: 'I am the true vine' (15:1). Against the backdrop of Old Testament revelation and the use of vine imagery in the Jewish culture of the day, this was a significant statement. He was making it clear that being part of God's fruitful vine was not a matter of national identity, political climate or religious fervour. It was first and foremost about himself, Jesus, and about being in relationship with him. That is a simple truth, but it is a vital truth. There is no such thing as Christ-less Christianity. To be part of God's Church, to have a place in God's family, and to enjoy the life that God offers, all have their beginning and ending with God's Son and with knowing him.

The second figure Jesus points to is his Father: 'I am the true vine, and my Father is the vine dresser' (15:1). Behind every great garden is a great gardener: someone who has planned, planted, pruned and produced everything that is seen on display. So it is with God the Father. He is the one whose eternal purpose lay behind the history of his people: the coming of his Son: and the purpose for which the Son had been sent. Everything we see in the Bible and everything fulfilled in the life of the church, is the outworking of the plan that the Father laid down in eternity and worked out in history.

The third group of people that Jesus identifies in these verses is those who believe on him: those who are 'branches' (15:5). What is interesting in this designation is the fact that Jesus clearly has two types of branches in view: those that are joined to the vine and are alive and fruitful (15:5) and those that are not joined to the vine and are dead and useless (15:6). Even though the members of this second group have some kind of outward, visible connection with Christ and his church, there is no living, vital union with him and therefore no true salvation. The departure of Judas is a case in point. Here was a man who could hardly have been closer to Christ in terms of appearances, yet could not have been further from Christ in terms of real spiritual experience.

The point is that fruitful Christian living is bound up in its very essence with a living faith-relationship with God through Christ. Without him we are nothing and can do nothing (15:5).

How It Is Achieved

The disciples would have been familiar with the fact that viticulture was a fine art involving much attention to detail. And as Jesus translates the image into spiritual experience, he shows his followers that a great deal of careful attention is needed in order to cultivate healthy and productive Christians and churches. It is clear from what he says that his Word is to play a central role in all that needs to happen.

This Word is the means of conversion (15:3, see also *1 Pet*. 1:23). It is the means of spiritual growth and development (15:7, see also *2 Tim*. 3:16–17). It is the key to our preservation (15:10). And it is sufficient for all that we need for life and godliness (15:15, cf. 2 Pet. 1:3). Jesus speaks of our response to his Word in terms of its remaining in us (15:4,7). He is pointing to the need for an abiding and unwavering confidence in that Word – a conscious commitment to all that God has revealed through Jesus. Jesus himself has demonstrated what that means in practice, under the most extreme conditions, by his unswerving commitment to the course mapped out in God's Word that led him to the cross. He simply would not take any other route.

Such faith in God's Word will of necessity express itself through obedience to the Word also (15:10). We are taught that the exercise of obedience cannot be separated from the love relationship between the believer and Christ. This time, interestingly, the order of love and obedience is the opposite to that in the previous reference (14:15). Just as the safety of a marriage rests upon adhering to certain ground rules that will head off temptation, so in Christ's marriage to his church, his laws are there to keep his people from straying into the seductive arms of others.

Jesus also points to the need for pruning in order for this spiritual life to flourish (15:2). The Father, like a master gardener, knows just when and how to cut off and cut back those elements in his people's life that do not belong, or which are not conducive to growth. The process may be painful, whether it takes place through his Word, by means of his servants, or by his providence, but it will always be worthwhile as it leads to a better and more profitable life in Christ. For those who are 'in' the Church, but who are not 'of' the Church, this will mean judgement (15:2). Their pretence, which may have fooled some, will never succeed in deceiving God. Sooner or later the truth will become apparent and their true relationship become clear in the most painful way imaginable (15:6).

In all of this the special love of Christ is pre-eminent (15:17). It is as the community of his people flourishes in mutual love that the evidence of true spiritual fruitfulness will come to light for all to see. Such fruitfulness cannot be artificially produced for it goes against the grain of sinful human nature. It will flourish among Christians if it truly flourishes between Christ and Christians in that loving, saving union that he alone establishes. This is the key to the most fulfilling and productive life possible.

34

A Most Painful Life

If the world hates you, know that it has hated me before it hated you. [19] If you were of the world, the world would love you as its own; but because you are not of the world, but I chose you out of the world, therefore the world hates you. [20]Remember the word that I said to you: 'A servant is not greater than his master.' If they persecuted me, they will also persecute you. If they kept my word, they will also keep yours. [21] But all these things they will do to you on account of my name, because they do not know him who sent me. [22] If I had not come and spoken to them, they would not have been guilty of sin, but now they have no excuse for their sin. [23] Whoever hates me hates my Father also. [24] If I had not done among them the works that no one else did, they would not be guilty of sin, but now they have seen and hated both me and my Father. [25] But the word that is written in their Law must be fulfilled: 'They hated me without a cause.' [26] "But when the Helper comes, whom I will send to you from the Father, the Spirit of truth, who proceeds from the Father, he will bear witness about me. [27] And you also will bear witness, because you have been with me from the beginning.

[1] "I have said all these things to you to keep you from falling away. [2] They will put you out of the synagogues. Indeed, the hour is coming when whoever kills you will think he is offering service to God. [3] And they will do these things because they have not known the Father, nor me. [4] But I have said these things to you, that when their hour comes you may remember that I told them to you. I did not say these things to you from the beginning, because I was with you (John 15:18–16:4).

The Christian life is not only fruitful it is also fraught. This is the sudden shift of emphasis that comes into Jesus' teaching at this point. Having spoken about the fulfilled and useful life found in fellowship with him, he now goes on to spell out the darker implications of being his disciple. The 'love' that characterizes relationships within the Church (15:17) sits in stark contrast to the 'hate' that will be directed against the Church by a hostile world (15:18). Life in fellowship with Christ will, by definition, be painful.

This is one aspect of the gospel that has been seriously overlooked and underplayed by many churches. The impression is given that to become a Christian is to embrace a life of ease. The opposite is the case. Jesus makes it clear elsewhere that following him involves self-denial and cross-bearing (*Mark* 8:34), and he makes it equally clear here that following him will bring opposition from the surrounding world.

As the storm clouds are gathering around the little group in the upper room, and as the arrest of Jesus and the dark sequence of events which that will trigger are imminent, Jesus gets the disciples ready. Not only do they need to be prepared for the trauma of seeing what will be done to their Master, they also need to be prepared for the trials and adversities that will become their own experience for the remainder of their lives in this world. What Jesus describes at some length in these verses, Paul states in one terse sentence, on the eve of his own execution. 'Everyone who wants to live a godly life in Christ Jesus will be persecuted' (*2 Tim.* 3:12).

This truth, of which Jesus warns his disciples, applies also to his people throughout all ages. It is something that all Christians need to grasp and come to terms with.

THE REASON FOR OPPOSITION

Very often people's expectations about life in God's kingdom, and their actual experience of the kingdom, are two very different things. This was certainly true when Jesus was on earth. There was a prevailing view, verging on triumphalism, that when Messiah appeared he would usher in another golden age for Israel of peace and prosperity of a kind unseen since the days of David. John has recorded the way that this expectation surfaced among the popular masses when the crowds tried forcibly to make Jesus their king after his miraculous feeding of the crowds (6:15). The same deep-seated hope was present in the disciples too. Even after all his teaching and all his sufferings on the cross, when Jesus was preparing to return to heaven, the disciples asked, 'Lord, will you at this time restore the kingdom to Israel?' (*Acts* 1:6). They still had not grasped the true nature of the kingdom into which they had been called. In his teaching on the night of his betrayal, Jesus leaves his followers and would-be followers in no doubt as to the cost of following him and the reason for this costly life of sacrifice.

It is primarily a matter of where we belong. Jesus says to his disciples, 'If you were of the world, the world would love you as its own' (15:18). He makes it clear that they did not belong to the world any more than he did. It was to become one of the most important truths in the self-understanding of God's people in the early decades of New Testament Christianity. Paul would see himself as being a citizen, not of Rome, but of heaven (*Phil.* 3:20). The writer to the Hebrews would speak of having no abiding place in this world, but rather, as one of God's pilgrim people, of looking for a better country and for a city that will last (*Heb.* 11:13–16). The words of the old Negro spiritual express the thought so well:

> *This world is not my home, I'm just a-passing through;*
> *My treasures are laid up, somewhere beyond the blue.*

Where we belong will have a profound effect on the way that we are treated.

It is not only a question of where we belong, but also of to whom we belong. Jesus speaks of the master-servant relationship that was so common in his day and in which the servant would receive the same treatment as his master, for good or ill (15:20–21). Indeed, Jesus traces it further back still (as he had done at other times) to his own relationship with the Father and the attitude of the crowds to him as a reflection of their attitude to God. Hence the opposition that Christians experience in the world has nothing do with whether or not they are nice people, or are kind to others; it is entirely because they bear the name of Jesus (15:21).

The third reason identified by Jesus as lying behind the opposition the disciples would face is found in the impact of truth on people's lives. Speaking of the light he brought through his presence and by his teaching, he describes the bitter antagonism in the hearts of his Jewish hearers and their increased guilt because of their reactions to the truth (15:22–24). Once again he stresses that responding to the gospel is not primarily a matter of the head, but of the heart. The unwillingness of the Jews to bow before the truth God embodied in the life of Jesus Christ was further evidence of their wilful rejection of God and all that was his. This rejection would inevitably be directed against the followers of Jesus as well.

All of this re-echoes the themes of darkness and light that have been running through John's Gospel. Just as Jesus is the Light of heaven, who has come into the darkened world and divided humanity into those who are drawn to him and those who are driven from him, so the same responses will drive the different reactions directed at his followers. The most striking thing about the opposition Jesus faced and, by extension, the opposition that Christians face, is that the world hates both 'without a cause' (15:25). It is not a matter of logic, but of sin.

THE REMEDY FOR OPPOSITION

Facing up to opposition is one thing. Being actually able to cope with it when it comes is another. All too often Christians have sought to cope, but on their own terms and in their own way, and not with the resources that Jesus has provided. There has always been the temptation to cope by simply running away and hiding, or by adopting a policy of 'live and let live' in an uneasy co-existence. Jesus sets out a completely different method of coping.

He points first of all to the work of the Holy Spirit: 'When the Helper comes . . . he will bear witness about me' (15:26). Once again Jesus calls the Spirit 'the Spirit of truth' and states that when he comes he will simply tell the truth as it really is. He will provide the divine testimony to Jesus and his work, however great the human efforts to discredit Christ's name.

The mounting opposition faced by the first disciples (and by many others since) would inevitably raise questions and doubts in their minds about the facts concerning Jesus and their understanding of all that had happened. When the Spirit came, he would bring out the truth and let the facts speak for themselves. When the Pharisees opted for lies and cover-up when news of the resurrection broke (*Matt.* 28:12–15), the Spirit's response was simply to point to an empty tomb and to scores of eyewitnesses to the risen Lord. There was no need for elaborate stories or concocted explanations. The facts were plain to see and the Holy Spirit bore witness to them.

Jesus points also to the unique testimony of the apostles themselves. They had been with Jesus from the beginning and it was their Christ-appointed task to relate simply what they had seen (15:27). Acting in conjunction with the Spirit, as Jesus has already mentioned, they were to provide the written testimony to Jesus as the Christ who would be the foundation stone of the Church through all ages (*Eph.* 2:20).

The remedy against opposition provided by Jesus for these men becomes also the abiding remedy for his people. The Church and her members stand against the hostility of the world, not through their own strength or guile, but on the unshakable testimony of the Spirit and the apostles, as found in the Word of Scripture. Empowered by God's Spirit and equipped with his Word, the Church has advanced against all the opposition that hell itself has thrown against it and has prevailed, and will continue to prevail until the end.

THE READINESS FOR OPPOSITION

Jesus explains why he has been dealing with these chilling issues: 'I have said all these things to you to keep you from falling away' (16:1). It was because of his great love for them and profound concern for their well-being that he warns them in advance of what to expect. In just the same way, his warning sounds in the ears of people scattered all over the world and throughout the centuries. Jesus wants his children to be fully aware of what awaits them in this world so that they might be fully prepared.

He speaks of opposition and persecution so intense that in some cases they would lead to martyrdom (16:2). This was to be the case for nearly all the men around the table that night. At the time that

John penned these words, some of them no doubt had already suffered death.

Again Jesus shows his concern for his children to understand why this experience occurs: it is because the persecutors 'have not known the Father, nor me' (16:3). No matter how kind and gracious as Christians they might be to others, or how much they are prepared to do in Christian service, there is an underlying antipathy against God in this world that will invariably lash out at anyone who belongs to him.

Basic training for any soldier involves the kind of briefings and drills that will leave them 'battle-ready', so that when the real attack begins they are prepared and have the wherewithal to cope. Similarly, every Christian soldier in Christ's army must be ready. Only when we fully understand that the life of discipleship is a life of conflict will we be able to stand when the conflict comes our way.

35

The Agent of Truth

But now I am going to him who sent me, and none of you asks me, 'Where are you going?' [6] *But because I have said these things to you, sorrow has filled your heart.* [7] *Nevertheless, I tell you the truth: it is to your advantage that I go away, for if I do not go away, the Helper will not come to you. But if I go, I will send him to you.* [8] *And when he comes, he will convict the world concerning sin and righteousness and judgement:* [9] *concerning sin, because they do not believe in me;* [10] *concerning righteousness, because I go to the Father, and you will see me no longer;* [11] *concerning judgement, because the ruler of this world is judged.* [12] *"I still have many things to say to you, but you cannot bear them now.* [13] *When the Spirit of truth comes, he will guide you into all the truth, for he will not speak on his own authority, but whatever he hears he will speak, and he will declare to you the things that are to come.* [14] *He will glorify me, for he will take what is mine and declare it to you.* [15] *All that the Father has is mine; therefore I said that he will take what is mine and declare it to you.* [16] *"A little while, and you will see me no longer; and again a little while, and you will see me"* (John 16:5–16).

A mong the many roles that the Holy Spirit fulfils, one of the most significant is that of God's Agent of truth: the one who brings home the truth of God to the hearts and minds of men and women. This aspect of his work has huge significance because 'truth' lies at the very centre of the liberating power of the gospel of the Son (8:32,36). All of this is even more relevant in an age in which the very concept of truth is ridiculed, but in which the deceiving lies of the devil are much appreciated.

Jesus is still reclining with his disciples around the table in the upper room, still giving them the briefing that will prepare them, not only for the trauma of the coming weekend, but for their life's-work. Once again he brings up the subject of the Holy Spirit and again his focus is on the Spirit of God as 'the Spirit of truth' (16:13). This is the thread that ties the teaching of this discourse together.

However, the way in which Jesus introduces the subject in this passage is somewhat intriguing. He begins by repeating the fact that he is going to the One who sent him, but he then proceeds to question the disciples about their failure to cross-examine him about his departure (16:5). The strange thing about this is that the disciples had indeed questioned Jesus about what lay ahead for him, on at least two occasions (13:36; 14:5). A possible explanation for this apparent inconsistency may be that the other instances did not involve questions arising from a real desire to understand what the coming days would mean for Jesus, so much as protests dressed up as questions expressing the disciples' frustration and fear.

Jesus wants these men to realize and appreciate that the joy and peace they have longed for as they have followed him can only come through the pain of what he must endure on the cross. The agony of Calvary is the necessary precursor to the joy of Pentecost. Only when that last crucial link in the chain of God's redemptive purpose had been put in place could the full blessing of God's salvation flow to the nations. That is why Jesus comments on the obvious grief that will engulf his followers when he departs (16:6), but then he puts it all in perspective by saying, 'It is to your advantage that I go away' (16:7). Only when Jesus had finished what the Father had sent him to do could the Spirit take that finished work and apply the joy of its achievement to the world.

These verses, then, have a foundational significance not just in our understanding of the work of the Holy Spirit in the world, but also of our understanding of the work of the gospel in the world. They give us an insight into three aspects of the work of the Spirit.

(1) HE CONFRONTS THE WORLD WITH THE TRUTH ABOUT ITSELF

The first major strand of the Spirit's work that Jesus identifies is the fact that 'he will convict the world concerning sin and righteousness and judgement' (16:8). This is clearly a summary statement that is further explained in what follows. Jesus is using the language of the law court and speaks about 'conviction' not merely as proving guilt in some dispassionate way, but as doing so in a way that touches the conscience. The Spirit does this quite simply by establishing the truth; specifically, the truth about sin, righteousness and judgement.

The Spirit convicts the world regarding sin because men do not believe in Jesus (16:9). There has been a fair amount of debate over whether unbelief is the most serious expression of sin, or whether it constitutes the very essence of sin. On balance it would seem to be the latter, because all sin has stemmed from man's original refusal to rest trustingly in God and in his revealed will. Refusal to believe in Jesus is synonymous with refusal to accept the truth of God.

This is borne out by what Paul says in the opening chapter of Romans. There he lays down the basis for the need of the gospel when he says that God's anger is revealed against those who 'by their unrighteousness suppress the truth' (*Rom.* 1:18) and who exchange 'the truth about God for a lie' (*Rom.* 1:25). Sin in its very essence is a denial of truth and therefore will express itself in a rejection of Jesus Christ, the Truth incarnate.

The convicting work of the Spirit, however, includes a conviction of righteousness as well (16:10). He will accomplish this, Jesus says, 'because I go to the Father'. This is Jesus' shorthand way of pointing to where true and objective righteousness is found. The brevity of the statement hides the depths it contains. Jesus is saying in effect that the Father will display the ultimate standard of righteousness in his vindication of the Son, when he is welcomed back into heaven. Having come as the righteous one from heaven; fulfilled all righteousness on earth; died in the place of unrighteous sinners on Calvary; and then been vindicated by God through the resurrection and ascension, Jesus becomes the benchmark of righteousness for all time.

The double edge in what Jesus says in this remark lies in the fact that the Spirit not only holds up the righteousness of God in Christ in order to expose and condemn, but he also reveals Jesus as the source of true righteousness. Paul again demonstrates in the Letter to the Romans that the hope of the gospel is the righteousness from God that has been made known in Jesus Christ (*Rom.* 3:21). Everyone who comes to trust in Jesus will receive this righteousness and find new peace with God.

This leads, quite naturally, to the third strand of the Spirit's convicting work, that which relates to judgement (16:11). The judgement of God, though future, has a very present dimension in that 'the ruler of this world is judged'. In a way that would become public through the supernatural events occurring at Calvary (*Matt.* 27:45,51–53), the devil's domain would be plundered and his condemnation displayed. This in turn would result in his dark kingdom being steadily pushed back as the gospel was to spread throughout the world. Through the preaching of the gospel the Holy Spirit exposes the lie of the devil and shows that he is already under condemnation.

In summary therefore, the Holy Spirit's work is to press home to the world the painful truth about itself and its destiny, and its urgent need to look to Christ to find salvation.

(2) HE MAKES KNOWN TO THE WORLD THE TRUTH THAT COMES FROM GOD

There are already signs in these chapters that the disciples were in shock over what Jesus was saying to them around the table that evening, so it is not surprising that he deals very gently with them. He tells them that, even though there is a great deal more he could say to them, he has no intention of overburdening them with more than was necessary at the time. However, he does pave the way for the most significant work in which the apostles would be involved: the completion of God's written revelation. They would be the instruments that God would use to complete the Scriptures, and in so doing they, along with the New Testament prophets, would become the foundation of the New Testament Church (*Eph.* 2:20).

Jesus was preparing these men for the unique role they would play in the revelation of truth for all time in the Bible; a role that they could only fulfil after the giving of the Holy Spirit at Pentecost. Jesus therefore says that when the Spirit comes, 'he will guide you into all the truth' (16:13). Two important points are found in this statement. The first is that the 'you' Jesus has in mind is not believers in general, but his apostles in particular – they would be involved in a non-repeatable process. The second is that the Spirit, when he came, would lead them into 'all the truth' – there would be no need of further revelation from God.

The universal application of what Jesus says here lies in the fact that the Bible is God's sufficient revelation for the whole world, through all history. Everything needed for faith and life is found in its pages. The only further aspect of the Spirit's work in relation to this is his illuminating of God's truth – a work that is necessary because of the darkened understanding of man in his fallen state (*Eph.* 4:18). In this sense, 'The Bible is the Spirit's greatest gift to the church!' (Melvin Tinker).

(3) HE REVEALS SUPREMELY THE TRUTH THAT IS EMBODIED IN CHRIST

Jesus' closing remarks in this section can easily be overlooked because they do not immediately appear to tie in with what he has said in the earlier verses. In fact these comments about the relationship between the Spirit and himself are what ties the entire section together.

What will be the substance of the revelation that is to be given by the Spirit through the apostles? What is the thread that will provide its unity? The answer is Christ: he is the central and unifying theme of Scripture from beginning to end. Just as the promise of the Christ is the unifying theme of the Old Testament, so the coming of the Christ and its significance will be the unifying theme of the New.

So Jesus says that the Spirit will bring glory to himself, the Christ, by taking what belongs to him and making it known through the apostles to the world by means of the Word (16:14–15). He will demonstrate how the truth of God written in Scripture is inseparable from the truth of God embodied in Christ.

In saying this, Jesus is holding out the key for us to know whether or not we have truly understood the message of the Bible. We need simply to ask, 'Has it led us to Christ?' Whatever moral, social, personal, or even theological insights it may give us, its ultimate purpose is to reveal Jesus!

The issues Jesus has been addressing were of such enormous moment that the disciples were no doubt reeling under their weight. They were being told that their lives were caught up in something that was quite beyond their comprehension, in something of infinite proportions. How could they be sure that these amazing words were really true? Jesus provides the answer. He gives them a sign; he tells them that the impossible will happen, and that when it does it will confirm the rest of the words he has spoken that evening. He says, 'A little while, and you will see me no longer; and again a little while, and you will see me' (16:16). He was of course referring to his imminent death and subsequent resurrection. When they witnessed the fulfilment of that remarkable prediction, they could be sure that everything else he had told them would be fulfilled as well.

36

Joy Comes in the Morning

So some of his disciples said to one another, "What is this that he says to us, 'A little while, and you will not see me, and again a little while, and you will see me'; and, 'because I am going to the Father'?" [18] So they were saying, "What does he mean by 'a little while'? We do not know what he is talking about." [19] Jesus knew that they wanted to ask him, so he said to them, "Is this what you are asking yourselves, what I meant by saying, 'A little while and you will not see me, and again a little while and you will see me'? [20] Truly, truly, I say to you, you will weep and lament, but the world will rejoice. You will be sorrowful, but your sorrow will turn into joy. [21] When a woman is giving birth, she has sorrow because her hour has come, but when she has delivered the baby, she no longer remembers the anguish, for joy that a human being has been born into the world. [22] So also you have sorrow now, but I will see you again and your hearts will rejoice, and no one will take your joy from you. [23] In that day you will ask nothing of me. Truly, truly, I say to you, whatever you ask of the Father in my name, he will give it to you. [24] Until now you have asked nothing in my name. Ask, and you will receive, that your joy may be full.

[25] "I have said these things to you in figures of speech. The hour is coming when I will no longer speak to you in figures of speech but will tell you plainly about the Father. [26] In that day you will ask in my name, and I do not say to you that I will ask the Father on your behalf; [27] for the Father himself loves you, because you have loved me and have believed that I came from God. [28] I came

from the Father and have come into the world, and now I am leaving the world and going to the Father."
[29] His disciples said, "Ah, now you are speaking plainly and not using figurative speech! [30] Now we know that you know all things and do not need anyone to question you; this is why we believe that you came from God." [31] Jesus answered them, "Do you now believe? [32] Behold, the hour is coming, indeed it has come, when you will be scattered, each to his own home, and will leave me alone. Yet I am not alone, for the Father is with me. [33] I have said these things to you, that in me you may have peace. In the world you will have tribulation. But take heart; I have overcome the world" (John 16:17–33).

There is a lovely verse in the Psalms that says, 'Weeping may tarry for the night, but joy comes with the morning' (*Psa.* 30:5). That truth well captures the mood and tone of what Jesus is saying here.

That Thursday evening had become dark and sorrowful in more ways than one for the disciples; but even more so for Jesus. Yet he was able to point them past the horizons of darkness that threatened to engulf them, and to the light and joy beyond. Just as Jesus was bracing himself for the ordeal he had to endure on the cross by looking to the joy that lay beyond (*Heb.* 12:2), so he directed his little band of followers to that same hope and certainty.

This passage not only paints on a broad canvas the picture of God's salvation coming into our world, it also provides the pattern for so much of our normal Christian experience. That verse mentioned above from the Letter to the Hebrews tells us that the unique experience of Jesus, as he faced the cross, becomes the pattern for all that trust in him in the struggles of this life. This brings us to one of the most vital elements of our Christian experience. What is it that constitutes 'the joy of God's salvation'? For too many Christians the answer to that question lies in cheap and ephemeral spiritual trinkets – the kind of things that cannot survive sorrow. Jesus had a far richer and more resilient joy in mind, and he wants his disciples to appreciate what it is and how it is received.

A JOY BORN IN PERPLEXITY AND PAIN

Jesus was very much aware of the mood around the table and the air of fear and foreboding that was beginning to stifle conversation. He responds by balancing the growing shadow of darkness with the promise of overwhelming joy (16:17–20).

He chooses an illustration from childbirth to make the point. The pain experienced by a woman in labour – no matter how intense – is forgotten because of the joy that follows in the life of a newborn child (16:21). So also will it be for the disciples; inevitably, they will weep and mourn and grieve over the events of the coming day, but their grief would most certainly turn to joy (16:22).

The pain and perplexity of their situation would be made worse because of the way the world (with all the depth of meaning that John invests in that word) would revel cruelly in Jesus' fate. But Jesus is being realistic: discipleship is anything but a pain-free existence. Indeed the irony of the Christian's calling is that the more he is caught up in the work of the kingdom, the more intense his struggle becomes. This is inevitable, because the work of the kingdom is the work of salvation.

At the same time Jesus stresses the hope and optimism of the gospel, reminding the eleven that their grief would turn to joy, and their joy would not be taken from them. Out of the pain and sorrow would emerge a joy that the world could never offer. It is a joy that has sustained countless Christians in the teeth of persecution throughout the whole history of the Church. True and lasting joy is born out of the intense struggles of the soul.

A JOY THAT GROWS THROUGH FELLOWSHIP WITH GOD

A recurring thread that runs through this conversation is Jesus' promise that he would see his disciples again. However comforting those words were, they still contain a certain ambiguity. Was this a promise referring to his resurrection, to his sending of the Holy Spirit, or to his return at the end of time? The answer may well be that he had all three in mind. Each of these events has its own unique contribution to make in the provision of joy in the Christian life.

The key to actually experiencing this joy, however, is explained in terms of a direct and personal relationship with God. All that Jesus would accomplish through his 'going away' would secure for his people a saving relationship with the Father (16:22–24). This relationship would not be wooden or static, but dynamic and constantly developing. In the case of the disciples themselves, the fellowship they had enjoyed with the incarnate Christ would lead into the richer, deeper fellowship with the invisible God.

The culmination of this relationship would be a joy that is 'complete': the very essence of the life for which we were created. The Westminster Divines captured this truth perfectly in the opening answer of their *Shorter Catechism*. It declares, 'The chief end of man is to glorify God and enjoy him forever.' That is the relationship in which true joy is found.

A Joy Nurtured by an Appreciation of the Gospel

Yet again in this memorable conversation, Jesus looks forward to the time when many of these things would become clearer (16:25). What had been true for the disciples in their experience of Christ would now become clear in their relationship with God. Jesus identifies two things that underpin a genuine relationship with God and which lie at the heart of a genuine appreciation of the gospel.

The first is that God loves those who love Jesus (16:26–27); those whose love, however faint, is expressed in a living faith that looks to him for salvation. Here is the great comfort and assurance of the gospel in all its simplicity: the promise of the Father to all who embrace the Son.

The other great truth is that Christ's intervention in this world has immeasurable consequences for everyone who believes (16:28). The free access to the Father, of which he speaks, and the liberty to make requests of God in the name of Jesus, all depended upon Christ's coming into the world and his completion of the work given him to do. This work that he had by now almost accomplished.

The immensity of the privileges of the gospel is inseparably connected to the enormity of Christ's achievement in salvation. The more we appreciate the latter, the greater will be our enjoyment of the former.

A JOY THAT IS NEVER PERFECT IN A FALLEN WORLD

The disciples, as they respond to Jesus' words, cannot refrain from the kind of well-intentioned, but shortsighted bravado that they had so often displayed on previous occasions. They brashly claim that all is now clear to them (16:29–30). Likewise, Jesus could not resist a touch of gentle sarcasm in what he says by way of reply: 'Do you now believe?' (16:31). And he immediately warns them with great solemnity that they had not really grasped matters at all (16:32). That very night they would scatter and abandon him in confusion and terror. Would these men never learn the truth about themselves and about their situation in the world? Would they never truly grasp the threat posed by the devil?

Jesus was warning them in advance that the joy of which he had been speaking would never be perfect in this imperfect world. Even the highest and sweetest moments of Christian experience would be tarnished by many other moments of blindness and failure. In that sense, the experience of these men is no different from that of every Christian through the ages. Christ takes us up into the breathtaking heights of the joy of salvation, but so often we in our weakness and folly plunge ourselves back into the sorrows that belong to this world.

A JOY THAT IS ONLY GUARANTEED THROUGH FAITH IN JESUS CHRIST

Jesus concludes this discourse, which has spanned four chapters, with a powerful statement: 'In the world you will have tribulation. But take heart; I have overcome the world' (16:33). He urges them to face up to the harsh realities of life in this world, while at the same time he assures them of the ultimate reality of who he is and what he has accomplished. Jesus is so certain of his victory that he uses the past tense while describing it.

Facing the greatest personal storm ever experienced in human history, Jesus says to his weak and fearful disciples, 'Trust me!' That invitation rings out through the ages to all who are caught up in the troubles of a fallen world or who tremble at the prospect of the judgement of the last day. The only way that there can be peace and joy in the face of such trouble and sorrow is through faith in the One who has overcome. He has endured, and the joy is now his. For those who entrust themselves to him, his joy will be theirs also.

No earthly joy compares to this lasting joy that is found in Jesus.

37

The Prayer That Changed the World

When Jesus had spoken these words, he lifted up his eyes to heaven, and said, "Father, the hour has come; glorify your Son that the Son may glorify you, ² since you have given him authority over all flesh, to give eternal life to all whom you have given him. ³ And this is eternal life, that they know you the only true God, and Jesus Christ whom you have sent. ⁴ I glorified you on earth, having accomplished the work that you gave me to do. ⁵ And now, Father, glorify me in your own presence with the glory that I had with you before the world existed.

⁶ "I have manifested your name to the people whom you gave me out of the world. Yours they were, and you gave them to me, and they have kept your word. ⁷ Now they know that everything that you have given me is from you. ⁸ For I have given them the words that you gave me, and they have received them and have come to know in truth that I came from you; and they have believed that you sent me. ⁹ I am praying for them. I am not praying for the world but for those whom you have given me, for they are yours. ¹⁰ All mine are yours, and yours are mine, and I am glorified in them. ¹¹ And I am no longer in the world, but they are in the world, and I am coming to you. Holy Father, keep them in your name, which you have given me, that they may be one, even as we are one. ¹² While I was with them, I kept them in your name, which you have given me. I have guarded them, and not one of them has been lost except the son of destruction, that the Scripture might be fulfilled. ¹³ But now I am coming to you, and these things I speak in the world, that they may have my joy fulfilled in themselves. ¹⁴ *I have given them your word, and the world has hated them because they are not of the world, just as I am not of the world.* ¹⁵ *I do not ask that you take them out of the world, but that you keep them from the evil one.* ¹⁶ *They are not of the world, just as I am not of the world.* ¹⁷ *Sanctify them in the truth; your word is truth.* ¹⁸ *As you sent me into the world, so I have sent them into the world.* ¹⁹ *And for their sake I consecrate myself, that they also may be sanctified in truth.*

²⁰ *"I do not ask for these only, but also for those who will believe in me through their word,* ²¹ *that they may all be one, just as you, Father, are in me, and I in you, that they also may be in us, so that the world may believe that you have sent me.* ²² *The glory that you have given me I have given to them, that they may be one even as we are one,* ²³ *I in them and you in me, that they may become perfectly one, so that the world may know that you sent me and loved them even as you loved me.* ²⁴ *Father, I desire that they also, whom you have given me, may be with me where I am, to see my glory that you have given me because you loved me before the foundation of the world.* ²⁵ *O righteous Father, even though the world does not know you, I know you, and these know that you have sent me.* ²⁶ *I made known to them your name, and I will continue to make it known, that the love with which you have loved me may be in them, and I in them"* (John 17:1–26).

The prayer that John records in this chapter is without question the most important prayer offered in the entire history of the world. It has often been called 'the great High Priestly prayer of Christ' because it was offered just before he made atonement for his people through his death on the cross. The significance of this prayer may be recognized by noting that it was offered on the eve of the greatest event in history; it is found in conjunction with the greatest message ever heard in history; and its contents involves the greatest experience that history can ever provide. Furthermore, every sentence within the prayer is bound up with the honour and glory of God.

Jesus' great concern, as the eternal Son of God, is that his Father might be seen and known for who he is, for what he is like, and for all that he has done. This helps us to appreciate more fully the reason why John saw fit to include this prayer in his Gospel. It is not just that the prayer was, and ultimately will be, fulfilled in its entirety so that it therefore provides an assurance that undergirds the truth of the gospel, but it also helps us to understand the gospel.

Too often people fail to understand the gospel properly because they try to squeeze it into the pattern of their own ideas about salvation. Almost invariably that means construing salvation as something purely man-centred. However, as we listen to Jesus pray in this chapter, it becomes abundantly clear that salvation is supremely God-centred, though it also contains unimaginable benefits for man. It brings home to us in the most powerful way possible that it is only when God is acknowledged in his true place in the world and in our lives, that all other aspects of life begin to fall into their proper place.

The prayer is made up of three parts. It begins with Jesus praying for himself; he continues with a prayer for the apostles, and he concludes by praying for all those who would truly embrace the apostolic message of the gospel. Each of these elements is vital to our understanding and experience of God's deliverance in Christ.

A Prayer for the Certainty of Salvation

As Jesus drew the discourse in the upper room to its conclusion, he sealed the evening of fellowship around the table with a prayer that is the culmination of all his teaching (17:1). He signals that the moment of fulfilment was almost upon him by saying, 'Father, the hour has come', and he also reveals the ultimate purpose of his coming by the words, 'Glorify your Son, that the Son may glorify you.' The climax of Jesus' coming and the greatest achievement of his work will be the recovery of God's glory in the world. It was not that God had somehow lost his essential glory, but that he had ceased to be honoured in his world by those who bore his image. What Jesus was about to accomplish on the cross would be the means of displaying the glory of God to a degree hitherto not seen, either in heaven or on earth. And here Jesus prays for the ultimate success of that mission.

This success would result in the glorifying of God by the achieving of salvation for his people. The fruit of Jesus' work in human terms would be seen in his obtaining eternal life for those that the Father had given him (17:2). The Father had planned salvation in eternity and chosen a people for himself (*Eph.* 1:4), and that plan would now be fulfilled by all that Jesus performed while on earth. The depth of love that lay behind the plan was about to be seen in the lengths to which God would go in order to fulfil it. Just as a parent's love is seen in the lengths he or she will go for the sake of his or her children, so the love of God is seen in that vicarious death on the cross for his chosen people. The essence of God's gift to his children is 'eternal life': a new and true life; a life that belongs to a different order and is of an altogether different quality.

Jesus provides the most thrilling definition ever given of this gift of life, when he says, 'And this is eternal life, that they know you, the only true God and Jesus Christ whom you have sent' (17:3). It is a life that consists of a new relationship with God through Jesus Christ. The knowledge that it involves is not that of detached academic awareness, but intimate personal communion – the knowledge of love. As will become clear in the rest of this prayer, Jesus is asking that his chosen people will be restored to a life of union and communion with God through him.

All of this will hinge upon Jesus' completion of the work which the Father has given him to do. So he prays that the Father will put his final seal of approval on the completed work which he, the Son, would offer up (17:4–5). By asking that he might be glorified with the glory that was his with the Father 'before the world existed' (17:5), he was praying that the glory revealed in his death would be sealed and vindicated by his resurrection and exaltation. This theme of his death was to become the new anthem of heaven (*Rev.* 5:12–14) and the supreme anthem of the redeemed on earth.

A Prayer for the Messengers of Salvation

In the central and dominant section of the prayer, Jesus commends his disciples to his Father's special care. He does so, not just because of the obvious bond of affection which he has for this small group with whom he had spent the past three years, but because of the unique role they would play in God's purpose in redemption. It was to these men that Jesus had revealed the Father and his will and it was to them that he had entrusted God's words in a particular way (17:6–8). He therefore makes them the particular focus of his prayer in that they would have an unique part to play in the spread of the gospel (17:9–10). Given the weakness of these men and the solemnity of the task entrusted to them, Jesus prays for three things.

He prays for their protection. He knows that he is soon to leave the world and to return to the Father, but the disciples were to remain in the world – with all its hostility towards God and his people – he therefore prays that they might be protected (17:11). Only the keeping power of God could sustain and preserve them through the rigours that lay ahead, not only as individuals, but also as an united body. Jesus would appear to be pointing to the oneness of the apostolic witness that would give such weight to their combined testimony. The fact that the testimony of these very different and uneducated men was so united is an evidence in itself of the divine character of their message.

Jesus also prays for their joy in all that lay ahead. He has already indicated to them that as long as they remained in the world they would have trouble (16:33), but his desire is that they might have a foretaste of the true and lasting joy of the world to come (17:13). That joy would derive from the sight of God's redemption perfectly accomplished in the work of Christ upon the cross. And the joy that Jesus requests for his apostles is the same joy for which he prays for all his children; it has its roots in the pain of Calvary, but will blossom in the never-ending pleasures of heaven.

The third element of Jesus' prayer for his disciples is for their sanctification (17:17). To be sanctified means to be set apart from the world for the Lord. Jesus repeats before God that these men are to remain in a world that is at odds with them and he prays for their safekeeping in that hostile environment (17:14–16). What is interesting is that their safety is bound up with their sanctity. They will be kept, not by blending in with their surroundings in a fallen world, but by being seen to be radically different. As the truth of God's Word is applied to their lives, so they will be seen to stand out for God. In one of the most curious statements of the whole prayer, Jesus goes on to say, 'For them I sanctify myself, that they too may be truly sanctified' (17.19). He is stressing that what is about to happen through his death on the cross will be the foundation of all that he will secure for the lives of his people. His death also is the guarantee that this remarkable prayer will be remarkably answered. He will consecrate himself to death in order that his followers might have a truly consecrated life.

A PRAYER FOR THE TRUE EXPERIENCE OF SALVATION

The final section of this great prayer considers the outworking of all that Christ and his disciples will accomplish through the proclamation of the gospel. It is a prayer for the actual experiencing of salvation in the lives of God's people. It is not merely a prayer for salvation to be experienced in a private and personal sense, but particularly that the shared life among God's people on earth would truly reflect the mystery of the shared life of God in heaven.

Jesus prays for all who will believe in him through the apostolic message of the gospel (17:20). The essence of his prayer is that 'they may all be one' (17:21). The unity within the diversity of God's people for which he prays is a reflection of the unity within the diversity of the Godhead. It is also a unity that is totally dependent on God. It can only come about as the people of God on earth share in the fellowship of Father, Son and Spirit in heaven.

The importance of this is very clearly expressed in the reasons Jesus attaches to his request. He asks that his people might be one 'so that the world may believe that you [the Father] have sent me' (17:21) and 'so that the world may know that you sent me and loved them even as you loved me' (17:23). The oneness of God's people is a vital ingredient to the credibility of the gospel! The ultimate answer to this prayer will be seen when every one of God's chosen people will have been gathered with Jesus in heaven, to see and to share in his glory forever (17:24).

The key to the fulfilment of this prayer is for Christ's people to be brought into a richer, deeper knowledge of God and therefore into a richer, deeper experience of God's love (17:25–26). This is the essence of the eternal life that Jesus came to secure.

38

The Cup and Its Consequences

When Jesus had spoken these words, he went out with his disciples across the Kidron Valley, where there was a garden, which he and his disciples entered. ² Now Judas, who betrayed him, also knew the place, for Jesus often met there with his disciples. ³ So Judas, having procured a band of soldiers and some officers from the chief priests and the Pharisees, went there with lanterns and torches and weapons. ⁴ Then Jesus, knowing all that would happen to him, came forward and said to them, "Whom do you seek?" ⁵ They answered him, "Jesus of Nazareth." Jesus said to them, "I am he." Judas, who betrayed him, was standing with them. ⁶ When Jesus said to them, "I am he," they drew back and fell to the ground. ⁷ So he asked them again, "Whom do you seek?" And they said, "Jesus of Nazareth." ⁸ Jesus answered, "I told you that I am he. So, if you seek me, let these men go." ⁹ This was to fulfil the word that he had spoken: "Of those whom you gave me I have lost not one." ¹⁰ Then Simon Peter, having a sword, drew it and struck the high priest's servant and cut off his right ear. (The servant's name was Malchus.) ¹¹ So Jesus said to Peter, "Put your sword into its sheath; shall I not drink the cup that the Father has given me?"

¹² So the band of soldiers and their captain and the officers of the Jews arrested Jesus and bound him. ¹³ First they led him to Annas, for he was the father-in-law of Caiaphas, who was high priest that year. ¹⁴ It was Caiaphas who had advised the Jews that it would be expedient that one man should die for the people. ¹⁵ Simon Peter followed Jesus, and so did another disciple. Since that disciple was known to the high priest, he entered with Jesus

into the court of the high priest, [16] but Peter stood outside at the door. So the other disciple, who was known to the high priest, went out and spoke to the servant girl who kept watch at the door, and brought Peter in. [17] The servant girl at the door said to Peter, "You also are not one of this man's disciples, are you?" He said, "I am not." [18] Now the servants and officers had made a charcoal fire, because it was cold, and they were standing and warming themselves. Peter also was with them, standing and warming himself.

[19] The high priest then questioned Jesus about his disciples and his teaching. [20] Jesus answered him, "I have spoken openly to the world. I have always taught in synagogues and in the temple, where all Jews come together. I have said nothing in secret. [21] Why do you ask me? Ask those who have heard me what I said to them; they know what I said." [22] When he had said these things, one of the officers standing by struck Jesus with his hand, saying, "Is that how you answer the high priest?" [23] Jesus answered him, "If what I said is wrong, bear witness about the wrong; but if what I said is right, why do you strike me?" [24] Annas then sent him bound to Caiaphas the high priest.

[25] Now Simon Peter was standing and warming himself. So they said to him, "You also are not one of his disciples, are you?" He denied it and said, "I am not." [26] One of the servants of the high priest, a relative of the man whose ear Peter had cut off, asked, "Did I not see you in the garden with him?" [27] Peter again denied it, and at once a cock crowed (John 18:1–27).

Perhaps the most remarkable thing about the Christian faith is that the greatest achievement of its founder was his death. Because this is so the Christian message focuses predominantly upon the cross of Jesus Christ. The gospel makes it clear that the death of Jesus was not an accident, nor a case of his being overtaken by events or circumstances. The death of Jesus lies at the very heart of the reason for his coming. Therefore if we are to receive any benefit from Christ's coming, we need more than anything else to come to terms with the meaning of his cross.

John (like the other Gospel writers) makes much of the fact that Jesus was fully aware of what awaited him that night and the next day. He did not shrink from the horrors that lay before him, but embraced them as the means by which his mission would be completed in obedience to his Father's will.

Even though his own disciples draw back at such a prospect and Peter tries to intervene violently to prevent his arrest, Jesus declares boldly, 'Shall I not drink the cup that the Father has given me?' (18:11). Drinking that 'cup' – referring to the cross and its sufferings – was the very essence of his mission. In these most difficult of circumstances, even as he treads the very path to Calvary, Jesus demonstrates three ever-present characteristics.

(1) His Total Control

When Jesus finished praying in the upper room with his disciples, they left together and he led them across the Kidron Valley to an olive grove – the garden of Gethsemane (18:1). It seems that Judas knew that he was likely to find Jesus there because, after having gone to alert the temple authorities, he then leads them to the grove to arrest Jesus (18:2–3). For a moment it seems as if Jesus has walked into a trap. But then John tells us, 'Jesus, knowing all that would happen to him, came forward and said to them, "Whom do you seek?"' (18:4). Whatever the disciples (and Judas particularly) may have thought, Jesus knew that nothing was happening that was not according to plan and within his sovereign jurisdiction.

Indeed, Jesus demonstrates his sovereign control in an even more startling manner. When the mob say that they are looking for Jesus of Nazareth, he answers (as the verse reads literally), 'I am' (18:5). The crowd understands perfectly what he means – once again he is asserting his deity – and they draw back and fall to the ground (18:6). It is not only the words of Jesus but his calm demeanour that fills them with dread.

Even when Simon Peter attempts to take control of the situation by attacking the high priest's servant with his sword, cutting off his ear, he only invites Jesus' rebuke. Then Jesus utters these solemn words, 'Shall I not drink the cup . . .?' (18:10–11). Though the 'cup' to which he referred was one of suffering on an unimaginable scale, it was a suffering that was in accord with the Father's purpose of salvation, and the Son would comply with that purpose to the very end.

It was only after the event and with the further insight and understanding that the Holy Spirit would give that Peter came to a full understanding of it. In his sermon on the day of Pentecost, he pointed to 'the definite plan and foreknowledge of God' as the key for realizing who was in control at Calvary (*Acts* 2:23). If such extreme circumstances as these were so essential to the mission of Christ, we can only conclude that there was no other way for God to redeem.

(2) HIS DRIVING CONCERN

What was it then that fuelled Jesus' determination to undergo such an ordeal, knowing everything that would be involved? Predominantly, it was the fact that it had been the Father who had placed this cup in his hands (18:11). Just as he had emphasized throughout his earthly ministry, Jesus again shows that his chief joy and pleasure was to do the will of the One who had sent him (4:38). No matter what it was to cost him, he knew beyond all shadow of a doubt that the will of God the Father was best in every way, and nothing would stop him obeying that will.

John gives us another major clue to help our understanding of Jesus' motives. As he describes what happened after Jesus had been bound and led away to Annas, the father-in-law of Caiaphas, John adds the comment, 'It was Caiaphas who had advised the Jews that it would be expedient that one man should die for the people' (18:14). This comment is clearly not necessary for John's description of the sequence of events. The only logical reason for its inclusion is that John deliberately inserts it in order to show that the unfolding developments must be understood against the larger backdrop of the purposes of God. This seemingly insignificant detail actually serves to put the whole scene in its true perspective.

It points in particular to Jesus as substitute, sacrifice and Saviour. Such a phrase, 'that one man should die for the people', would be instantly recognizable to any Jewish reader as the language of atonement. The key theme in the understanding of the work of Jesus, announced first of all by John the Baptist when he cried out, 'Behold, the Lamb of God, who takes away the sin of the world!' (1:29), was now about to reach its fulfilment. The death that Jesus was about to die was the death of a sacrificial victim making perfect atonement for the sin and guilt of his people.

This was the driving concern that had led the Son of God from heaven and into a fallen world. This was the concern that brought him through thirty years of preparation in the obscurity of Nazareth. This was what had directed the course of his earthly ministry over the past three years. This now was the driving concern that was about to bring him through the darkness of the coming hours. The concern that if there was to be reconciliation between a holy God and a sinful race, a perfect sacrifice was needed, and only he himself was qualified and authorized to become that sacrifice.

(2) His Extraordinary Compassion

Jesus' devotion to his Father and obedience to his will are sufficient in themselves to explain why he was willing to endure what he did on the cross, but John shows that there was something even greater at work. Jesus was motivated in a most extraordinary way by his love for his people.

We see this in his commitment to the eleven disciples in the midst of all that was happening, and his obvious concern for their welfare. When he might understandably have been preoccupied with concern for himself in the face of the trial ahead of him, Jesus is eager to ensure that his followers are safe. John adds another detail (18:8, 9) that reveals Christ's carefulness that no harm should come to his disciples, so that the statement which he had prayed to his Father might be fulfilled, 'Of those whom you gave me I have lost not one.'

This commitment on Jesus' part stands out all the more strikingly when it is contrasted with the fickle resolve of Peter. Though he had been eager to display his bravado in the safety of the upper room and in the turmoil of events in the garden, yet, when his commitment to Christ was placed under sharp scrutiny in the high priest's courtyard, it crumbled in the most shameful fashion. But this failure of Peter only highlights further Christ's loving commitment. The final detail of the incident, after Peter's third denial, 'At once a cock crowed' (18:27), powerfully reminds us that even this tragic failure was not outside the bounds of Christ's knowledge and purpose. What Jesus had forewarned (13:38), was very quickly fulfilled. But Jesus' loyalty to Peter did not waver.

In many ways the story of this disciple crumbling under cross-examination, when compared to the unwavering endurance of Jesus under the severest scrutiny, serves only to magnify the loving resolve that kept Jesus true to his mission. The fact that Annas questioned Jesus, not only about his teaching, but also about his disciples (18:19), stresses Christ's relationship with his followers. The fact that they had deserted him and that their main spokesman was in the process of denying him might be reason enough for Jesus to distance himself from them; but he would make no such betrayal.

Here was a Saviour who was loyal to his flock, not because they were faithful to him, but because of his unconditional love for them. He would be faithful in life and he would prove faithful even unto death until he had finally obtained for them everything which he had promised.

39

What Is Truth?

Then they led Jesus from the house of Caiaphas to the governor's headquarters. It was early morning. They themselves did not enter the governor's headquarters, so that they would not be defiled, but could eat the Passover. ²⁹ *So Pilate went outside to them and said, "What accusation do you bring against this man?"* ³⁰ *They answered him, "If this man were not doing evil, we would not have delivered him over to you."* ³¹ *Pilate said to them, "Take him yourselves and judge him by your own law." The Jews said to him, "It is not lawful for us to put anyone to death."* ³² *This was to fulfil the word that Jesus had spoken to show by what kind of death he was going to die.*

³³ *So Pilate entered his headquarters again and called Jesus and said to him, "Are you the King of the Jews?"* ³⁴ *Jesus answered, "Do you say this of your own accord, or did others say it to you about me?"* ³⁵ *Pilate answered, "Am I a Jew? Your own nation and the chief priests have delivered you over to me. What have you done?"* ³⁶ *Jesus answered, "My kingdom is not of this world. If my kingdom were of this world, my servants would have been fighting, that I might not be delivered over to the Jews. But my kingdom is not from the world."* ³⁷ *Then Pilate said to him, "So you are a king?" Jesus answered, "You say that I am a king. For this purpose I was born and for this purpose I have come into the world— to bear witness to the truth. Everyone who is of the truth listens to my voice."* ³⁸ *Pilate said to him, "What is truth?"*

After he had said this, he went back outside to the Jews and told them, "I find no guilt in him. ³⁹ *But you have a custom that*

I should release one man for you at the Passover. So do you want me to release to you the King of the Jews?" *40* *They cried out again, "Not this man, but Barabbas!" Now Barabbas was a robber* (John 18:28–40).

In this first stage of Jesus' trial before Pilate there is more going on than meets the eye. The key to unlock the layers of meaning present is found in the question Pilate asks towards the middle of the proceedings, 'What is truth?' (18:38). It is possible that he is asking that question in all sincerity as one who is genuinely perplexed as to what is really true in a world that is filled with deceit. However, it is more likely that these are the words of a hardened cynic. Pilate was typical of the empire that he represented and which was already beginning to rot from within because of its moral inconsistencies. The fact that pragmatism and expediency became the decisive factors in the trial would seem to indicate that Pilate had few principles in his approach to life. Yet, here is the intriguing thing about these events: the disciples and friends of Jesus who had some awareness of what was happening, might be thinking that things were going horribly wrong in that courtyard, and under the authority of such a man, but the truth was very different. In reality, 'Both the Jewish accusers and the Roman judge are actors in a drama scripted by a divine planner' (Raymond Brown).

Behind the shameful façade of a caricature of Jewish and Roman justice, another form of justice is unfolding. The glory of the gospel is that the hand of God is at work in all these events and the purpose of God is being fulfilled in all that transpires. The crucial requirement for those reading these trial proceedings is an appreciation of the larger stage. We need to understand where the truth really lies.

A True Justice

Everything about this trial, begun under the cover of darkness and continuing into the early light of dawn, simply reeks of injustice. Quite apart from the dubious legality of the Jewish leaders' earlier actions that night, we note the injustice of their determination to have Jesus killed at all costs. Here is the utter hypocrisy of these religious leaders. They were fastidious in their refusal to become ceremonially impure by stepping into a Gentile's house (18:28), but thought nothing of the moral impurity of their plotting. Then, when confronted with a simple legal question as to the charges being levelled against Jesus (18:29), they provide a convoluted answer that, under normal circumstances, would have had them driven from the court. It finally becomes clear that they are determined to execute Jesus regardless of right or wrong (18:31). They are demanding what is in effect a legalised lynching. Pilate's pragmatic and politically devious handling of the case compounds matters further.

Any reader with the least sense of natural justice would cry out in disbelief at the way the trial of Jesus unfolds. In the light of the commentary on the life of Jesus provided by John in this Gospel, we are here seeing the final all-out effort of those engulfed in spiritual darkness to swallow up the one true light of the world. It is when we bear this in mind, along with all the other clues that John has given, that we realize how carefully we must analyze matters if we are to understand their full significance.

Once again it is a comment by John that alerts us to the truth behind the events of that morning. He reminds his readers of a prediction by Jesus concerning his death, and notes that it is only by means of these present events that such words could be fulfilled (18:32). Jesus would not die by stoning, but rather by crucifixion. He would die in a way that was particularly offensive to Jewish eyes, by being hung on a tree: a way that marked him out as being under God's curse (*Deut.* 21:23). It may well have been that for the shrewder members of the Sanhedrin, looking for a semi-legitimate way to dispose of Jesus, this might have been considered a bonus. Not only were they getting rid of this man, but they were doing so in a manner that would tarnish his memory among the Jewish population.

But here lies the irony of this situation. It was precisely God's intention to lead his Son to this point and to exactly this method of execution. God wanted the world to know that Jesus was indeed under the judicial curse of the Covenant God. The true justice being carried out on that day was God's eternal justice. In contrast to the injustice of earth stands the justice of heaven. The apostle Paul was to express it years later, 'Christ redeemed us from the curse of the law by becoming a curse for us, for it is written, "Cursed is everyone who is hanged on a tree"' (*Gal.* 3:13).

A True Kingdom

As Jesus stood before Pilate on the steps of his official residence, it appears that the governor had gleaned enough from the accusers to realize that Jesus was being charged with sedition. So the very first question in his cross-examination is, 'Are you the king of the Jews?' (18:33). (It is interesting to note, from the parallel accounts of Jesus' trial, that the Jews had accused him before the Sanhedrin of being the Messiah (*Matt.* 26:63), but before Pilate they accuse him of a claim to kingship.) Pilate is taken aback when Jesus responds to his question by saying, 'Do you say this of your own accord, or did others say it to you about me?' (18:34). This angers the judge, but it does not deter Jesus from continuing with an affirmation of his kingship, but in a way that shows its true nature. His is a throne and realm that pose no threat politically to Pilate or to Rome (18:36).

Jesus emphasizes this point by explaining that to understand the true character of his kingship and kingdom one needs to understand who he really is and why he came into the world (18:37). He has not come to set up just another political realm on earth, because his kingdom is 'not of this world' (18:36) and therefore it does not operate on the same principles as earthly powers.

It is at this point that Jesus makes his boldest assertion: 'Everyone who is of the truth listens to my voice' (18:37). That statement introduces us to the second great element of the drama unfolding on this stage. Behind the petty territorial rivalries of the Jews and the Romans, we see the timeless splendour of the kingdom of God, and Jesus, its king. All who have a genuine part in that true and lasting kingdom recognize this and gladly lay aside the passing concerns of this world, taking their stand instead with Jesus and his kingdom.

Throughout the trial, Jesus' composure and commanding presence dominate the proceedings of the court. It is clear from what is said and from the way that events unfold that it is not the Jews nor the Roman governor who are in control of events, but Jesus. He is the true king and the title deeds to his kingdom are in the process of being sealed through all that is taking place. This is the kingdom that will outlast all others.

A True Release

The paradox and irony of the situation becomes ever more apparent as matters develop. Pilate, clearly uneasy with the way the trial is proceeding and having declared to the Jews that he finds no basis for the charge against Jesus (18:38), tries another ploy so as to be able to release Jesus. He reminds the Jews of the custom of releasing a prisoner to mark the Feast of Passover (18:39). He offers to release Jesus. But the crowd calls for the release of a man called Barabbas instead – a man known to be an insurrectionist (18:40). Pilate's plan fails, but God's plan is being accomplished.

There is a certain irony even in the name of the prisoner in question. 'Barabbas' means 'Son of the Father', the designation that Jesus had used for himself in relation to God (8:54). It also seems (according to tradition) that the man's first name was Jesus. So here are two men before Pilate, both called 'Jesus, Son of the Father'. The one is a rebel; the other, the perfect Son. The latter is sentenced to death, and the former is released!

The ugliness of this miscarriage of justice is put in the shade by the beauty of God's accomplishment in it. Peter captures it perfectly when he says, 'Christ also suffered once for sins, the righteous for the unrighteous, that he might bring us to God' (*1 Pet.* 3:18). Here is the greatest truth of all: the truth of the gospel that brings hope even to those who stand condemned before the bar of heaven. The events of that Friday in Jerusalem led not merely to one rebel being released from prison, but to the release of millions across the world and throughout history.

The question, 'What is truth?', is the most penetrating question we will ever face in this world. It confronts us with the painful revelation about ourselves, that we have 'exchanged the truth about God for a lie and worshipped and served the creature rather than the Creator' (*Rom.* 1:25). It is only when we see through the deceitfulness of the devil and look instead to the truth embodied in Jesus that we find the true and lasting life for which we long.

40

'Suffered under Pontius Pilate'

Then Pilate took Jesus and flogged him. ² And the soldiers twisted together a crown of thorns and put it on his head and arrayed him in a purple robe. ³ They came up to him, saying, "Hail, King of the Jews!" and struck him with their hands. ⁴ Pilate went out again and said to them, "See, I am bringing him out to you that you may know that I find no guilt in him." ⁵ So Jesus came out, wearing the crown of thorns and the purple robe. Pilate said to them, "Behold the man!" ⁶ When the chief priests and the officers saw him, they cried out, "Crucify him, crucify him!" Pilate said to them, "Take him yourselves and crucify him, for I find no guilt in him." ⁷ The Jews answered him, "We have a law, and according to that law he ought to die because he has made himself the Son of God." ⁸ When Pilate heard this statement, he was even more afraid. ⁹ He entered his headquarters again and said to Jesus, "Where are you from?" But Jesus gave him no answer. ¹⁰ So Pilate said to him, "You will not speak to me? Do you not know that I have authority to release you and authority to crucify you?" ¹¹ Jesus answered him, "You would have no authority over me at all unless it had been given you from above. Therefore he who delivered me over to you has the greater sin."

¹² From then on Pilate sought to release him, but the Jews cried out, "If you release this man, you are not Caesar's friend. Everyone who makes himself a king opposes Caesar." ¹³ So when Pilate heard these words, he brought Jesus out and sat down on the judgement seat at a place called The Stone Pavement, and in Aramaic Gabbatha. ¹⁴ Now it was the day of Preparation of

the Passover. It was about the sixth hour. He said to the Jews, "Behold your King!" [15] They cried out, "Away with him, away with him, crucify him!" Pilate said to them, "Shall I crucify your King?" The chief priests answered, "We have no king but Caesar." [16] So he delivered him over to them to be crucified. So they took Jesus (John 19:1–16).

The Apostles' Creed – one of the greatest summaries of the essentials of Christian truth – contains the statement that Jesus 'suffered under Pontius Pilate', but the inclusion of that statement has raised major questions. Some have found this reference to a pagan Roman governor in such a sacred statement of faith to be offensive, so why was it included?

At one level it simply demonstrates that this crucial element in the life and work of Christ was historical and not a fictional product of myth and legend put together by the Early Church. Here was an event that was public and official. Presumably there was a record of proceedings. Certainly there was a significant number of people there who witnessed what took place. This was a real event that actually happened. All of this is vital to the gospel, because salvation is not only about what God has said, but particularly about what God has done. Christian hope rests ultimately on the historical fact that God, in the person of his Son, has intervened in human history to bring about the redemption of his people.

But there is another reason why this statement is in the Creed. Those who drew up the wording of this creed saw fit to rank the sufferings under Pilate alongside the virgin birth, the suffering of the cross, and the reality of the empty tomb, as an integral part of Christ's saving accomplishment. Just as all the other elements of his incarnation and ministry underpin the certainty of salvation, so also does the suffering Jesus endured under this Roman official. That being the case, we need to make sure that we appreciate the meaning of these events.

Their importance lies in the fact that they open up for us a window on truths that have far greater significance than the circumstances of the various individuals in the court. We are again being provided with glimpses of realities that have eternal consequences for us all.

MAN AND THE STATE OF HIS HEART

The very first verse of this chapter confronts us with the beginnings of what turns out to be an ugly catalogue of human hatred, brutality, cruelty and violence. We witness the savagery of the soldiers, the cruelty of Pilate and the frenzied animosity of the Jews (19:1–6). Jesus is subjected to scourging, ridicule and the pain of gross injustice. Through it all we are a given a sobering view of what seemingly decent people are capable of doing.

Although in one sense the savagery of the soldiers is typical of men who were trained to fight and kill, yet their behaviour was sanctioned and encouraged by members of the ruling and religious establishments of the day. Behind this atrocity were respectable members of the community. It brings to mind the chilling facts that came to light from Nazi death camps during the Second World War. Many of the people involved in those crimes against humanity were in their peacetime employment members of respectable professions of banking, teaching, the civil service, etc. They were ordinary people who to all appearances were decent citizens, yet they had it in their hearts to inflict the most wicked forms of cruelty upon fellow human beings.

In an even more sobering way these events make us realize how the entertainment industry through the ages has thrived upon the portrayal of violence and upon different forms of exploitation. It taps into the depravity rooted in every man, woman and child. The horror and ugliness of sin is far more insidious than we can ever begin to imagine.

As we look more closely at this passage, we see that the three sets of participants in the proceedings – the military ruler, the spiritual leaders, and the crowd – shared one thing in common: they were united in their hatred for God, his truth, and his Son. Even when Pilate realised that he was dealing with someone who was more than just a man, he did not stop or change his course of action (18:7–11). All that was done against Jesus was done with the full awareness that he was the Son of God. We are reminded again of that sobering theme that runs throughout this Gospel: 'People loved the darkness rather than the light, because their deeds were evil' (3:19). This is the verdict of God. This is human nature as it really is.

No matter how much we may try to downplay this painful reality, the fact remains. As Paul puts it, man in his natural state is hostile to God (*Rom.* 8:7). He does not exist in a state of polite and benign neutrality, but one of sinister enmity. The desire of these people to murder God is the same desire that lurks deep in every person. Such is the grip this hatred has on our heart. We are powerless in ourselves to change it.

JESUS AND THE STRENGTH OF HIS LOVE

In the midst of these proceedings, Pilate, the pragmatist, trying to find a politically expedient solution to the problem in his courtroom, presents Jesus to the crowd and says, 'Behold the man!' (19.5, as the verse reads literally). It is one of those many statements that we find in this Gospel that can be read in different ways.

There can be little doubt that, on face value, it was another example of the Roman governor's cynicism. Jesus, after the treatment he had received, was the picture of weakness and brokenness. He had been deprived of sleep, been placed under extreme duress, his flesh had been flayed and his face disfigured by the crown of thorns – he surely no longer posed any threat to the Jewish authorities!

Yet at the same time Jesus was the very picture of strength itself, despite the ravages to which he had been subjected. Even at this stage of the trial he comes across as being in control. Although he has supernatural power at his fingertips and the authority of heaven on his side, he chooses not to invoke either for his defence. Instead, out of unspeakable love for those he came to save, he enters fully into their suffering and the consequences of their sin, not just so as to empathize truly with them (though this he does), but rather that he might truly atone for them.

Again, in the wider context of John's record, this cynical pronouncement of Pilate stands in contrast to the great declaration of John the Baptist: 'Behold the Lamb!' (1:29). Here was the sacrificial offering that God had prepared for making atonement for the sin of the world. Far from being the helpless victim on the verge of being crushed by men, Jesus is the loving victor on the verge of being vindicated by God. His silence (19:9) was not that of indignation or helplessness before Pilate, but rather of acquiescence to the perfect will of God. He knew that only by walking the painful road the Father had set before him, could his people be forgiven and set free. What kept him fixed on that course of unbelievable suffering? It was the strength of his love for those he came to save.

GOD AND THE WONDER OF HIS GRACE

The third great aspect of this passage is the evident presence and purpose of God that is seen in the proceedings. In anger and frustration with Jesus, Pilate says, in effect, 'Don't you realize that I have power either to free you, or crucify you?' (19:10). To this Jesus replies, 'You would have no power over me if it were not given to you from above' (19:11). He is saying in effect that neither Pilate nor the mob is in control of what is happening that day; there is an infinitely higher power at work in it all.

This of course raises the obvious question: If God really was in control, why did he allow such cruelties? The only possible answer is that this is how things had to be. This was the fulfilment of that which Isaiah had prophesied seven centuries earlier: 'It was the will of the LORD to crush him: he has put him to grief' (*Isa.* 53:10). All of this was happening in perfect accord with God's set plan and purpose (*Acts* 2:23). If that is indeed the case, what purpose did God have in mind that he allowed his Son to endure such torment?

Once more a clue to the answer is found in the text. After describing for us the way that the governor capitulated to the intimidation of the mob, the episode ends with the bald statement, 'So he [Pilate] delivered him over to them to be crucified' (19:16). Here is the final act of an unscrupulous judge. But, while commenting on what happened from a later vantage point, Paul has this to say: 'He who did not spare his own Son, but gave him up for us all, how will he not also with him graciously give us all things?' (*Rom.* 8:32). We see here the most gracious act of the most glorious Judge of all the earth! God did to his own Son what he ought to have done to his enemies, in order that from now on he need never act in such a way towards those who trust in him. This was the beginning of that supreme spiritual transaction that underwrites the gospel and provides the legal warrant for its message.

In the midst of all the perversity of the thoughts and actions of the men involved in these proceedings, the words of Joseph to his brothers come ringing back. In response to their injustice he said, 'You mean evil against me, but God meant it for good, to bring it about that many people should be kept alive' (*Gen.* 50:20).

Why does the church affirm that Jesus 'suffered under Pontius Pilate'? It is because that suffering was an essential part of the legal proceedings of the court of heaven. It is on the basis of those proceedings that God's salvation is now offered to sinful men.

41

'He Was Crucified, Dead and Buried'

And he went out, bearing his own cross, to the place called the place of a skull, which in Aramaic is called Golgotha. ¹⁸ *There they crucified him, and with him two others, one on either side, and Jesus between them.* ¹⁹ *Pilate also wrote an inscription and put it on the cross. It read, "Jesus of Nazareth, the King of the Jews."* ²⁰ *Many of the Jews read this inscription, for the place where Jesus was crucified was near the city, and it was written in Aramaic, in Latin, and in Greek.* ²¹ *So the chief priests of the Jews said to Pilate, "Do not write, 'The King of the Jews,' but rather, 'This man said, I am King of the Jews.' "* ²² *Pilate answered, "What I have written I have written."*

²³ *When the soldiers had crucified Jesus, they took his garments and divided them into four parts, one part for each soldier; also his tunic. But the tunic was seamless, woven in one piece from top to bottom,* ²⁴ *so they said to one another, "Let us not tear it, but cast lots for it to see whose it shall be." This was to fulfil the Scripture which says,*

"They divided my garments among them,
and for my clothing they cast lots."

So the soldiers did these things, ²⁵ *but standing by the cross of Jesus were his mother and his mother's sister, Mary the wife of Clopas, and Mary Magdalene.* ²⁶ *When Jesus saw his mother and the disciple whom he loved standing nearby, he said to his mother, "Woman, behold, your son!"* ²⁷ *Then he said to the disciple, "Behold, your mother!" And from that hour the disciple took her to his own home.*

[28] After this, Jesus, knowing that all was now finished, said (to fulfil the Scripture), "I thirst." [29] A jar full of sour wine stood there, so they put a sponge full of the sour wine on a hyssop branch and held it to his mouth. [30] When Jesus had received the sour wine, he said, "It is finished," and he bowed his head and gave up his spirit.

[31] Since it was the day of Preparation, and so that the bodies would not remain on the cross on the Sabbath (for that Sabbath was a high day), the Jews asked Pilate that their legs might be broken and that they might be taken away. [32] So the soldiers came and broke the legs of the first, and of the other who had been crucified with him. [33] But when they came to Jesus and saw that he was already dead, they did not break his legs. [34] But one of the soldiers pierced his side with a spear, and at once there came out blood and water. [35] He who saw it has borne witness— his testimony is true, and he knows that he is telling the truth— that you also may believe. [36] For these things took place that the Scripture might be fulfilled: "Not one of his bones will be broken." [37] And again another Scripture says, "They will look on him whom they have pierced."

[38] After these things Joseph of Arimathea, who was a disciple of Jesus, but secretly for fear of the Jews, asked Pilate that he might take away the body of Jesus, and Pilate gave him permission. So he came and took away his body. [39] Nicodemus also, who earlier had come to Jesus by night, came bringing a mixture of myrrh and aloes, about seventy-five pounds in weight. [40] So they took the body of Jesus and bound it in linen cloths with the spices, as is the burial custom of the Jews. [41] Now in the place where he was crucified there was a garden, and in the garden a new tomb in which no one had yet been laid. [42] So because of the Jewish day of Preparation, since the tomb was close at hand, they laid Jesus there (John 19:17–42).

Having followed John's account of the life and work of Jesus, we come at last to the cross: the most significant moment in the history of redemption. It is no cliché to say that the cross is the very crux of Christianity – it is the one event on which all others in Christ's work of salvation depend.

It is for this moment that the whole of the Bible has been preparing us. From the time of the Fall, throughout the whole Old Testament revelation, God was leading his people towards that day when he would send a Saviour and through him bring about salvation for all time. Similarly, from the moment of the conception of Jesus in the womb of the virgin Mary, right through to the climax of his ministry in Jerusalem, the Gospels have been preparing us for this – his death, and everything that it would achieve.

Given the climactic importance of this event and the weight it carries in the gospel record, here is a point where we are compelled to pause and ponder; to gaze upon the One who was crucified for sinners so that we might understand the salvation he has secured. Most importantly of all, here is the point where we are called upon to make our response to Christ and to his gospel, if that salvation is to be ours. We cannot however make any sense of this sombre event by means of our own understanding alone; we need Scripture to be our guide. With that in mind, it is worth asking what particular viewpoint John gives us, as compared with the testimony of the other Gospel writers?

Interestingly, John avoids the low-point of the cross – that moment when Jesus cried out in his forsakenness – and focuses instead on the fulfilment of the cross. He notes particularly that Jesus after passing through the darkest and deepest point in his sufferings was already conscious of his triumph before he finally gave up his spirit and died. This clear emphasis in John's account of the cross is shown by the way, in quick succession, he uses three words that share the same root. He speaks of Jesus knowing that all things were 'completed' and that the Scripture needed to be 'fulfilled' (19:28), and, in common with the other Gospel testimonies, he records the victory-cry of Jesus, 'It is finished' (19:30). In other words, John wants us to realize that in God's language of redemption, the cross spells completion. The deliverance that God had planned in eternity and promised in history was now brought to fulfilment at Calvary.

REQUIREMENTS FULFILLED

At the very heart of John's account of the crucifixion, Jesus is described as 'knowing that all was now finished' (19:28). This ties in with a sequence of statements throughout the section signalling the fulfilment of scriptural expectations (19:24, 28, 36, 37). In other words the experience of Jesus on the cross was following a course that had been mapped out beforehand in the Old Testament. Everything that God had revealed concerning his plan of salvation was reaching its culmination in these dark hours on the cross.

The great frustration for those who lived during the days of Old Testament revelation was that they could see that God had laid down the requirements for salvation, but they looked in vain for someone who met those requirements fully. Now, in full public view, a chain of events was unfolding in which each link connected perfectly with the details God had made known in advance concerning his promised Redeemer.

Indeed, Jesus himself was profoundly aware of every development even as he hung on the cross in mortal agony. He, more than any other, was conscious that everything that he was enduring was 'according to plan'. This truth hits us from the very beginning of the account. As Jesus makes that final trek towards his death, no detail is accidental; everything is pervaded by the predictions of the Old Testament Scriptures.

As Jesus carries his own cross (19:17), there is an immediate echo of the covenant curse of God resting upon him (*Deut.* 21:23). As he is taken 'out' to the place where he would die, we are reminded of the sacrifice for sin that was taken 'outside the camp' (*Exod.* 29:14) because of its uncleanness. When Jesus is crucified, although he is among thieves, there is a public record that he is crucified as a 'king' (19:19) – it is God's Anointed One who here suffers. Right down to the point at which his clothing is taken from him and divided among the soldiers (19:24), the Old Testament echo is heard, this time from David's cries to God (*Psa.* 22:18). At every point throughout their duration these dark sufferings of Jesus are illuminated, both for himself and for ourselves, by the light of God's Word. His sufferings are anything but meaningless; they are the fulfilment of the greatest purpose the world has ever known: the purpose of God in salvation. In his life Jesus had fulfilled all righteousness on behalf of his people, now in his death he was making perfect atonement for their sins. Everything was complete. God's just requirements for salvation were being satisfied.

REDEMPTION ACCOMPLISHED

Having primed us with references to the fulfilment of Scripture and indicated that Jesus was fully aware of all that was being accomplished, John now records Christ's cry of triumph: 'It is finished!' (19:30). The English translation of this word is not the most helpful, as it suggests defeat – the cry of a man who has been beaten. The word actually used by Jesus had quite the opposite meaning. It might be rendered more literally, 'It is accomplished!'

In one sense it is a strange utterance to make, given that he had not yet actually died and that the resurrection and the divine vindication which it represented, had still to take place, and that both are essential for redemption. However, Jesus had passed through the lowest point of his passion, he had plumbed the depths of the suffering he had to endure, and was already rising from the hell to which he had been exposed. The only moment he had ever known when he could not call God 'Father' was over, and even as he prepares for death he is able, as Luke indicates, to take once more that term of intimate communion upon his lips (*Luke* 23:46).

Therefore, knowing that the worst had been accomplished he had confidence that God would enable him to complete what remained. He would 'taste death for everyone' (*Heb*. 2:9) and he would rise for all his people (*1 Cor*. 15:22). Having passed through the point of greatest crisis in his sufferings, his mission was as good as over, and he could proclaim his triumph to the world. His shout of accomplishment was the cry for which creation had been waiting since the fall of Adam. The fact that this victory was announced in the face of death and in the midst of darkness was in itself significant. It demonstrated the divine certainty in the accomplishing of redemption.

The consequences are immeasurable. People now need not look anywhere else. All that is necessary for salvation is found here in the sacrifice made by Jesus Christ and the reconciliation to God that he alone guarantees.

'He Was Crucified, Dead and Buried'

RESPONSE REVEALED

John concludes his account of the cross by tying all the threads together. He does not allow his readers to remain as merely detached observers to these events. He draws everyone in by underlining the response that such truths demand. He says, pointing (almost certainly) to his own personal presence at the cross, 'He who saw it has borne witness – his testimony is true, and he knows that he is telling the truth – that you also may believe' (19:35). He calls his readers to respond by faith.

Some have wondered why John seems to lay so much stress on the fact that he was an eyewitness to these events, given that there were other eyewitness accounts already in circulation and enjoying widespread acceptance. It may well have been because, at this later stage of the New Testament period, there were already those who were downplaying the importance of the historicity of these events, and were reducing them to the level of symbol. That has been the recurring problem with the interpretation of the events of Calvary by some throughout the ages: they view the cross either as having some mystical power or as being merely a powerful example. John refuses both interpretations. For him the cross can only have saving significance if Christ actually accomplished something during the dark hours in which he hung there. John wants us to know that something unique took place on that barren hillside outside Jerusalem that day: Jesus secured salvation. The Son of God actually fulfilled something that no-one else could possibly do: he paid the price of sin and secured the way back to God. The only response that will ensure the experience of this great salvation is that of faith in him and all that he has done.

We have a glimpse of that response of faith in the closing verses of the chapter. Joseph of Arimathea and Nicodemus (the one who had been a secret disciple for fear of the Jews) came to Pilate and asked permission to bury Jesus' body. Their faith was not one that had full possession of the facts, nor a full understanding of all that was involved – but it was still a saving faith. They were prepared, at great risk to themselves, to publicly declare that faith in Jesus Christ and to take their stand with him.

42

A Woman's Testimony

Now on the first day of the week Mary Magdalene came to the tomb early, while it was still dark, and saw that the stone had been taken away from the tomb. ² So she ran and went to Simon Peter and the other disciple, the one whom Jesus loved, and said to them, "They have taken the Lord out of the tomb, and we do not know where they have laid him." ³ So Peter went out with the other disciple, and they were going toward the tomb. ⁴ Both of them were running together, but the other disciple outran Peter and reached the tomb first. ⁵ And stooping to look in, he saw the linen cloths lying there, but he did not go in. ⁶ Then Simon Peter came, following him, and went into the tomb. He saw the linen cloths lying there, ⁷ and the face cloth, which had been on Jesus' head, not lying with the linen cloths but folded up in a place by itself. ⁸ Then the other disciple, who had reached the tomb first, also went in, and he saw and believed; ⁹ for as yet they did not understand the Scripture, that he must rise from the dead. ¹⁰ Then the disciples went back to their homes.

¹¹ But Mary stood weeping outside the tomb, and as she wept she stooped to look into the tomb. ¹² And she saw two angels in white, sitting where the body of Jesus had lain, one at the head and one at the feet. ¹³ They said to her, "Woman, why are you weeping?" She said to them, "They have taken away my Lord, and I do not know where they have laid him." ¹⁴ Having said this, she turned around and saw Jesus standing, but she did not know that it was Jesus. ¹⁵ Jesus said to her, "Woman, why are you weeping? Whom are you seeking?" Supposing him to be the gardener, she said to him, "Sir, if you have carried him away, tell me where you have laid him, and I will take him away." ¹⁶ Jesus said to her, "Mary." She turned and said to him in Aramaic, "Rabboni!" (which means Teacher). ¹⁷ Jesus said to her, "Do not cling to me, for I have not yet ascended to the Father; but go to my brothers and say to them, 'I am ascending to my Father and your Father, to my God and your God.'" ¹⁸Mary Magdalene went and announced to the disciples, "I have seen the Lord" – and that he had said these things to her (John 20:1–18).

John's account of the resurrection of Jesus is dominated by the testimony of Mary Magdalene (20:1). Although there were two female companions with Mary on the morning she went to the tomb (*Mark* 16:1), John is especially interested in what Mary saw. And even though Peter and 'the other disciple, the one whom Jesus loved' (John presumably) were involved (20:2–10), this is only because Mary had alerted them to what she has seen.

This emphasis by John on a woman's testimony to the resurrection is interesting, particularly when we consider the male-dominated world to which he was writing. What special contribution does Mary make to the record of the risen Christ? The answer may well lie in the fact that her testimony not only confronts us with the historicity of what happened, but also with the unique benefits it provides to those who embrace it. In other words, it is not just that her testimony concerns the occurrence of a wonderful event, but the occurrence of a wonderful event that has great personal implications.

Indeed, the way that John introduces Mary's testimony is in itself a picture of how people are brought to faith in the risen Saviour. John says that Mary came to the tomb 'while it was still dark' (20:1). Mark, however, says that it was 'when the sun had risen' (*Mark* 16:2). There is no necessary contradiction between these accounts – Mary set out before sunrise and joined her companions by the time it was light – but John is laying hold particularly on a factual detail in order to make a spiritual point. Throughout his Gospel, physical darkness has been a symbol of spiritual darkness. So here again he is pointing to the fact that Mary was still stumbling around in spiritual darkness as she tries to come to terms with what had happened two days earlier. The journey that brings us to faith begins, by definition, in darkened understanding. It is only the revelation of the risen Christ that finally brings us into true and lasting light. Mary's testimony bears witness to three important aspects of the resurrection:

(1) THE REALITY OF CHRIST'S RESURRECTION

John Calvin shares the view that John has a particular interest in Mary's testimony that contrasts with the other eyewitness accounts. His reason has to do with the fact that the resurrection of Jesus has so often been dismissed as myth, or some kind of fabrication of the disciples, or of the early church. Recent centuries of scholarship have seen a decided shift towards this view in many theological circles. The influence of rationalism, and the disdain in the academic world for the supernatural, have led many theologians to regard the accounts of miraculous events in the Bible as having some rational explanation, or else as being fables.

This tendency has always existed. Matthew draws attention to the way the Pharisees tried to discredit the reports of the resurrection by bribing the guards and telling them to spread the story that Jesus' body had been stolen (*Matt.* 28:12–15). It is also clear from Paul's lengthy comments on this subject to the Corinthian church that, within twenty years of the resurrection, some Christians even were embracing the idea that the resurrection had not been a physical event. Paul shows the seriousness of what is at stake by declaring that if Christ did not rise, then the whole message of the gospel collapses (*1 Cor.* 15:14). It stands to reason, therefore, that this vital fact must be established and must be able to withstand the severest of scrutiny.

In connection with this, Calvin remarks, 'It is strange that a more competent witness could not be found.' He is not being disdainful of Mary in saying this; rather he is making a somewhat sarcastic jibe at those who suggest that the gospel account of the resurrection is some kind of invention. If the resurrection was indeed an elaborate concoction of the early Christian community, then Mary was a bad choice if their story was to have credence. For one thing, as a woman, her evidence would have been inadmissible in a Jewish court and furthermore, she was a woman with a disreputable past, having been involved in a life of prostitution. Her testimony therefore would have been tarnished.

The only logical conclusion is that John calls Mary to testify simply because her testimony is genuine. She really did see and hear what she says she did. Her experience is another example of fact being stranger than fiction. The last thing that Mary expected to find as she went to tend the body of Jesus that morning was a tomb that was empty. When she gets there therefore and finds that the stone covering the entrance of the grave had been removed, her initial reaction is panic (20:2), then perplexity (20.13), but then finally to pause for thought (20.15–16).

John wants us to appreciate that she is being taken from the darkness of despair, through the half-light of seeing God's fingerprint upon what had happened, and to the absolute certainty that what she was seeing was true and not some horrible illusion. This is the very essence of conversion as the hope of the gospel lays hold of the despairing souls of men. If Jesus is dead, then hope is dead; but if he is indeed alive, then there is real hope!

(2) The Focus of Christ's Love

The central section of this passage records the personal encounter that took place between Mary and the risen Lord (20:10–16). The most striking thing about it is the very gentle and personal character of the meeting.

Mary was still utterly overwhelmed by grief. The anguish of Jesus' death was compounded by the horror of the thought of his grave being plundered by grave robbers and we see her wailing as she peers into the empty tomb (20:11). She sees two angels inside the tomb, but obviously does not understand who they are at this stage. But then she turns and sees someone else beside her – someone that she assumes is the gardener – and she asks him if he has removed the body (20:14–15). Jesus responds to her by simply uttering one word: 'Mary!' (20:16). That simplest of gestures became the turning point of her life. Jesus made himself known to her in a way that dealt with the depth of her need.

Here is the good and gentle Shepherd that John has already spoken of – the one who 'knows his sheep by name' (10:3, 27). He lovingly reaches out to this one poor wounded sheep in a way that speaks of the bond that existed between them. Here is the one relationship that transforms everything.

Although Jesus had accomplished something of universal significance that had implications for the entire human race, we see by his behaviour here that this in no sense eclipses the personal dimension involved. His people are not mere numbers in a book, they are individual people with individual needs, and he knows them through and through.

It is at this point that Mary's darkness is banished and light comes flooding in to her life. The gospel assumes for her a degree of personal significance that she had never realized until this moment. She sees that the glorious resurrection of Jesus was not just for the world as a whole, but for her as a person. Mary was the first of countless millions to be brought face to face with the resurrected Christ, not merely as a clinical fact of history, but as the ultimate fact of life.

(3) The Scale of Christ's Accomplishment

The amazing conclusion to John's account of this first resurrection appearance is found in Jesus' explanation to Mary and in what he tells her to do. Mary was at first relieved because she thought that things were to be restored to the situation before the awful events of the previous week, but Jesus indicated that matters had moved on from that point. Mary had embraced Jesus in a gesture that showed how glad she was that he was back, but Jesus said, 'Do not cling to me, for I have not yet ascended to the Father; but go to my brothers and say to them, "I am ascending to my Father and your Father, to my God and to your God"' (20:17).

He was saying in effect, 'I must bring my mission to completion.' All that Jesus had accomplished on earth had to end with the vindication of his return to heaven and his enthronement in glory. Only when the Father above had put his seal on Jesus' achievement could its benefits begin to flow to his people below. The fact that Jesus speaks of 'my Father and your Father . . . my God and your

God', emphasizes evocatively the possibility for fallen sinners like Mary to be brought back into living fellowship with God. The risen and exalted Christ is the key to a restored and everlasting relationship with God.

Jesus goes further. Not only does he explain all this to Mary, he commissions her to make the first public announcement of it: she is to go and tell the disciples. It is as though the Queen had taken a poor girl, rescued from a life on the streets, and commissioned her to announce the Queen's arrival at a Mansion House banquet! Such is the dignity and glory that Jesus confers upon those who trust in him. They come to share his glory.

The resurrection is the keystone that holds the arch of the gospel and the Christian faith in place. It is amazing that Jesus hands the announcement of this keystone to a woman; she is to be the very first person to put it in place. Such is the wonder of the gospel and the depth of Christ's love. But Jesus did not merely do that once; he does it daily as he calls others not only to embrace the same message, but to take it to the world as the one message of hope for all mankind.

43

'That You May Believe
That Jesus Is the Christ'

On the evening of that day, the first day of the week, the doors being locked where the disciples were for fear of the Jews, Jesus came and stood among them and said to them, "Peace be with you."

[20] When he had said this, he showed them his hands and his side. Then the disciples were glad when they saw the Lord. [21] Jesus said to them again, "Peace be with you. As the Father has sent me, even so I am sending you." [22] And when he had said this, he breathed on them and said to them, "Receive the Holy Spirit. [23] If you forgive the sins of anyone, they are forgiven; if you withhold forgiveness from anyone, it is withheld."

[24] Now Thomas, one of the Twelve, called the Twin, was not with them when Jesus came. [25] So the other disciples told him, "We have seen the Lord." But he said to them, "Unless I see in his hands the mark of the nails, and place my finger into the mark of the nails, and place my hand into his side, I will never believe."

[26] Eight days later, his disciples were inside again, and Thomas was with them. Although the doors were locked, Jesus came and stood among them and said, "Peace be with you." [27] Then he said to Thomas, "Put your finger here, and see my hands; and put out your hand, and place it in my side. Do not disbelieve, but believe." [28] Thomas answered him, "My Lord and my God!" [29] Jesus said to him, "Have you believed because you have seen me? Blessed are those who have not seen and yet have believed." [30] Now Jesus did many other signs in the presence of the disciples, which are not written in this book; [31] but these are written so that

you may believe that Jesus is the Christ, the Son of God,
and that by believing you may have life in his name (John
20:19–31).

T he remainder of chapter twenty contains the record of two
further resurrection appearances: the first to ten of the disciples
on the day the resurrection took place, the other a full week later, to
all eleven disciples, but with a particular focus on Thomas. The
climax of the chapter, however, and indeed of the entire Gospel
comes at the end. There John tells us his reason for writing: it is that
his readers 'may believe that Jesus is the Christ, the Son of God, and
that by believing [they] may have life in his name' (20:31). He will
not allow people to read what he has written in any casual manner.
He presses home upon them the full force of what God has revealed
and done through Jesus and calls for the response of faith. The last
verse of the chapter, therefore, gives us a vantage point from which
to view the whole Gospel, and from which also to work backwards
through the verses that immediately precede it.

This last verse is a fitting climax to all that has been said up to
this point. The significance of the resurrection and the impact that
the post-resurrection appearances have had on Jesus' followers
contribute immensely to its force. Its conclusions are viewed against
the backdrop of the incidents leading up to it. These incidents
emphasize how important it is to understand what is involved in the
faith, and they highlight several factors that distinguish true saving
faith from a faith that is merely an acknowledgement that certain
things are true.

A CLEAR OBJECTIVE

'Faith' must be one of the most vacuous and slippery terms in the
vocabulary of religion. Often it is used to mean something that is an
end in itself. For many people, a profession of having 'faith' (whatever
they might mean by that), is sufficient for them to assume that they
are safe as far as God is concerned. But faith in itself means nothing.
Faith in 'faith' cannot save, because faith without an object is a
nonsense. There must always be someone, or something, in which
faith is placed.

John is unequivocal as to what that object must be if faith is to lead to salvation. Faith must be placed in Jesus; in particular it must be placed in Jesus, 'the Christ', who is none other than 'the Son of God' (20:31). He could hardly be more specific, and at the same time he could hardly be more expressive of the power that lies in this Saviour.

John has spent twenty chapters looking at the historical figure of Jesus of Nazareth and piecing together the clues as to his identity. He now finally stands back and points to the finished picture that these clues present. Who is this Jesus? When all the evidence is set out and all his pronouncements put alongside, what do they point to? The facts speak for themselves. They declare Jesus of Nazareth to be none other than the Son of God and Saviour of the world – the Anointed One that God had promised from the beginning of time and for whom his people had been waiting. Like a barrister presenting a carefully argued court case, John has begun his account of the gospel by telling the 'jury' what he intends to prove. He has spent the bulk of his time recording the facts and marshalling his arguments; and now presents the inescapable conclusion to which all these arguments point.

All the evidence speaks for itself. The carpenter's son from Nazareth is actually the Son of God from heaven. The facts call not merely for assent, but for trust. If what John has recorded is indeed true, then there is no other response that we can make than to believe in this Jesus. If Jesus is the Christ, he must be acknowledged as such, or else we must face the consequences.

John confronts his readers with a person to whom no one else in all the history of the universe can be compared. He is truly unique and the facts about his identity, and all that he has done, are compelling. They challenge everyone to think again as to who or what they are trusting for the deepest issues in life, and they point to Christ as the only sufficient object for saving faith.

A Solid Foundation

The argument against such a faith sometimes claims that it is just the spiritual equivalent of the story of the emperor's new clothes. This is the story in which an emperor is deceived by a pair of unscrupulous 'tailors' into believing that a 'suit' they have made him is magnificent, when in fact it is non-existent! It is the argument of the schoolboy who, when asked to define faith, said that it was 'believing what you know isn't true'. For many people, that is what they perceive faith to be: nothing more than a giant leap in the dark.

However, just as faith that has no clear objective is folly, so also is a faith that has no firm foundation. In bald terms, why trust in Jesus as opposed to Allah, or Buddha, or an off-shore bank account, or in the 'certainties' of the academic world? John's response is again to point to the absolute uniqueness of Jesus, not just in terms of what he did and what he said, but in the way that God accredited him.

He points in particular to the role of the miraculous signs that he performed in the presence of his disciples during his earthly ministry (20:30). These, John says, lie at the heart of the written record of his book. They bring us back to that distinctive pattern of God's revealing himself by both word and deed throughout the Scriptures. Fresh revelation from God is always coupled with fresh mighty works. This pattern becomes strongest in New Testament revelation as it points to Jesus and attests the uniqueness of his identity and the truth of his claims (*Acts* 2:22; *Heb.* 2:1–4). The purpose of John, in keeping with that of the other New Testament writers, is to provide a foundation that is solid enough to bear the weight of faith.

The fact that the resurrection is the final sign that John records is crucial in this, not least for the disciples themselves. There was no more daring prophecy that Jesus could have made than to claim that he would die and then rise again, but this is what he had repeatedly told his disciples would happen. To forecast one's death is conceivable, but to forecast one's subsequent resurrection and to specify the time when it would occur, is something altogether different. More than anything else, this one prediction would either make, or break Jesus' credibility. John's point, of course, is that it proved absolutely true and that even Thomas, the sceptic, was forced to acknowledge its veracity.

When facts of such enormity have been established beyond any doubt, especially in the face of death, that last enemy that all must face, there can be no securer foundation on which faith can rest in hope of life eternal.

ENCOURAGEMENT

The beauty of Jesus' own role in all this is that he was perfectly aware of the weakness of faith in his followers and the need for their faith to be nurtured and encouraged. This had been true with Mary, and the gentle way with which Jesus had dealt with her, we find repeated in his treatment of the disciples – especially Thomas. When faith, instinctively and in one sense rightly, holds back with a healthy caution, Jesus gently persuades of the need to receive him fully.

He demonstrates this first of all by emphasizing their need for peace. He had promised them in the upper room that peace would be one of the special gifts he would leave with them after the completion of his work (14:27; 16:33). Now that his mission was accomplished, he greets them, on three occasions, in a way that emphasizes that this promised peace was now secured (20:19, 21, 26). He uses a familiar Hebrew greeting that speaks of the entire well-being that comes through fellowship with God. Through his death and resurrection Jesus had secured that fellowship and was now encouraging his disciples to recognize that the promises had become a reality and that they should trust him.

Jesus also highlights the need for faith by linking it to the need for pardon. He repeats his promise to equip his followers with the gift of the Holy Spirit so that they might fulfil the task he had given them to do, and says, 'If you forgive the sins of anyone, they are forgiven; if you withhold forgiveness from anyone, it is withheld' (20:23). This is an enigmatic statement that is bound up with the apostolic proclamation of the gospel and the response it evokes from its hearers. The implication of these words seems to be that those who respond by faith to the apostolic testimony to Christ will be forgiven, while those who reject their testimony will not. Here is further encouragement for a response of faith to these truths.

The final encouragement to believe has to do with our need for God's blessing to rest upon our lives. As Jesus concludes his words to Thomas he connects belief in himself with the obtaining of blessing from God (20:29). A life resting in the fullness of God's favour can only be found through faith in God's resurrected Son. Even though for the vast majority of his children, unlike Thomas and the disciples, this will involve simply trusting in the promise of God, nevertheless, the blessing of God will be exactly the same.

RESILIENCE

Jesus in no way minimizes the fact that faith will face struggles of many different kinds. So he lovingly addresses the weakness of faith in his followers. This is seen in the way that he reveals himself to these men, not just miraculously, but in a way that demonstrates his concern for them.

We see it especially in the way that he deals with Thomas and in what he says to him (20:27). Even though Thomas had expressed his doubts about the claims the other disciples had made of seeing Jesus alive again (20:24–25), Jesus does not rebuke or ridicule him for his faithlessness. Instead he leads him through his doubts into one of the greatest confessions of the New Testament. He acknowledges Jesus in the most personal terms as: 'My Lord and my God!' (20:28). Though he had questioned the testimony of his fellow apostles and doubted its veracity (20:25), he now discovered that it was entirely true. It is the trustworthiness of that apostolic testimony that undergirds the gospel message itself (20:29). The blessing that Thomas had received in a tangible way through meeting the risen Christ, every believer receives through faith.

The need for a resilient and persevering faith is seen in the way that John words the mission-statement of his Gospel at the end of the chapter. The tense he uses for 'believe' (20:31) is one that carries the sense of 'go on believing'. The life of faith will invariably involve struggle, and the true faith that leads to salvation is that persevering faith that holds on to Christ to the end.

A TRUE SENSE OF DIRECTION

What is the end to which faith finally leads? Jesus has given one answer in terms of the promise of peace, pardon and blessing. John sums it up in the words, 'that by believing you may have life in his name' (20:31). Jesus had already declared that he had come in order that those who believe in him might have life and have it to the full (10:10). He had defined that life in its essence as being 'eternal life' – a life that consists of union with God through union with Christ

(17:3). Now John makes it clear that this life becomes ours, not in some mystical or mysterious manner, but in the 'name' of Jesus; that is, entirely by his merits and on his account. It comes by virtue of all that Jesus is and all that he has accomplished.

In a world in which, for many, 'life is what you make it', the promise of the gospel is of a life that consists of what Christ can make it. Given the brokenness and emptiness of life, here is the greatest reason to believe in the Christ of the gospel.

44

May I Return to the Beginning?

After this Jesus revealed himself again to the disciples by the Sea of Tiberias, and he revealed himself in this way. ² *Simon Peter, Thomas (called the Twin), Nathanael of Cana in Galilee, the sons of Zebedee, and two others of his disciples were together.* ³ *Simon Peter said to them, "I am going fishing." They said to him, "We will go with you." They went out and got into the boat, but that night they caught nothing.*

⁴ *Just as day was breaking, Jesus stood on the shore; yet the disciples did not know that it was Jesus.* ⁵ *Jesus said to them, "Children, do you have any fish?" They answered him, "No."* ⁶ *He said to them, "Cast the net on the right side of the boat, and you will find some." So they cast it, and now they were not able to haul it in, because of the quantity of fish.* ⁷ *That disciple whom Jesus loved therefore said to Peter, "It is the Lord!" When Simon Peter heard that it was the Lord, he put on his outer garment, for he was stripped for work, and threw himself into the sea.* ⁸ *The other disciples came in the boat, dragging the net full of fish, for they were not far from the land, but about a hundred yards off.*

⁹ *When they got out on land, they saw a charcoal fire in place, with fish laid out on it, and bread.* ¹⁰ *Jesus said to them, "Bring some of the fish that you have just caught."* ¹¹ *So Simon Peter went aboard and hauled the net ashore, full of large fish, 153 of them. And although there were so many, the net was not torn.* ¹² *Jesus said to them, "Come and have breakfast." Now none of*

the disciples dared ask him, "Who are you?" They knew it was the Lord. [13] Jesus came and took the bread and gave it to them, and so with the fish. [14] This was now the third time that Jesus was revealed to the disciples after he was raised from the dead (John 21:1–14).

As we move into the final chapter of John's Gospel, we find ourselves brought full circle in the relationship between Jesus and his disciples. The chapter may well have been a kind of appendix that John chose to add, because the last verse of the previous chapter bears all the marks of being the climax and conclusion of all that the apostle had written. However, that does not mean that this closing chapter is in any sense out of kilter with the previous chapters. Quite the reverse; for when we compare John's record of this memorable day that Jesus spent with the apostles just before his ascension, with the record in the other Gospels of the very first beginnings of his time with them, there are unmistakable similarities.

There is an obvious echo here of that occasion when Jesus formally called some of these men to follow him, so that they might become 'fishers of men' (*Mark* 1.16–17). That too took place on a beach by Galilee and may even have been this very same beach where they were breakfasting. There is a similarity also between the miracles that took place on these two occasions (see also *Luke* 5:1–11). As Jesus prepares to launch these men upon their life's-work, for which he had been preparing them the last three years, he brings them back to where it all began. He reminds them of how they were called and what they had been promised. Now, having fulfilled all that was required, he gets ready to commission them for service.

The way that John records the incident gives us a particular insight into what was going on. The section is bracketed by two distinctive comments: 'Jesus revealed himself again to his disciples' (21:1) and, 'This was now the third time that Jesus was revealed to his disciples after he was raised from the dead' (21:14). The word translated 'revealed' carries the sense of 'was manifested'. It conveys more than a mere superficial encounter. Through the miracle, and during this breakfast on the beach, the disciples were being given an even deeper understanding of Jesus, of their relationship with him, and of his purpose for their lives. Here was a crucial exercise in the reinforcing of the disciples' faith and it tallies exactly with what John has written about the purpose of his Gospel. As we saw in the last chapter, his desire was for people not only to believe, but to 'go on believing' (20:31). That ability to continue believing in Jesus is intimately bound up with knowing Jesus. So Jesus here emphasizes four vital truths about himself to his followers so that they themselves might be strengthened to go on believing.

SOVEREIGN LORD

John tells us that one of the last things Jesus did in his disciples' company before his return to glory was to perform a miracle. It could be argued that there was no further need of miracles to testify to his identity and message. The resurrection was the greatest of all signs and could not be superseded. But Jesus knew how fragile the faith of his followers was and he was eager to strengthen it. So he performs a miracle that surely struck a chord deep in their hearts.

It was a miracle designed to confirm their faith by taking them back to familiar ground. Here were the disciples, still reeling after the events of the past few weeks, and still fearful because of the mood in Jerusalem (their release from such fear was still to come), so Jesus provides miraculous reassurance for them. They had gone to Galilee because Jesus had sent them there (*Matt.* 28:7; *Mark* 16:7) and while they were waiting for Jesus to join them, they went fishing (21:2–3). However, having fished all night, they had caught nothing. As they head for shore they see a figure on the beach in the early morning light. He hails them and asks how they are doing, then tells them to try again, this time throwing their nets on the right side of the boat. The result was an incredible catch of fish (21:4–6).

This was a most poignant lesson for the disciples. 'In the Gospels, the disciples never catch fish without Jesus' help!' (Raymond Brown). They cannot even do the thing they are supposed to be good at without his involvement. Jesus was pressing home what he had taught them in the upper room: 'Apart from me you can do nothing' (15:5). Here is a fundamental truth for living the Christian life. Along with the disciples, we need to recognize Jesus' lordship over the whole of life. There is no area from which we can afford to exclude him.

This is exactly how the disciples react. The one whom Jesus loved exclaimed, 'It is the Lord!' (21:7). Peter responds with a gesture of religious awe, covering himself up and throwing himself into the sea to swim to Jesus. Jesus was revealing to them again his sovereign control over the very elements of nature and over the lives of his people, and the only possible response was adoration.

LOVING SERVANT

As the disciples struggle on to the beach with their enormous catch of fish, they find Jesus with a fire burning and breakfast cooking, but none of them dares to ask, 'Who are you?' (21:8–12). Having just displayed his sovereign lordship, Jesus immediately displays his willingness to serve. This was the same Jesus who had donned the servant's apron to wash their dirty feet in the upper room. Now he had become the camp cook and was ready to fill their hungry stomachs.

We are reminded again of the great paradox and glory of the gospel. The one who is Lord of the universe enters our world, not to be served by his creatures, but to serve them (*Matt.* 20:28). It is the key not only for understanding the majesty of Jesus' mission, but also for appreciating the depth of our need.

This was an axiomatic truth that needed to be embedded firmly in the apostles' minds. Jesus had come to minister to the needs of his people, because they could not meet those needs by themselves. Hence this seemingly trivial provision of a meal on a beach was but another reminder that Christ had taken care of their greatest need: the need of their souls. Because Jesus has taken care of what matters most through his death upon the cross, we can be sure that he will take care of everything else that matters; all we need to do is to trust him.

EXTRAVAGANT PROVIDER

The net is hauled on to the beach and the catch counted, and we are told that 153 large fish had been brought to shore (21:11). In other words, this was no mere subsistence miracle but proof that Jesus is perfectly able to do 'immeasurably more than all that we ask or think' (*Eph.* 3:20) – he does not operate by half-measures.

There have been many complicated and fanciful attempts to explain the significance of this miracle. Many have involved a prediction as to the success of these 'fishers of men' as preachers of the gospel. Jerome, for example, took the number 153 to represent the nations of the world and saw this as the extension of God's kingdom to all people. However, all such explanations are unnecessary. The only clue we need is the one that Jesus himself had given earlier in the Gospel. It is the truth of his great promise, 'I came that they may have life and have it abundantly' (10:10).

John underscores this same truth in his first letter when he penned the words, 'See what kind of love the Father has given to us, that we should be called the children of God!' (*1 John* 3:1). The love of God towards his people through his Son is a love that knows no limits.

This truth was especially important to the disciples at this time when their feelings of insecurity and vulnerability were not being helped at all by the thought of Jesus' imminent departure. That simple meal within smelling distance of the catch of a lifetime said it all! The One to whom we pray, 'Give us this day our daily bread', is more than able to supply all our needs. We need to appreciate that Jesus is not just a faithful, but also an extravagant Provider.

INTIMATE FRIEND

Even the simple meal that they shared that morning was a lesson in itself. Far from being an opportunity to dispense with the customary etiquette of dining in a more formal setting, Jesus carefully follows the respected Jewish practice of giving thanks for the food before giving it to the disciples (21:13). He was demonstrating in a way that the disciples would have understood fully that a meal together is more than just a matter of sharing food with one another, it is an act of fellowship with God.

Here, as Jesus, the Son of God incarnate, dines with these men on the beach, he is confirming the fellowship of the past, despite their desertion, and assuring them of his intimate friendship for the future.

Through this little incident, Jesus is strengthening the bond between himself and his disciples, preparing them further for the work that lies ahead. True discipleship rests upon precisely this same point: living fellowship with Christ.

45

Restored and Reinstated

When they had finished breakfast, Jesus said to Simon Peter, "Simon, son of John, do you love me more than these?" He said to him, "Yes, Lord; you know that I love you." He said to him, "Feed my lambs." ¹⁶ He said to him a second time, "Simon, son of John, do you love me?" He said to him, "Yes, Lord; you know that I love you." He said to him, "Tend my sheep." ¹⁷ He said to him the third time, "Simon, son of John, do you love me?" Peter was grieved because he said to him the third time, "Do you love me?" and he said to him, "Lord, you know everything; you know that I love you." Jesus said to him, "Feed my sheep. ¹⁸ Truly, truly, I say to you, when you were young, you used to dress yourself and walk wherever you wanted, but when you are old, you will stretch out your hands, and another will dress you and carry you where you do not want to go." ¹⁹ (This he said to show by what kind of death he was to glorify God.) And after saying this he said to him, "Follow me."

²⁰ Peter turned and saw the disciple whom Jesus loved following them, the one who had been reclining at table close to him and had said, "Lord, who is it that is going to betray you?" ²¹ When Peter saw him, he said to Jesus, "Lord, what about this man?" ²² Jesus said to him, "If it is my will that he remain until I come, what is that to you? You follow me!" ²³ So the saying spread abroad among the brothers that this disciple was not to die; yet Jesus did not say to him that he was not to die, but, "If it is my will that he remain until I come, what is that to you?"

[24] This is the disciple who is bearing witness about these things, and who has written these things, and we know that his testimony is true. [25] Now there are also many other things that Jesus did. Were every one of them to be written, I suppose that the world itself could not contain the books that would be written (John 21:15–25).

The finale of John's Gospel is not merely a tagged-on account of an isolated incident, it is a significant event that neatly ties together many of the threads John has been weaving throughout its chapters. Earlier in this book we drew attention to the fact that John was not just writing a potted biography of Jesus, but was calling for a response to him by faith (1:12–13). This call to faith has been restated and reaffirmed in the climax to his gospel record (20:31). He has made it clear that his objective in writing is to call people to discipleship. And so, as the spotlight falls on Peter in these closing verses, we find in him a beautiful picture of a disciple in the making.

Followers of Jesus are not made and perfected in an instant. Although conversion is instantaneous and that new relationship with God that it involves is established irrevocably in that moment, the process of moulding and shaping a disciple takes a lifetime. That is a vital and thrilling fact to remember. Salvation in biblical terms not only has a past tense but a present and a future tense as well. A Christian is not only someone who has been saved, but someone who is being saved, and is yet to be saved, in the sense that his or her salvation will be perfected finally in glory to come.

So, as John draws his Gospel to its end he shows Jesus dealing with his people and making them into what he wants them to be. He does not promise some magical or mystical experience to transform them in an instant. Instead he engages with them intimately and personally, and through this unique relationship they are made new. If it is true in a lesser sense that when a man or woman gets married, he or she become a new person by virtue of their new relationship, how much more is this the case in our spiritual marriage to Christ.

The way that Jesus deals with Peter in these verses displays the beauty and the sensitivity of Jesus' dealings with his children.

RESTORED

Clearly, the background to this exchange on the beach over breakfast is Peter's threefold denial of Jesus on the night of his arrest (18:15–27). That was the absolute low point in Peter's relationship with his Lord and even though in one sense he knew there had been a restoration, there was understandably an underlying fear that irreparable damage had been done. There is no record of any clearing of the air between them before this point, and in light of Christ's wider teaching, we know that sin and failure cannot be dealt with simply by brushing them under the carpet. Peter realized from his own experience that, for true reconciliation to take place, the offending issues had to be addressed and resolved.

It is striking to note the weight that Scripture attaches to the need for reconciling all breakdowns that occur in relationships, not just in our relationship with God, but also with our fellow Christians. Jesus has pointed to the way that broken fellowship impinges upon effective worship (*Matt.* 5:23–24) and Paul will later indicate that broken communion between believers will have an impact on communion with God (*1 Cor.* 11:17–34). Here we see Jesus taking the lead in restoring a follower who has lapsed.

Jesus does not address Peter by the name by which he had been known for much of the past three years, but reverts to his original name: 'Simon son of John' (see also 1:42). It is as though Jesus is taking him back to the beginning and starting afresh. There follows a threefold exchange that revolves around two different words for 'love' and two different words for 'know', not distinguished in the translation we have been using (21:15–17). There is no need to regard this as some kind of cryptic code that needs to be deciphered. It is simply an indication of Jesus' thoroughness in dealing with Peter's condition. He is meticulous in working through, not just the surface issues, but also the deeper ones lurking within.

The different words for 'love' reflect the different aspects that love entails; it involves both the head and the heart. The different words for 'know' refer to awareness and perception. Put together they show us what Christ is looking for and working for in the lives of his followers; namely, a total and a consistent response to him. Jesus seeks to impress upon Peter the true dynamics of relationship with himself. Peter, like many believers, could easily have fallen prey to the mentality, 'I have sinned, therefore I am sidelined', but Jesus shows him that this is not the case. He shows him afresh the same grace of forgiveness that he had revealed at the outset and that he had maintained throughout their time together. The power of this restoring grace is demonstrated dramatically in the difference between the Peter of the Gospels and the Peter we meet in the book of Acts and in his letters.

For God's children, failure is never final. The whole purpose of the gospel is restoration and nothing will stand between God and the fulfilment of that great end.

REINSTATED

The fact that Jesus focuses primarily on a relationship that needs to be restored shows the vital link between relationship with Christ and service in his kingdom. We cannot serve him if we do not know him. This helps to clarify the importance of humility in this whole equation. Before his fall, Peter had been self-absorbed, self-confident and self-exalting, and all of these traits seriously impaired his ability to serve Christ effectively. Now, as the relationship between the Master and the disciple is both restored and deepened, the way is opened for him to be reinstated to Christ's service.

Useful service to God depends upon a vital relationship with God. The only way that vital relationship can be established is not through what we can do for him, but only through what he has done for us in Christ. When something is broken, it has to be fixed before it can function. The same is true for our broken humanity. The heart of its problem is a broken relationship with God. Only when that has been put right through the redeeming and reconciling work of Christ can we begin to function in the way that God intended.

This truth is demonstrated in Peter. The reinstatement to his calling as an apostle and servant of Christ can only take place after he has been restored to fellowship with him. As Jesus responds to each of Peter's affirmations of his love for him, he uses different permutations of the same picture: the image of caring for a flock. There is no need to tie ourselves in knots looking for some hidden meaning in all this, Jesus is merely painting a comprehensive picture of a shepherd's work. Peter was being reinstated to the task of caring for all of God's people in all of their many and diverse needs.

Perhaps the most amazing element of this is the way it relates to Jesus himself and his role as the Good Shepherd (10:11). The work that Jesus was entrusting to Peter was nothing less than an extension of the work in which he himself was involved.

REDIRECTED

Throughout this interview Jesus is shaping Peter for a task in which the key qualification is love; a love characterized by humility, dependence and obedience. Jesus brings all of this into sharp focus by saying, 'Follow me!' (21:19). These were words that took Peter back three years to the beginning of that precious relationship (*Matt.* 4:18–19). This was the call that had first redirected his whole life and the call that would now bring him back on track after he had strayed so grievously. Jesus, on this occasion, repeats the call, 'Follow me . . . follow me!' (20:19,22). Peter's life was being turned around and redirected.

The call of Christ in the gospel is by definition one that must redirect our lives. Sin has set us going in the wrong direction – it has turned us in towards ourselves instead of out towards God. God's grace in the gospel however turns us in repentance away from sin and self, and back towards himself through faith in Jesus Christ his Son. Even though this is a call that when heard the first time has decisive consequences (as was true for the disciples), it still rings in our ears every day, and constantly summons us away from all that would distract us and pull us from God. It calls us, like Peter, to a life of undistracted discipleship to Christ.

When Peter then, with traces of his old self still rising to the surface, asks, 'What about this man?' (21:21), Jesus in effect answers, 'That is none of your business!' We are not called to look at other people and at God's dealings with them, we are called to look to God and follow wherever he may choose to lead us in his service. It is the same truth that we find presented in the Letter to the Hebrews where, under the most painful of circumstances, God's people are called to fix their eyes on Jesus and run with perseverance the race that is mapped out before them (*Heb.* 12:1–3). The faith to which we are called in the gospel is not that of trusting at just one point in our lives, but a trusting that will completely reorder and redirect our lives forever.

So ends John's account of Jesus. He brings it to a conclusion with the most overt reference yet to himself as the unnamed author of the work (21:24), and with the comment that he could have written so very much more (21:25). The whole Gospel bears the hallmark of his burning desire – a desire expressed so well in Charles Wesley's words:

> *O that the world might taste and see*
> *The riches of His grace;*
> *The arms of love that compass me*
> *Would all mankind embrace.*

Group Study Guide

This Study Guide has been prepared for group Bible study, but it can also be used individually. Those who use it on their own may find it helpful to keep a note of their responses in a notebook.

The way in which group Bible studies are led can greatly enhance their value. A well-conducted study will appear as though it has been easy to lead, but that is usually because the leader has worked hard and planned well. Clear aims are essential.

AIMS

In all Bible study, individual or corporate, we have several aims:

1. To gain an understanding of the original meaning of the particular passage of Scripture;

2. To apply this to ourselves and our own situation;

3. To develop some specific ways of putting the biblical teaching into practice.

2 Timothy 3:16–17 provides a helpful structure. Paul says that Scripture is useful for:

(i)   teaching us;

(ii) rebuking us;

(iii) correcting, or changing us;

(iv) training us in righteousness.

Consequently, in studying any passage of Scripture, we should always have in mind these questions:

What does this passage teach us (about God, ourselves, etc.)?

Does it rebuke us in some way?

How can its teaching transform us?

What equipment does it give us for serving Christ?

In fact, these four questions alone would provide a safe guide in any Bible study.

PRINCIPLES

In group Bible study we meet in order to learn about God's Word and ways 'together with all the saints' *(Eph.* 3:18). But our own experience, as well as Scripture, tells us that the saints are not always what they are called to be in every situation – including group Bible study! Leaders ordinarily have to work hard and prepare well if the work of the group is to be spiritually profitable. The following guidelines for leaders may help to make this a reality.

Preparation:

1. Study and understand the passage yourself. The better prepared and more sure of the direction of the study you are, the more likely it is that the group will have a beneficial and enjoyable study. Ask: What are the main things this passage is saying? How can this be made clear? This is not the same question as the more common 'What does this passage "say to you"?', which expects a reaction rather than an exposition of the passage. Be clear about that distinction yourself, and work at making it clear in the group study.

2. On the basis of your own study form a clear idea *before* the group meets of (i) the main theme(s) of the passage which should be opened out for discussion, and (ii) some general conclusions the group ought to reach as a result of the study. Here the questions which arise from 2 Timothy 3:16–17 should act as our guide.

3. The guidelines and questions which follow may help to provide a general framework for each discussion; leaders should use them as starting places which can be further developed. It is usually helpful to have a specific goal or theme in mind for group discussion, and one is suggested for each study. But even more important than tracing a single theme is understanding the teaching and the implications of the passage.

Leading the Group:

1. Announce the passage and theme for the study, and begin with prayer. In group studies it may be helpful to invite a different person to lead in prayer each time you meet.

2. Introduce the passage and theme, briefly reminding people of its outline and highlighting the content of each subsidiary section.

3. Lead the group through the discussion questions. Use your own if you are comfortable in doing so; those provided may be used,

developing them with your own points. As discussion proceeds, continue to encourage the group first of all to discuss the significance of the passage (teaching) and only then its application (meaning for us). It may be helpful to write important points and applications on a board by way of summary as well as visual aid.

4. At the end of each meeting, remind members of the group of their assignments for the next meeting, and encourage them to come prepared. Be sufficiently prepared as the leader to give specific assignments to individuals, or even couples or groups, to come with specific contributions.

5. Remember that you are the leader of the group! Encourage clear contributions, and do not be embarrassed to ask someone to explain what they have said more fully or to help them to do so ('Do you mean . . . ?').

Most groups include the 'over-talkative', the 'over-silent' and the 'red-herring raisers'! Leaders must control the first, encourage the second and redirect the third! Each leader will develop his or her own most natural way of doing that; but it will be helpful to think out what that is before the occasion arises! The first two groups can be helped by some judicious direction of questions to specific individuals or even groups (*e.g.* 'Jane, you know something about this from personal experience . . .'); the third by redirecting the discussion to the passage itself ('That is an interesting point, but isn't it true that this passage really concentrates on . . . ?'). It may be helpful to break the group up into smaller groups sometimes, giving each subgroup specific points to discuss and to report back on. A wise arranging of these smaller groups may also help each member to participate.

More important than any techniques we may develop is the help of the Spirit enabling us to understand and to apply the Scriptures. Have and encourage a humble, prayerful spirit.

6. Keep faith with the schedule; it is better that some of the group wished the study could have been longer than that others are inconvenienced by it stretching beyond the time limits set.

7. Close in prayer. As time permits, spend the closing minutes in corporate prayer, encouraging the group to apply what they have learned in praise and thanks, intercession and petition.

STUDY 1: John 1:1–18

AIM: To appreciate the main contours of the gospel as mapped out by John and to recognize why they are essential to salvation.

1.   How does the opening verse of this Gospel give us an immediate sense of the scale of what is involved in God's salvation?

2.   John gives us a profound insight into the eternal existence of Jesus Christ (1:1–4). What does he tell us about who he is, what he has done, and what he gives to all mankind?

3.   The themes of light and darkness are prominent throughout this Gospel and are introduced from the outset by a play on words (1:5). How does this help us to understand the constant conflict between Jesus and the world during his ministry?

4.   John the Baptist was a key figure in the lead–up to the beginning of Jesus' earthly ministry. What are we told about the warrant for his work (1:6); the work he was sent to do (1:7); and the wider significance of his work (1:7–9)? In what way does his testimony still stand today?

5.   What are we told in advance about the negative reaction that Jesus would meet when he came into the world and what was so surprising about this reaction (1:10–11)? What does this teach us about our human nature?

6.   What is promised to those who respond to Jesus by faith, and what lies behind this response (1:12–13)?

7.   As John brings his Prologue to its climax, what does he want us to know from the outset about the true identity of Jesus (1:14–18)?

For STUDY 2: Read John 1:19–51 and chapters 4–5 of the commentary.

STUDY 2: John 1:19–51

AIM: To see the main thrust of John the Baptist's testimony about Jesus and to understand how that testimony is used to start drawing people to him.

1.   What was John's testimony and why was it so important for Jewish people who had lived with the promised hope of the Old

Testament Scriptures (1:19–28)? Why should his reference to the prophecy of Isaiah (1:23) make the Jews realize something significant was about to happen in God's calendar?

2.   Given the Old Testament background to all that was happening, how are we to understand the Baptist's description of Jesus as 'the Lamb of God' (1:29)? What is unique about Jesus that allows John to speak in this way (1:30–31)? In what way does this have a universal relevance?

3.   How did John recognize that Jesus was the One that God had sent and what was so momentous about the designation he gave him (1:32–34)?

4.   What drew the two disciples of the Baptist mentioned here to follow Jesus (1:35–39)? Why do you think that their interest in Jesus was aroused and in what way does that help us to appreciate how people are drawn to Jesus today?

5.   When Andrew returned from spending a day with Jesus, what was the first thing he did (1:40–42)? What can we learn from this about the way we should be affected by a personal meeting with Jesus?

6.   As Jesus begins to call these men to follow him, what do we learn from the calling of Nathanael and the response that he made to Jesus (1:43–51)?

For STUDY 3: Read John 2:1–25 and chapters 6–7 of the commentary.

STUDY 3: John 2:1–25

AIM: To understand how verbal testimony about Jesus is strengthened by the testimony of miracles and to see the impact this has on those who witnessed the miracles.

1.   John places great emphasis on the fact that the miracles Jesus performed were also 'signs' (2:11). How does this detail help us to appreciate the deeper significance of the miraculous side of Jesus' ministry (cf. *Acts* 2:22; *Heb.* 2:3–4)?

2.   This is the first place where Jesus talks about his 'time' and when it would come (2:4). What was this referring to, and how does

it affect the way that we are meant to understand Jesus' reason for coming into the world?

3.   It is significant that even though this miracle is not recorded in the other Gospels, it was the first miracle Jesus performed (2:11). What can we learn from the Old Testament background to this event (*Isa.* 25:6) that helps us to appreciate the joy of redemption that Jesus brings?

4.   As the scene changes from Cana to Jerusalem, why is Jesus so incensed by what was happening in the temple (2:12–17)?

5.   How does Jesus' reference to the sign that he would give to prove his authority, provide a direct challenge to the empty ritual of Jewish worship in his day (2:18–22)? In what way can the Christian faith be reduced to mere ritual without reality (look at *2 Tim.* 3:5)?

6.   Why does Jesus not welcome the 'faith' of those who responded to him in Jerusalem during the Passover Feast (2:23–25)? How might similar 'faith' manifest itself in the church today?

For STUDY 4: Read John 3:1–36 and chapters 8–10 of the commentary.

STUDY 4: John 3:1–36

AIM: To see how Jesus challenges religion that is merely superficial and confronts us with God's answer to man's deepest need.

1.   There is clearly a connection between the superficial religion that Jesus encountered among the Jews during the Passover Feast and what he found in Nicodemus. How does Jesus begin to raise questions in this man's mind that Nicodemus had never considered before (3:1–3)? What does this teach us about our natural spiritual state (look at *Eph.* 2:1)?

2.   When Nicodemus asks Jesus about what it means to be 'born again', how does Jesus make it clear that without God's intervention we are lost and without hope (3:4–8)?

3.   How does Jesus show Nicodemus that he is uniquely qualified to reveal these things and in what way does he point to the cross as the ultimate proof of this (3:9–15)?

4.   John adds his own explanatory comment at this point (3:16–21). What does this teach us about our legal standing in the sight of

God; firstly, in terms of human nature, and secondly, by reason of what Christ secures for those who trust him?

5.   Why is John the Baptist neither jealous nor angry when it becomes clear that Jesus is gaining a larger following than himself (3:22–30)? In what sense does it make his joy 'complete' (3:30)?

6.   What makes Jesus utterly unique and worthy of the trust of those whom he calls to himself (3:31–35)? In the light of this, what are the inevitable and justifiable consequences that flow from the way that we respond to Jesus (3:36)?

For STUDY 5: Read John 4:1–42 and chapter 11 of the commentary.

STUDY 5: John 4:1–42

AIM: To observe Jesus engaging a woman whose life has been ruined by sin and to understand how he restores, not only her, but many others as well.

1.   Given that there was no obvious geographical necessity for Jesus to travel through Samaria on this journey, what are we to make of the statement, 'Now he had to pass through Samaria' (4:4)? How might this help us to maintain a deeper daily awareness of God's providence in our lives?

2.   How does the simplicity of Jesus' question to this woman belie the significance of the fact that he was asking the question at all (4:6–9)? In what way should this make us think about the kind of barriers we are prepared to cross as we look for opportunities to bring the gospel to others?

3.   In your own words, describe the way in which Jesus steered this conversation from a request for a drink to God's answer for our deepest needs in life (4:10–26). Can you think of other ways that we could use natural situations in order to show people their supernatural need?

4.   What is the core truth that Jesus teaches this woman about God (4:21–24)? What is the key fact that Jesus reveals about himself (4:25–26)?

5.   What can we learn from the next section about the importance of doing God's will and the place of evangelism in so doing (4:27–38)?

6.   Why do you think the woman's testimony, 'He told me all I ever did,' stirred such extraordinary interest in Jesus among the villagers (4:39–42)? How does that same truth about Jesus continue to work itself out in practice today?

For STUDY 6: Read John 4:43–5:15 and chapters 12–13 of the commentary.

STUDY 6: John 4:43–5:15

AIM: To catch a glimpse of how the healing miracles of Jesus depict the spiritual restoration he came to bring.

1.   Why do you think John colours the welcome Jesus seemed to receive in Galilee with Jesus' comment about a prophet having no honour in his own country (4:43–45)? Does this say anything about the kind of motives that lie behind some apparently positive responses to the gospel?

2.   What was it that made the royal official trek the twenty–five miles from Capernaum to Cana to see Jesus and what lay behind the persistence of his pleadings (4:46–49)? How does this give us a glimpse of where our deepest need in life really lies?

3.   Where do we find the key to the man's response to Jesus (4:50)? In what way is this a pattern for every true response to Christ?

4. How was the official's faith vindicated and what effect did this have on him and the other members of his household (4:51–53)? Suggest ways in which personal faith can have wider effects in the lives of other people.

5.   As the scene changes from Galilee to Jerusalem and involves a large crowd of disabled people, what can we learn from the question that Jesus asks the lame man (5:1–6)? How does this probe the deepest longings of our hearts?

6.   What can we learn from Jesus' sovereign intervention in this man's life and what he later says to him about his sin (5:7–9,14–15)? Does this in any way help us to appreciate more fully the way that Jesus deals with us?

7.   Why was there controversy surrounding this miracle and was it justified (5:9–13)?

For STUDY 7: Read John 5:16–47 and chapter 14 of the commentary.

STUDY 7: John 5:16–47

AIM: To see how the ugly truth about human nature is demonstrated in the way people react to Jesus.

1.　　How does the controversy over Jesus' attitude to the Jewish Sabbath begin to reveal the dark truth about human nature (5:16–18)?

2.　　How does Jesus respond to his persecutors (5:19–23)? What does this teach us about the only way that we can truly relate to God?

3.　　Why is it so important to understand the relationship between Jesus and God the Father (5:24)? How should this affect not only our own personal response to the gospel, but the way we react to other people's responses?

4.　　What gives Jesus the authority to speak as he does about 'life from the dead' and in what sense is he using that expression in these verses (5:25–27)? In what way does he take this teaching to a different level in the verses that follow (5:28–30)? How are these two lines of thought connected?

5.　　Try to identify the five strands of testimony or evidence to which Jesus points in support of his momentous claims (5:31–47). In what way were these significant for his original Jewish audience and how are they significant for us?

For STUDY 8: Read John 6:1–24 and chapter 15 of the commentary.

STUDY 8: John 6:1–24

AIM: To recognize that Jesus brings the power and provision of a future world into the present, but is so easily misunderstood as he does so.

1.　　There are many details in this section that point to a link between Jesus and Moses. Why do you think John wants to emphasize this connection? What significance would it have for his Jewish readers and does it say anything to a wider audience?

2.   Why do you think Jesus puts Philip on the spot by asking him how they could feed such a vast crowd (6:5–6)? What does this say about the limits of human resources, not just in the face of practical needs, but especially with reference to those that are spiritual?

3.   What does Jesus teach us as he performs this miracle (6: 7–13)? How does the provision made on that one day in history relate to the eternal provision he makes in eternity?

4.   What was wrong with the way the people reacted to Jesus after this miracle (6:14–15)? Is it still possible today to try to press Jesus into roles he never intended to fulfil?

5.   Bearing in mind what has been said already about the wider links in this passage, what are we to make of the events that followed the miraculous meal (6:16–24)? How does this help us to appreciate Jesus as the true deliverer that God promised to send?

For STUDY 9: Read John 6:25–71 and chapters 16–17 of the commentary.

STUDY 9: John 6:25–71

AIM: To understand the explanation Jesus gives for the miracle of the feeding of the five thousand and see how this touches the very heart of the gospel.

1.   The miracle of providing bread for thousands is followed by a discourse about the way that Jesus is actually bread for millions. How does Jesus shift the crowd's attention from the miracle to the One who performed it (6:26–29)? Why is this of vital importance to the way we understand Christ's miracles?

2.   How does Jesus answer the request for a sign to justify his claims (6:30–33)? What are we to make of the fuller explanation he provides (6:34–40)? How does his references to God the Father and his sovereign role in redemption bring this teaching into sharp focus for everyone?

3.   Why did Jesus' answer offend the Jews and in what sense does it continue to be offensive in all ages and in every culture (6:41–42)?

4.   How are we to understand the imagery that Jesus uses of his being the 'Bread of Life' (6:43–51)? Even though Jesus had not yet instituted the Lord's Supper, do you think the language he uses is meant to point forward to the meaning of that sacrament (6:52–59)?

5.   Why do you think these sayings of Jesus were so offensive, even to many of those who had been his followers up to this point (6:60–66)? Is there still an offence in this aspect of the gospel that will cause many who claim to be Christians to baulk at what it truly means to follow Christ?

6.   What can we learn from the way that Jesus confronts the Twelve; from Peter's response; and from Jesus' comment about a betrayer (6:67–71)?

For STUDY 10: Read John 7:1–24 and chapter 18 of the commentary.

STUDY 10: John 7:1–24

AIM: To see how Jesus counters the widespread misunderstanding about who he was and what he came to do.

1.   What was wrong with the way Jesus' brothers perceived the mission he was pursuing on earth (7:1–5)? How can the same kind of misunderstanding today prevent people from grasping the gospel, especially in the cluttered marketplace of world religions?

2.   How does Jesus' repeated reference to 'the right time', in his answer to his brothers, help to show them that there is something far bigger at stake than his private personal agenda (7:6–9)? Why is this crucial to an accurate understanding of the gospel?

3.   In what ways do the mixed reactions to Jesus among the Jews of his day reflect the mixed reactions to him throughout history (7:10–13)?

4.   How does Jesus explain his extraordinary ability to teach (7:14–19)? How does this demonstrate that a genuine understanding of Jesus' teaching will never leave us with only a mere code of ethics or system of belief?

5.   How are we to explain the vitriolic reaction that Jesus' answer provoked among the crowd (7:20)? Was this reaction exclusive to the Jews of his time or does it have a wider expression?

6.   In what way does Jesus turn the tables on his Jewish detractors (7:21–24)? How does this help us to see that part of our task in persuading people of the truth of the gospel is to show the inconsistency of what they believe themselves?

For STUDY 11: Read John 7:25–53 and chapter 19 of the commentary

STUDY 11: John 7:25–53

AIM: To grasp the fact that people are deeply divided in their reactions to Jesus and see how hard we are by nature in our attitude to God.

1.   Why is the question of the authority that lies behind Jesus and his teaching so important (7:25–27)? In an age when the issues of truth and authority have fallen prey to relativism and pluralism, does this question still matter and, if so, how should we address it?

2.   In what way does the exchange that follows serve to confirm the truth about who Jesus really is (7:28–36)? Can you think of examples of people who have at one time been bitterly opposed to Jesus, but have finally come to put their faith in him?

3.   What do we learn about Jesus and about the salvation promised in the gospel from his pronouncement on the last day of the Feast (7:37–39)? In what sense is there a timelessness and universal appeal in the language he uses?

4.   How do we make sense of the continuing division in reactions to Jesus after all he has said and done (7:40–44; look at 3:3,5; 6:44)? How should this affect the way we pray for the gospel to spread and actually pursue the task of evangelism?

5.   How does the bitter reaction of the Jewish leaders serve to prove what John has been saying about light and darkness in the Gospel so far (7:45–49; see also 1:5; 3:19–21)?

6.   What made Nicodemus risk his position among the Jews by speaking up for Jesus (7:50–53)? What does this teach us about the fact that true believers will never be able to conceal their faith in Christ?

For STUDY 12: Read John 8:1–59 and chapters 20–21 of the commentary.

STUDY 12: John 8:1–59

AIM: To see how Jesus addresses the problem of a hardened heart by exposing not only the enslaving power of sin, but also the liberating power of grace.

1.   In the episode in which the Jewish leaders bring an adulterous woman to Jesus for him to judge her, what comes out as the most sordid sin in all that happens (8:1–11)? Why do you think that Jesus in his teachings is more scathing about hypocrisy than any other sin?

2.   What are we to learn from the way that Jesus dealt with the woman in question (8:9–11)? How should this affect our personal response to Jesus and his Word, and how also should we deal with others who have fallen into sin?

3.   What does Jesus want us to learn when he says, 'I am the Light of the world' (8:12)? Can you think of ways in which that truth about Jesus is brought to bear on people's lives throughout the world?

4.   How does Jesus respond to the challenge the Pharisees issue concerning the validity of his testimony (8:13–26)? What future event does he point to as the ultimate proof that his claims are true and why is this so significant (8:27–30)?

5.   What does Jesus say about the enslaving power of sin and how it manifests itself and to where does he point us to find deliverance (8:31–41)? How is this true both in conversion and in our progress in the faith?

6.   Why is Jesus' further response to the Pharisees so alarming, not just for the Pharisees, but for all people (8:42–47)?

7.   In the heated exchange that follows, what is it that drives the Jews to the point of trying to stone Jesus and are they justified in this (8:48–59)? What implications arise from this incident?

For STUDY 13: Read John 9:1–41 and chapters 22–23 of the commentary.

STUDY 13: John 9:1–41

AIM: To follow Jesus' further exposure of the depth of our spiritual need as he deals with blindness, both physical and spiritual.

1.   How does the initial encounter with the blind man and the exchange between Jesus and the disciples set the scene for what is about to happen (9:1–5)? In what way does this immediately take us beyond this one man and his personal need and towards the universal need of all people?

2.   How does the mighty work that Jesus performs in restoring sight to the blind man (9:6–12) endorse his mighty words in the claims he makes about himself? Why is it still important to recognize the connection between what Jesus said and what he also did?

3.   What can we learn about the strength of the Pharisees' case against Jesus from the kind of argument they invoke (9:13–17)? How would you respond to a person who was raising that kind of objection to Christ and the gospel?

4.   Why do the blind man's parents respond to the Pharisees in the way they do (9:18–23)? How can fear of what others might do – especially in religious circles – prevent people from trusting in Christ today? What would you say to a person holding back from Jesus for those reasons?

5.   What are we to learn from the path by which Jesus brought the blind man beyond physical healing to true conversion (9:24–38)?

6.   In what way does the final exchange between Jesus and some of the Pharisees highlight the solemn responsibility that goes with the privilege of having the light of God's truth (9:39–41)?

For STUDY 14: Read John 10:1–42 and chapters 24–25 of the commentary.

STUDY 14: John 10:1–42

AIM: To see the love and gentleness of Jesus as he is revealed as God's perfect Shepherd and to note, yet again, the negative reaction that this provokes in his hearers.

1.   What is the connection between this chapter and the teaching it contains and the preceding incident involving the blind man and the Pharisees (10:1–6)? In what ways do people still need to be alert to those who are not true shepherds of God's flock?

2.   What did Jesus mean when he called himself 'the gate' (10:7–10)? What does this teach us about the way of salvation; about how we experience the blessings of salvation; and about the nature of the salvation he provides?

3.   How does Jesus prove himself to be the 'Good Shepherd' (10:11–18)? What kind of response to him does this draw from us?

4.   Why do you think that many Jews were so extreme in their denunciation of Christ (10:19–21)? Is this a symptom of a more widespread reaction against him?

5.   How does Jesus respond to the request that he explain plainly whether or not he is the Christ (10:22–30)? Why do you think he answers in this way?

6.   How does Jesus justify his claim to be God in answer to the Jews' determination to stone him (10:31–39)?

7.   What do we learn from the contrast between the reaction of the Jews in Jerusalem and that of those in the region beyond the Jordan (10:40–42)? What was one of the main factors in the difference between these two responses?

For STUDY 15: Read John 11:1–44 and chapter 26 of the commentary.

STUDY 15: John 11:1–44

AIM: To see how Jesus deals with death and shows, by word and deed, that he alone has power to conquer it.

1.   How does Jesus deliberately use the crisis over Lazarus' serious illness to give this incident a significance that would go far beyond the experience of one family (11:1–6)? In what way would this lead to glory for God and for Jesus?

2.   How does the reluctance of the disciples to go with Jesus to Bethany emphasize the way that the fear of death holds everyone hostage (11:7–16, see also *Heb.* 2:15)? In what ways does the fear of death display itself in people's experience today?

3.   In what way does Jesus take his followers' understandings of who he is and what he came to do on to a different plane by means of his words here (11:17–27)? Why are these truths so vital for a full enjoyment of the Christian life?

4.   What can we learn about Jesus' reaction to Mary's grief, and his response at the tomb of Lazarus (11:28–38)? What makes Jesus' reactions different from any merely human expression of grief?

5.   Why does Jesus preface this miracle with a very public prayer (11:39–42)? To where does this prayer direct us in our quest for true hope in the face of death, and how might this be expressed in practical terms in the way we deal with death and dying?

6.   How does the miracle lend weight to the sound of Christ's words (11:43–44 and 11:25–26)? How does this event impact upon the consistent teaching of Jesus about his own death and resurrection, and on the way that his predictions would be perceived by disciples and Jews alike?

For STUDY 16: Read John 11:45–12:19 and chapter 27 of the commentary.

STUDY 16: John 11:45–12:19

AIM: To see how the reactions of one woman in a small village and a huge crowd in a large city, bear testimony to all that has been revealed about Jesus up to this point.

1.   The raising of Lazarus provided the strongest evidence yet that Jesus' claims were authentic. What effect did this have upon those who witnessed this miracle and those who heard reports about it (11:45–47)? How does this help us to appreciate that there is more to saving faith than simply knowing the facts about Jesus?

2.   How did the members of the Sanhedrin react to the news they heard about events in Bethany (11:47–48)? What solution did Caiaphas propose and how did this serve only to demonstrate that the unfolding situation lay in the hands of One higher than themselves (11:48–57)? In what way does this encourage greater confidence in the message of the gospel (look at *Acts* 2:23)?

3.   Jesus was invited to a meal in the home of Mary, Martha and Lazarus. While he was there, Mary anointed his feet with expensive perfume. What reaction did this provoke from Judas Iscariot, and what did that reveal about his motivations and concerns (12:1–6)? How did Jesus rebuke Judas for his cynicism (12:7–8)?

4.   In what way was Mary's testimony to Jesus an expression of a wider conviction that was growing among ordinary Jewish people, and how in turn did that serve only to infuriate the leaders even further (12:9–11)?

5.   When Jesus rode into Jerusalem on a donkey, many of the people who welcomed him did not fully appreciate the significance of what they were saying about him. Nevertheless, they were giving Jesus the highest recognition that Jews could give. What do we learn about Jesus from the Old Testament quotations that were used to acknowledge him (12:12–16)?

6.   What is the effect of the straightforward testimony of those who saw what Jesus did in raising Lazarus (12:17–19)? What can we learn from this about the way God has promised to honour the witness we bear to his Son?

For STUDY 17: Read John 12:20–50 and chapter 28 of the commentary.

STUDY 17: John 12:20–50

AIM: To listen carefully to Jesus as he explains the necessity of his death and warns of the eternal consequences of refusing to believe in him.

1.   Do you see any connection between John's report of the Pharisees' complaint (12:19) and the fact that foreigners come seeking an audience with Jesus (12:20–22)? In what way does this take the gospel out of a merely Jewish context and give it universal significance?

2.   Jesus finally announces that his hour has come (12:23). What does this mean, firstly, for himself (12:23–24); and also for his followers and the kind of service to which they are called (12:25–26)? How do you explain the element of necessity in both these strands of teaching?

3.   How does Jesus give us a glimpse of the horror of what lay ahead for him (12:27)? How does God provide the encouragement he needs, and the testimony to the crowds, and shows that the work of the cross will not be in vain (12:28–33)?

4.   How does Jesus give his message an additional urgency in the face of the gathering storm (12:34–36)? Is there a wider application of his words in every age of history?

5.   How does John explain the persistent unbelief of the Jews despite all the evidence that was staring them in the face (12:37–41)? In what way should this humble us before God to appreciate the salvation of believers, and to pray for God to show mercy to those outside the kingdom?

6.   Despite widespread rejection, many people came to put their trust in Jesus (12:42–43). What warning does Jesus issue to those who still refuse to believe, and how does this warning serve also as an opportunity for grace (12:44–50)?

For STUDY 18: Read John 13:1–38 and chapters 29–30 of the commentary.

STUDY 18: John 13:1–38

AIM: To watch Jesus as he demonstrates in an acted–out parable the purpose of his coming and to see how his love shines against a backdrop of betrayal and denial.

1.   How does John introduce this next major section of his Gospel (13:1)? How does this help us appreciate, not only what Jesus does as he washes the disciples' feet, but everything that happens in the upper room that night? How is this accentuated by what is said about Judas (13:2)? What does this teach us about the nature of Christ's love?

2.   What was so striking about Jesus' gesture of foot–washing and the way it was performed (13:3–5; contrast 12:12–16)?

3.   How does Jesus use Peter's objections in order to explain more fully the truth that lay behind this action, concerning his relationship with these men (13:6–11)? How does this help us understand the

once-for-all nature, and the daily dimensions, of fellowship with Christ?

4.   In what way does Jesus expect his followers to emulate the kind of behaviour he has just modelled for them (13:12–17)? Can you think of ways that we can show this service in our relationships within the church and in our dealings with the wider world?

5.   What do we learn about the dynamics of sin from Jesus' disclosure that Judas would betray him, and from the way Judas reacts (13:18–30)? Although there is something quite unique in what was happening here, is there anything that we can learn about the way sin takes hold of a person's life and literally controls him to death?

6.   Jesus turns again to his disciples to warn them of his imminent departure. What is surprising, but significant, about the command he gives in face of his ominous announcement (13:31–35)? How does this affect the priorities we have as we live for Christ and seek to serve him?

7.   How is Jesus' love for Peter displayed in the rebuke he gives him (13:36–38)? How does the fullness of Christ's knowledge affect the pain of Peter's failure when it happens, and are there any lessons we can learn about dealing with our own sin and failure?

For STUDY 19: Read John 14:1–31 and chapters 31–32 of the commentary.

STUDY 19: John 14:1–31

AIM: To understand the nature of the comfort that Jesus promises his followers through his assurances of heaven in the future and of the promise of the Holy Spirit in the present.

1.   The disciples are clearly showing signs of being troubled by what they are hearing in the upper room. How does Jesus give them reason to rise above their doubts and fears (14:1–4)? How do these words continue to bring hope and comfort to Christians through all ages?

2.   What should we make of the doubts that Thomas expresses (14:5)? How should Christians handle the doubts they experience?

3.   In what way does Jesus' answer to Thomas provide an assurance that links the present with the future (14:6–7)? How are we to understand what Jesus says about his being 'the way, the truth and the life'?

4.   How does knowing Jesus lead us into knowledge of God the Father (14:8–14)? In what sense will those who know God through his Son do 'greater things' than Jesus has done (14:12)?

5.   How do we express a genuine love for Jesus (14:15)? In what way does this statement provide a safeguard against legalism?

6.   In what special way does the promise of the Holy Spirit provide reassurance for the disciples in the present world (14:16–21)?

7.   What is the connection between the peace that Jesus gives, the promise of the Holy Spirit, and the teaching that the Spirit will provide (14:22–31)? How does this help us to understand what lies at the heart of the Holy Spirit's work in the life of believers?

For STUDY 20: Read John 15:1–16:4 and chapters 33–34 of the commentary.

STUDY 20: John 15:1–16:4

AIM: To discover the key to a truly fruitful and effective life in this world and to see that this does not mean that life will be free from trouble and pain.

1.   How do the pictures of the vine, its branches and a gardener, help us to understand better the dynamics of Christian experience (15:1–4)? In what way do they help us to appreciate more fully the place of God's discipline in his dealings with his children?

2.   Remaining or abiding in Christ is the key to fruitful Christian living. What does this mean in practical terms (15:5–8)? What are we to make of the branches that are 'thrown into the fire and burned'?

3.   What are the links in the chain of love that Jesus describes in these verses (15:9–17)? How is the love of God expressed in the relationships within his family? What might this mean in practice for you as a member of your church?

4.   Jesus says, 'The Father will give you whatever you ask in my name' (15:16). How does the context of that promise help us to understand what it means?

5.   Many Christians struggle with the fact that following Christ means hostility from other people. What does Jesus tell his disciples that enables them to understand why this should be so (15:18–25)? How does this connect with the joy of suffering for the gospel? (see also *James* 1:2–4, *1 Pet.* 1:3–7)

6.   In what way will the Holy Spirit help the disciples in particular, and all the followers of Christ generally, to cope with opposition and fulfil the work that God gives them to do (15:26–27)? How does this apply in a world where many people no longer believe in absolute truth?

7.   Why was Jesus saying these things to his followers (16:1–4)? How are Christians tempted to 'go astray' today and how can these same truths keep that from happening?

For STUDY 21: Read John 16:5–33 and chapters 35–36 of the commentary.

STUDY 21: John 16:5–33

AIM: To see how Jesus prepares his disciples for the trouble they would face by explaining how the Holy Spirit will help and equip them for the work they must do.

1.   Many people think that the Christian life was far easier for the disciples who were with Jesus when he was on earth. Why, then, does Jesus say that it is for the good of the disciples that he is going away (16:5–7)?

2.   What three aspects of the Holy Spirit's work does Jesus identify and what does each of them mean (16:8–11)? How do these truths affect our attitude to the spreading of the gospel?

3.   Jesus says that when the Holy Spirit comes, 'he will guide you into all truth' (16:12–15). Why must this statement apply in a special way to the apostles? In what sense does it have relevance to all of God's people?

4.   How do Jesus' comments about being seen no longer and then being seen again both confuse and encourage the disciples (16:16–24)? What are the levels of meaning that Jesus builds into that statement? How will this lead to the disciples' joy being made complete (16:24)?

5.   What reassurance is found in the closing remarks of Jesus' discourse in the upper room (16:25–32)? How do they show that God's strength is made perfect in our weakness?

6.   Why should Christians take heart from the fact that Jesus has 'overcome the world' (16:33)? What effect should this have on us as we face the daily struggles of living in this world?

For STUDY 22: Read John 17:1–26 and chapter 37 of the commentary.

STUDY 22: John 17:1–26

AIM: To be encouraged by the prayer that Jesus offers before his death, when he prays that his sacrifice might accomplish everything that God intends it to.

1.   Jesus talks about the cross as being the time for glory (17:1). In what sense did the cross bring glory to God the Son, and glory to God the Father? How should this affect our worship?

2.   How are we to understand the essence of eternal life (17:2–3)? In what way is this connected to Jesus' sacrifice on Calvary?

3.   Why does the cross mark the pinnacle of Christ's work in the world, and what proves that this is so (17:4–5)? What does this say about the place of the cross in authentic Christian experience?

4.   What does Jesus pray for in relation to his disciples (17:6–12)? Why is this prayer so significant for the gospel?

5.   How will it be possible for the disciples to know joy in full measure even though they continue to live in a world that is hostile to them (17:13–19)? How does this help us to appreciate what is involved in sanctification?

6.   What is Jesus' prayer for all who will believe in him through the apostolic testimony in the gospel (17:20–26)? Why does Jesus

place so much emphasis on the oneness of his people? How should this affect our attitude to those things that divide us from other believers?

7.   What is the goal of Jesus' ongoing work in the life of his people (17:25–26)?

For STUDY 23: Read John 18:1–40 and chapters 38–39 of the commentary.

STUDY 23: John 18:1–40

AIM: To appreciate the importance of Jesus' trial, not just as a fact of history but as an integral part of the gospel.

1.   The account of Jesus' arrest is seen from two very different perspectives: that of Jesus and that of his disciples. How does Jesus' statement, 'Shall I not drink the cup that the Father has given me?' (18:11), help us to understand the whole episode (18:1–11)? What does the expression 'cup' teach us about the ordeal that Jesus was facing (see *Isa*. 51:17,22)?

2.   Why does John deliberately repeat his comment about Caiaphas as Jesus is taken away to be tried by the Jews (18:12–14)? In what way does this affect our understanding of the trial and its outcome?

3.   John tells us about the first of Peter's three denials (18:15–18). What do we learn from this about our natural weakness in the face of temptation, even when we have been pre–warned by God's Word?

4.   In what way do the opening exchanges of Jesus' trial serve to prove his innocence from the outset (18:19–24)?

5.   The obvious innocence of Jesus is put alongside the clear guilt of Peter (18:19–27). How does this reinforce the fact that Jesus was on trial as God's substitute for sinners (see *1 Pet*. 3:18)?

6.   In what way does Pilate's question, 'What is truth?' (18:38), become the pivot on which the whole trial before this governor turns (18:28–40)? Point to ways in which it highlights the grace and justice of God against the background of the corruption and injustice of Pilate's court.

For STUDY 24: Read John 19:1–42 and chapters 40–41 of the commentary.

STUDY 24: John 19:1–42

AIM: To look with renewed wonder and appreciation at the sacrifice that Jesus had to make to secure the redemption of all who believe on him.

1.   Why do you think the Apostles' Creed includes the affirmation that Jesus 'suffered under Pontius Pilate' (19:1–16)? Why is Pilate's verdict so important, not only in the court proceedings, but to the gospel (19:4)?

2.   What is ironical in the charge the Jews were levelling against Jesus (19:7, cf. *Gen.* 3:5)? What does this say about the nature and whereabouts of the real guilt in this situation?

3.   Who was actually in control of events on that day (19:8–11, cf. *Acts* 2:23)? Where does this lead us in our understanding of what is happening?

4.   What can we learn from the love of Jesus on the cross as contrasted with the backdrop of the bitterness and hatred of those who put him to death (19:17–27)?

5.   In what way are the Scriptures used as the key to our understanding of the suffering of Christ on the cross (19:28–37)? Given the widespread misunderstanding of the crucifixion, why is this point so important?

6.   Why is the account of the burial of Jesus so necessary in the gospel record (19:38–42)? In what way are those involved in his burial a living testimony to the power of the gospel, even before Jesus had been raised from the dead?

For STUDY 25: Read John 20:1–31 and chapters 42–43 of the commentary.

STUDY 25: John 20:1–31

AIM: To see the gentle grace of Jesus as he appears after the resurrection to his dispirited followers and the response of worship which ensues.

1.   Why do you think John gives such a prominent place to a woman's testimony in his account of the resurrection (20:1–18)? What does this prominence, emphasized to a religious world in which women were second–class citizens, reveal about the grace of God?

2.   How does the obvious shock and surprise of the disciples at the sight of an empty tomb help to prove that the early church did not fabricate the resurrection story (20:1–9)?

3.   What do we see of the love of Christ in the way that he dealt with Mary in her grief and confusion over the empty tomb (20:10–18)? In what way does this show him to be the true Shepherd of God's sheep (look at 10:27)?

4.   In what way does Jesus after the resurrection invest with new meaning the peace promised in a traditional Hebrew greeting (20:19–23)? What part does the resurrection play in the experience of assurance in the Christian life (see *Rom.* 4:25)?

5.   Why is Thomas' failure to accept the testimony of his fellow apostles, and the events that follow a week later, so significant in establishing the reliability of the gospel message (20:24–29)? In what sense is there greater blessing for those who accept that testimony without the need for physical proof (20:29)? How has this encouraged believers throughout the ages?

6.   What reason does John give for writing his Gospel, and for writing it in the way he did (20:30–31)? How do you respond to his invitation?

For STUDY 26: Read John 21:1–25 and chapters 44–45 of the commentary.

STUDY 26: John 21:1–25

AIM: To see how Jesus prepares, equips and commissions his disciples to carry out the mission they were to perform in the world as they served him.

1.   How does the final chapter of John's Gospel bring us full circle with respect to Jesus' method of calling and preparing his band of apostles for their unique ministry (21:1–14, see *Mark* 1:16–17, *Luke* 5:1–11)? In what way did this preparation encourage the apostles before Jesus returned to heaven?

2. How do the miraculous catch of fish, and the breakfast on the beach, reinforce what the disciples already know about Jesus? In what way do these truths help us today?

3. What did Peter learn through the painful exchange with Jesus after the meal that morning (21:15–19)? How did that conversation pave the way for true restoration to a useful life of service for the apostle? Can you think of examples that show how this whole experience made Peter a different man? How might God sanctify to us our sins and failures?

4. How does the way that Jesus deals with Peter provide a fitting conclusion to a book intended as an explanation of the meaning of the gospel in terms of transformed lives?

5. John, in this chapter, comes as close as he does anywhere in the Gospel to actually naming himself (21:20–24). How does he point to the need for everyone to exercise submissive trust in Jesus?

7. In what way does the final verse of the Gospel bring John's record of Jesus to a conclusion on a note of praise and wonder (21:25)? What effect has your study of this Gospel had on you?

FOR FURTHER READING

J. CALVIN (trans. J. Pringle), in *Calvin's Commentaries*, Grand Rapids: Baker Book House, 1979.

D. A. CARSON, *The Gospel According to John*, Leicester, UK: IVP, 1991; Grand Rapids, USA: W. B. Eerdmans, 1991.

W. HENDRIKSEN, *The Gospel of John (New Testament Commentary)*, London: Banner of Truth, 1959.

G. J. KEDDIE, *John*, Vols. 1 and 2 , Darlington: Evangelical Press, 2001.

B. MILNE, *The Message of John*, Leicester: IVP, 1993.

J. C. RYLE, *Expository Thoughts on the Gospels: John, Vols. 1–3*, 1869, 1873; republished, Edinburgh: Banner of Truth, 1987.